# ALCHEMY OF A WARRIOR'S HEART

*William "Rev. Bill" McDonald JR.*

Foreword by
Gayle Lynds

*Photo by Richard Munn (England 2016)*

Cover design by Mario Arturo
www.marioarturo.com

Book cover photography Shutterstock Images

Interior layout by Tom Heffron

**Alchemy of A Warrior's Heart**
Copyright 2018 by William H. McDonald Jr.
All rights reserved.

No part of this book may be reproduced, stored in a retrieval system, or transmitted by any means, electronic, mechanical, photocopying, recording, or otherwise, without written permission from the author. Permission is granted to use quotes for media publications, books, or reviews, as long as the author and this book are referenced.

Photo Credits: *Arden Kamille Varnel, David Schulz, Henry Sanchez,& Richard Munn*

*Sacred Owl Publishing*
Elk Grove, CA 95624

SBN-13:978-1723378164
ISBN-10:172337816X

Printed by CreateSpace, An Amazon.com Company

1 Spirituality 2 Inspirational 3 New Age 4 Metaphysical 5 Memoir

First Edition

# Dedicated to
# Yogiraj Satgurunath Siddhanath

*Photo by David Schultz (India 2010)*

# Contents

**Foreword** — *vii*

**Introduction** — *xiii*

*Part One*
**DESTINATION: INDIA 2004** — *1*

*Part Two*
**LESSONS FROM THE HEART** — *39*

*Part Three*
**THE GURU FINDS ME** — *69*

*Part Four*
**LEARNING TO SERVE** — *111*

*Part Five*
**BACK HOME AT THE ASHRAM** — *133*

*Part Six*
**LIFE OR DEATH - DECISIONS OF THE HEART** — *169*

*Part Seven*
**DON'T GIVE UP HEART** — *191*

*Epilogue*
**LAST WORDS AND THOUGHTS** — *ccxxv*

**About the Author** — *ccxxvii*

**Acknowledgements** — *ccxxxi*

# Foreword

## by Gayle Lynds

The first time I saw Bill McDonald was in 2006, on the doorstep of a house where I was staying in San Francisco. He was a jaunty, handsome man in jeans and jacket. He wore a brown Panama hat; his closely cropped beard graying. Behind him, his pickup truck was parked at the curb. With his warm smile and unassuming manner, few would guess the rich spiritual life he led, or the thousands of people he'd helped. I was one of them. Because of him, I was transforming my life.

There is the public me, and there is the private me.

The public me writes spy thrillers; international political novels in which espionage, greed, ambition, and violence play large roles.

The private me believes in love, kindness, and otherworldly experiences.

As a child, I "flew" at night, often up to the ceiling across from the bed I shared with my grandmother. Other times, I'd fly to towns I'd never seen. Within a week of this flight, our little family would pile into our car to go there, to that very place, to visit friends I'd never met, except in my flying dreams.

Once, as my father was driving us into one of those towns, I sat up in the back seat and announced, "We've been here before." It had taken me a while to build up the courage to admit this sort of thing.

"No," my father said, correcting me. "This is the first time." My father, a tall man with a baseball cap on his head to shade his eyes from the Iowa sun, drove west.

But my mother glanced back at me, asking curiously, "Why do you think we've been here?"

"It's me," I tried to explain. "*I've* been here." I was probably five years old. All I knew about my nighttime flying was one moment I was cozily in bed, and the next galumphing across the countryside, preparing to rise above the treetops. Sometimes I merely flew softly upwards in my bedroom, aware of a gentle rocking. I'd look down at Grandma and me sleeping together, wondering how I'd gotten up in the corner. In daylight hours, fully awake, I'd flap my arms and try to soar up to the clouds.

"What's the name of the town?" Dad asked, quizzing me to see if I was lying.

I really did not know, but I recognized the white snowball hydrangeas lining the front of a blue Victorian house, and the ball field in the next block, and the concrete wall fronting a line of bungalows on the left.

"You should turn here," I told him matter-of-factly, then spilled the beans. "I saw all of this in a dream."

He shook his head. "Lucky guess."

Grandma was sitting in the back seat beside me. "Dreams aren't real," she said firmly.

Dad turned the car onto the street I'd indicated, and soon we were at the cape-style house I remembered.

As we left the car, my mother hugged me. My feelings were hurt and she wanted to comfort me. But in my mind, my grandmother's words echoed, a warning: "Dreams aren't real." Years later, when I was in my twenties and home alone in the kitchen with my mother, I remembered the incident and her compassionate hug.

"Do you fly at night?" I asked curiously, but also a little fearfully. I was opening myself up to disbelief and ridicule.

Mom was a heavyset woman with soft cheeks and a light tread. In the kitchen, she always wore an apron.

She assessed me. "Not anymore," she admitted. "Do you?"

*She'd flown, too!* "When I was little, I did a lot. Not much now. Why did you stop?"

"Your grandma," Mom answered, a bit sad. "I told her about it when I was five or six years old. Her answer then, as was with you, was, "Dreams aren't real." Afterwards, I couldn't get off the ground again. Oh, how I loved flying…"

As we talked, it occurred to me we'd never revealed our nighttime journeys to anyone until now. Keeping the secret had haunted us, and somehow stunted us. The years passed. I gave birth to two wonderful children, divorced, remarried, acquired two equally wonderful stepchildren, and worked hard to support my family by doing what I love, writing novels. I've been lucky to have published a number of them. During that time, I continued to fly sporadically, particularly when I was stressed. And, too, I found myself drawn to what I called psychic phenomena—tarot, astrology, numerology, life readings—that sort of thing.

# FOREWORD

In August 2005, my second husband died. Our children, adults now, came home. When the phone rang, we'd pick up an extension and say hello, but all we'd hear was empty silence, no human voice to answer, not even a dial tone to say someone had ended the conversation. Other times, we'd be on the phone talking with a friend and static would erupt so loudly we couldn't continue. The phone problems were making us crazy.

Over the next month, the phone company came twice. Each time the telephones would return to normal for a few days, then the static and eerie silences would resume. Finally, after the repairmen's third visit, the phones stabilized.

While this was going on, I was also having trouble with the lamp next to my husband's side of the bed. The light would flicker, making it hard to read at night. So, I replaced the bulb. The lamp still flickered. I figured it probably needed to be rewired. A friend did it, and the lamp worked fine again…for a while.

For years, I'd been giving endorsements to help sales of novels I enjoyed. That winter, the wife of one of the authors of those books asked me to read a memoir by her friend Bill McDonald, with the idea of endorsing it, too. She said Bill was a Vietnam vet, a poet, and a writer who counseled many people, including troubled vets. The title of his memoir in those days was *A Spiritual Warrior's Journey*. It's available again, revised, and with a new title: *Warrior: A Spiritual Odyssey*.

By then I'd read quite a bit in the psychic/spiritual field. A few books were terrific, others not so much. And I often had a sense they were more about psychic phenomena than about spiritual growth, despite claiming the opposite. I wasn't excited about reading another one.

Still, for some unfathomable reason, I agreed to do it. The memoir arrived in the mail, accompanied by a hand-written note from Bill offering condolences for the loss of my husband. Beneath his signature was a phone number and an invitation to call anytime I wanted to talk.

His niceness wasn't going to sway me, I decided. I tossed the book onto my mailing desk. Soon piles of papers migrated to settle over it—out of sight and out of mind. I focused on my own work. When the memoir was visible again, I felt a pang of guilt, and so carried it upstairs, where it ended up atop the stack of books and magazines on my bedside table. Soon it was buried there, too.

Life went on.

A couple of months later, the memoir resurfaced. I didn't want to read it… and I no longer remembered why.

When I settled in into bed and opened Bill's book, I found myself caught up in his childhood experiences of spiritual development, as he navigated the terrors and misfortunes of a highly dysfunctional family. He wrote with sensitivity and insight.

The next night, I took the book with me so I could continue reading, while waiting in a restaurant for a friend. When she and I finished our meal, it was nearly ten o'clock. She left, and I stopped outside to fish through my purse for my keys. The sidewalk was busy with people enjoying the lovely California evening.

My keys found, I drove home.

I was getting ready for bed when I looked inside my purse for Bill's memoir. My throat tightened. His book was gone. I called the restaurant. No one had seen it.

Panicking, heart racing, scenarios twittering through my head, I ran to my car and drove there.

With welcomed relief, I spotted the book, illuminated on top of a decorative brick wall. Despite all of the people passing by, it was where I'd put it when I'd searched for my keys.

Palatable relief filled me. Anyone could easily have walked away with it.

*At last*, I got the point: I'd been trying to lose the book, yet now I didn't want anything to happen to it. It was a treasure.

I read late that night, and awoke and read until I finished the next afternoon. What a remarkable experience. I wanted to call Bill to tell him how much his book meant to me.

Still, I waffled for two days.

Finally, on Mother's Day 2006, I dialed the number in his note.

A vibrant male voice answered. I introduced myself.

"Did you know I was going to call?" I asked curiously.

"Actually, I thought you'd call yesterday," he said.

With laughter, our first conversation began. We talked for four fascinating hours. Bill describes our chat in the pages of this book, *Alchemy of a Warrior's Heart*, but I'll add two more pieces important to me.

About an hour into our conversation, the rich fragrance of roses flowed through my room, in what could only be described as a river. The scent was a lush perfume unlike anything I'd ever inhaled, reminding me of my mother, who'd loved roses just as I do. About the same time, the illumination from my two bedside lamps, which had been glowing steadily, dimmed then brightened in perfect unison. In a stately fashion, the lights continued to lower and rise, lower and rise. I told Bill about the rose river and my wayward lamps, but he made no comment; just chuckled as if he knew exactly what was happening.

Over the years, Bill and I have talked and met periodically. I was humbled when Bill asked me to write this Foreword. In spiritual matters, I remain a novice. But because of Bill, I know more, am open to more, and live a far more spiritual and happy life. My self-doubts have turned into belief, and my fears of being ostracized have transformed into confidence. I continue to be blessed. I fell in love and married again. My husband and I live in Maine, where we both write and have collaborated on short stories. Beside my side of the bed is the lamp from ten years ago that a friend rewired. Since then, it's been rewired twice more, and yet its light continues to flicker sporadically. I no longer worry about it. I simply accept and enjoy the mystery of it.

Bill is truly a spiritual warrior. His modesty and honesty are renowned. In our conversations over the years, he's told me many of the stories in this book. In a way, I became a distant and very fortunate eye-witness. As you read, you'll live Bill's adventures as they happened. You'll marvel at his unusual experiences, resonate with his doubts, and revel in his spiritual discoveries. There are tales of panthers, cobras, holy men, miraculous healings, outlaws, Babaji's Cave, a boat ride on the Ganges River, the Om Café, dead yogis, premonitions of death, out-of-body experiences, visualizations, owls, the Lodi zoo, Mount Shasta, the blue lotus feet of a guru, and the world's largest, one-piece, solid mercury stone, sometimes called the Philosopher's Stone. To see the stone, you'll *have* to travel to Gurunath's Forest Ashram in India. But after experiencing this book, I think you'll very much *want* to go there for yourself.

In the beginning, I told you what Bill looked like when we first met in 2006. These days his beard is shot with silver, but his face looks younger than ever. His eyes even twinkle. His walk is robust. His mind is a wonder of clarity. He's lived many lives, many times.

I envy you. You're about to begin what may be your first great exploration with Bill. Bon voyage!

**Gayle Lynds**
September 2017
Portland, Maine

*Gayle Lynds is an award winning novelist who has had many of her thriller books on the New Times Best Selling List. More importantly, she is one of my best friends.*

# Introduction

When I was a much younger man, I was a door-gunner/crew-chief on a Huey helicopter during the Vietnam War. I have always felt the presence of saintly beings surrounding and protecting me, even before I went off to war. No matter what happened to me on the various battlefields of life, I rest-assured someone was always looking after me. Desire to discover that 'someone' fueled my life-quest.

In the sixth decade of my life journey, a saintly Himalayan guru captured my heart and radically changed most everything I held true. Not only did I find a living spiritual master, but I uncovered a friendship deeper than the ocean. In addition, I learned he was a part of the same spiritual lineage as my guru, Paramahansa Yogananda.

This book is an account of the spiritual adventure leading me to find this living spiritual master. More accurately, my voyage placed me in his path so he could find *me*. The contents deal with many paranormal and supernatural events that took place over a ten-year period, during which I faced imminent death on several occasions. This period began with a trip to India. It was the first of many, and the fulfillment of a lifelong dream. It opened my heart to a new, mystical world and a higher level of thought.

This book does not attempt to detail teachings or steal the thunder of any gurus. It simply asks you to sit beside me as I tell you stories of a spiritual awakening. These stories are presented chronologically without interjecting hindsight, so the mystical insights may be revealed to you one by one as they were to me as I lived them. The book does not pass any judgments. I present only how I felt and saw things at the time without any later day revisions.

The most important thing in life is LOVE. I think from my heart and enjoy my experiences without the need to dissect and understand them. Like a child, I accept the Divine beings, healings, out-of-body experiences, mind-reading, having two bodies, visions of the future and the past, altered states, powers over nature, moving objects with the mind, time travel, near-death experiences, and LOVE beyond measure that have become a part of my life. The only thing I truly understand is LOVE. I *know* LOVE, when I get it and when I give it.

For a period of six weeks, when my youngest grandchild, Gianni, was three years old, he had nightly visions of a lofty saint-like yogi. His disclosure received my full attention. I listened intently as he spoke of having visits from "his friends" Babaji, Shri Yukteswar, Lahiri Mahasaya, and others, including Paramahansa Yogananda. After this, I had my own visions and dreams of meeting this lofty saint-like yogi master, a being who ended up transforming every aspect of my emotional, spiritual, and physical self. That he changed my life, is a massive understatement.

The last several years of my life have been a series of spiritual lessons that came quickly to me. The lessons are universal in scope and, if one has an open mind and heart, they might personally benefit from reading about my experiences.

Although this book has a beginning and end; in the present now of this reality, the spirit of the narrative continues to unfold. Until one truly finds enlightenment there are no endings. May you be sufficiently inspired on your own personal journey, to someday find your own man or woman of God who teaches and transforms you. This story is how I know I found mine.

**Rev. Bill McDonald**

*Part One*

# DESTINATION: INDIA 2004

### Love is the Most Important Thing

All through my life I'd envisioned traveling to India. There were several times it almost happened, but money, time, the Vietnam War, family, work, even a national emergency and ban on travel had taken turns standing in the way.

My earliest Indian dreams were always about exploring the places of holy men and meeting those I'd only read about in Paramahansa Yogananda's classic book *Autobiography of a Yogi*.

Raised in a severely dysfunctional family, I left home following high school graduation in 1964, headed to the Hawaiian Islands, with my sights set on continuing to India. Instead, in 1965, after returning to California, I hitchhiked across the USA and flew to Western Europe. My youthful heart figured I would find an easterly passage to India. But once again, I returned to the states and ended up in the U.S. Army. My tour-of-duty (October 1966-67) took me to Vietnam to fly combat missions with "*The 128th Assault Helicopter Company*" as a door gunner/crew chief.

I'd briefly considered volunteering for another year's duty in Nam, to qualify for thirty days of extra leave with free transportation to anywhere in the world. I could go to India! But after being shot down, crashing in my helicopter several times, and being wounded and almost captured, the free trip didn't feel like the best idea.

I returned to civilian life near the end of 1968 and went home to the San Francisco Bay Area, married my former high school sweetheart, Carol, and settled into an adult life of work and family. The dream of traveling to India became a long-range desire, but the pull was powerful.

From my earliest memory, the inherent knowledge of God and spirituality were deeply rooted in me, allowing me to experience a great number of otherworldly events. Meditation and the practice of spiritual mentorship through a guru was paramount.

Years flew by, and not without a few health issues. Nevertheless, ongoing spiritual experiences continued to point me to India.

I've always responded to the pain of others, spiritually and literally. Therefore, at the end of several years of speaking engagements, the making of a documentary, and actually 'grasping' my heart when my son told me he and his lovely wife had decided to divorce (I worried for my grandson, Spencer), I knew for me to be there for those I loved, I needed to follow my destiny and discover something in India. It was my dharma.

Several months later an opportunity opened for me to once again embrace my lifelong dream. I talked my old veteran friend, Dave Gallo, into traveling with me. I then tied up loose ends, obtained my visa, and purchased the ticket.

Those loose ends included finally meeting with actor Danny Glover. His agent had contacted me a couple of years before when Mr. Glover was making a movie about a PTSD Vietnam veteran. Danny had been visiting my old web site *The Vietnam Experience* and reading my stories and poetry to better understand the character he would be playing in that movie. At the time, I was busy helping make a documentary film *In the Shadow of the Blade*.

The flight to India was long and arduous. Dave and I were totally exhausted by the time we landed in Delhi and cleared customs. It was about 2:30 in the morning local time when we found our beds. I was so keyed up to *finally* be in India, I woke before sunrise and took off for an early morning walk with Dave.

We wandered to a city park where a group of Sikhs practiced yoga in the early morning sun. We engaged in a friendly conversation with them and were invited to join their ritual. They extended invitations for us to come to their homes to meet their families and share a meal; a friendly and fortuitous beginning.

It turned out these men were part of a group known as *"The Blood Society"* and had been gathering at the city park every morning for over two decades. Comprised of the movers and shakers of the business and political worlds, with a few poets and authors thrown into the mix, they represented a strong collective who had both money and power.

The yoga routine included several laughing exercises. Everything was harmonious as the ritual workout wound down. Then the leader of the group took out a copy of a book which listed in order of importance, all those things the group believed in. He smiled, then read them all to me in a loving way, beginning with the most important principle of their society: physical exercise and health. He continued through the list, including education and employment; a most noble and thoughtful listing of the society's principles. The morning was almost too good to be true.

Then he handed me the book, opened to the items he'd just read, and asked me which one of the principles of the society I understood to be most important. He then stood back, expecting me to choose from the list.

That's when the other shoe dropped.

I looked at him and spoke without censoring, "The most important thing in life is love. Without love, then health, money, and education mean absolutely nothing." My homily included what I had intended to be a sincere discourse about the importance of love on our spiritual journey.

He snatched the book from my hands and began reading it aloud and with great volume, shouting the words at me. One might have thought I'd just attacked him on every level. Such was not my intention. I had come from and with love. Eventually, when he'd yelled long and loud enough to convince me to understand the error of my words and recant, he stopped.

I shrugged my shoulders as an indication I held firm to my convictions. The man and his entire group turned away from us. We stood alone in the park, uninvited to their homes, a meal, or their fellowship. I'd offended them…with love.

Dave was amused by my ability to piss off so many important people in such record time. He wondered out loud what I might do for an encore, given we'd just started the trip.

For the next three weeks we wandered around India, ending up in the Himalayan Mountains hundreds of miles from Delhi. We drove to a spot where we could hike up to the snowline, where I could do something I'd always wanted to do: eat a handful of snow from those lofty, spiritual peaks (a leftover desire from a younger time in my poetry phase).

I was also searching for that wise, old proverbial guru who could answer all my spiritual questions; him sitting cross-legged on some mountaintop, waiting for me. I even had an idea of what this master would look like and how he would act.

Throughout the hike, the skies became dark and stormy. Lightning flashed across the peaks and black clouds quickly surrounded us. A light rain began to fall, so we headed back to the car and had the driver continue along the mountain road. Soon, I became interested in an old temple located on a hill beside the narrow, bumpy road. I asked our driver to stop while Dave complained about why I wanted to see yet another old temple. After all, we'd seen several dozen already, clearly more interesting than this one, and it wasn't even in our guidebook. The temple itself looked like it had weathered many centuries of use.

We parked the car and we followed a large procession of spiritual pilgrims who were heading across a rough and well-worn stone courtyard toward the temple. We joined hundreds of people making their way in the rain. Although we attempted to blend in, being an old American with a long white beard, jeans, sandals, Indiana Jones hat, and walking stick, we may have stood out from the others slightly. Under a covered area, on the left side of the temple, was an odd assortment of sadhus (wandering holy men) holding begging bowls, sitting next to a smoky campfire. I was later told they were probably Nath yogis. But at the time of the temple visit, I hadn't a clue what that meant.

The leader of this group of sadhus was a small guru wearing an orange jacket with a *Nike* trademark swish on it. He wore a loincloth wrapped around his waist and lower areas. All the men were covered with ashes from the fire, and their hairstyles varied from braids and dreadlocks to the wild, bad-hair-day hair of fight promoter Don King.

The apparent guru stood, then reached out his dirty hand in my direction. He yelled, calling me "American Babaji" and motioned for us to join the group. He kept on waving to us, indicating he wanted us to come over and talk. I hesitated, but Dave seemed interested.

The moment we sat, they passed around a huge smoking pipe loaded with some unknown drug, reminiscent of a *Cheech and Chong* movie.

Dave looked at the pipe and said, "Hey, when in Rome, do as the Romans do!"

I passed on the opportunity of smoking the dope, but Dave, very willing to be a good guest, took the pipe and inhaled a deep breath of whatever was burning inside the pipe's bowl. He grinned from ear to ear and muttered an "oh yeah" and something about it being "some good stuff."

I have always been uptight and extremely rigid about drugs. In many a conversation, with Dave and others, I have expressed my opinion that there is no value in using drugs in one's search for self-realization. Dave, on the other hand, was more open to the possibility of enhancing one's spiritual experiences with drug use. At times, he'd pointed out the long history of the traditional use of drugs by Native American shamans and various tribal witch doctors for vision quests. However, his arguments always fell upon my deaf ears.

I found myself sitting in the midst, of a bunch of dopers talking total nonsense. Their recitations were spoken as if they held some great spiritual wisdom, including topics of nature spirits and demons. They mentioned the sun had a consciousness. I laughed to myself at such an absurdity; that in my journey to find the "guru-on-the-mountain-top experience" I'd found myself at the feet of an intoxicated guru and his motley crew of inebriated followers. These men obviously had very little to teach me about my own personal search for God.

As I listened to the group babble on for almost an hour, I decided the experience would go down as a wasted afternoon with hollow memories of a bunch of unwashed, uneducated, homeless guys masquerading as holy men. With enough of their nonsense filling my time, I asked respectfully of the guru what advice, or sage wisdom, he might give me that he had gained from his years of meditation and mountain wandering. But before the guru could answer my question, the most intoxicated man in the group yelled out to his guru to allow him to answer. The guru looked at his spaced-out devotee, who could barely speak any comprehensible English and was basically falling into the fire pit, and waved his approval.

I could hardly contain myself, almost laughing out loud. I was about to receive an answer to an important life question, from the least qualified man in the group and perhaps the least qualified 'holy man' in the entire galaxy. I figured God was having some great fun at my expense.

Sitting back, I waited for the madman's wisdom; folded my arms across my chest and nodded for this doped-up fool to bring it on. If nothing else, it'd be good for a laugh later.

The ash-covered fool looked towards me in the best way he could, given his eyes were rolling around unfocused. And yet again, he almost tumbled into the fire pit. Then, he spoke, in perfect English, saying, "The most important thing in life is love. Without love: then health, money, and education mean absolutely nothing."

He continued speaking the exact words I'd spoken my first morning in India.

The exact words!

Unable to fathom what was occurring, I muttered a series of incomprehensible syllables, amounting to a stream of "whats." *Who was this fool?* I had always believed I could easily tell a highly evolved spiritual person from someone who was worldly. My paradigm was shattered by this seemingly, feeble minded, holy man. One thing was for certain, I could not deny the wisdom of what he had stated.

I looked at Dave enjoying a long inhalation from the enormous pipe. His face was one broad ear-to-ear smile; totally in his own world and very much enjoying it. Faced with the realization that my views on the Divine were confined and narrow, I had to observe all human souls with the possibility any or all could be a saint, a sage, an angel, or even God.

The experience was an indicator the trip to India would change my thinking in ways I could never—even in my shocked, shattered state—imagine. And the journey had only just begun.

## Highway Collision

One of our first nights driving around India took us north towards Pakistan. We were on our way to visit the Golden Temple, running a little late due to our driver having stopped at a small roadside temple of the monkey god, Hanuman.

Dave and I had made fun of him for his needing to stop to give a quick prayer for our safety on the road that night. Even though it was all in good humor, the driver did speed up to make up time.

In India, like a few other countries, they drive on the left side of the road, so everything in the car is the reverse of what we are used to in the United States. Though it doesn't change the overall effect, the re-orientation provides a strange feeling. My view from the passenger seat gave me a front row view of all the dangers coming at our small car. Dave was in the back. We moved along at about sixty miles-an-hour as we dodged oncoming vehicles who were using our lane to pass other vehicles. Darkness had fallen and there were no streetlights to illuminate the highway. All we could see was what was directly in front of our headlights.

Suddenly, out of nowhere, appeared an old yogi directly in front of our speeding car. He was clad in a basic loincloth and had long, white hair and a white beard. Being short and chubby, he reminded me of Santa Claus. As he stood there, like a target, our driver tensed and prepared for the impending collision; too late to avoid hitting him at sixty mph. Ten feet ahead, and closing, I could see his bulging eyes as we readied for contact.

But that is not how it works. Ask anyone who has been in an accident and they'll say time stands still. Perhaps our miraculous brains compute at such a high speed, on so many levels, it appears that way. There seems to be time for thoughts to extend into contemplations on various solutions.

So, my perception was that time stood still. Everything went into ultra-slow-motion as we approached his body, seemingly frozen in front of our eyes. I asked God to protect him. The driver prayed to his monkey God for the same. Dave prepared for impact. So, surreal. Then, just as we should have hit him…he disappeared!

We looked back, and there he was, standing at the side of the road, unharmed. He continued to look at us as we almost slowed to a stop. Then he smiled a strange smile and scampered off into the darkness. We took a collective deep breath and stared at each other, each acknowledging what had happened was impossible. We had not hit him. We had not turned the car out of his path. He'd vanished, and then reappeared on the other side of the road. It did not make any sense.

I mumbled something about thanking God, but our driver reminded us it was his stopping off at the roadside temple and his fortuitous prayers to the monkey god for protection that saved the man and us from any harm. I wasn't sure about the powers of his monkey god, but I do know what we saw, what we experienced, involved things beyond our understanding. How did time go so slowly? It almost stood still. How did the man get instantly transported out of harm's way? None of us had any answer then, nor do I today. The whole thing sent chills up my spine.

## Babaji's Cave

My heart's foremost desire on my journey was to visit Babaji's Cave. This is where the spiritually historic meeting of 1861 took place between the deathless Avatar, Babaji, and a yogi master named Lahiri Mahasaya, as recorded in the great spiritual classic, *Autobiography of a Yogi* by Paramahansa Yogananda.

The spiritual importance of that meeting, and the significance of who Babaji is, cannot be fully explained in this story. Briefly, Babaji is an immortal being who has been around since the beginning of this world cycle, helping mankind with its spiritual evolution. It is said and believed he has taught spiritual techniques such as Kriya Yoga to all the great spiritual masters throughout all of earth's history, including Jesus, Buddha, Moses, and Krishna. It was in this very cave the lost practice of Kriya Yoga was given back to the world by the grace of Babaji, to his disciple Lahiri Mahasaya. The sacredness of this cave cannot be overstated. I experienced an intuitive and profound need to find and meditate in this cave. It was a lifetime dream to find this sacred space and sit where these two cosmic souls had their Divine reunion.

Right from the start of our trip I'd been working on a way to locate and get to the cave. The general starting point was in Ranikhet, a small town nestled in the forested foothills of the Himalayan Mountains. I had gathered some casual reference points—nearby landmarks—and a general location of the YSS Ashram that served as the gatekeeper to the cave.

The swamis who ran the ashram had the keys to the cave. Sadly, they had to install a barred door to prevent vandals and other non-serious visitors from entering. The ashram tightly controlled access, and unless one was a sincere follower of Yogananda or one who practiced Kriya Yoga, entrance was forbidden. The ashram truly functioned as the spiritual guardian of this sacred cave. We would have to visit the ashram, receive permission and directions, then locate the cave.

Despite my planning and research, the ashram *itself* was not so easy to find. Thankfully, with the greatest of Divine luck, we finally found it hidden away in a little Himalayan village down an extremely rough road. The ashram stood behind two massive gates.

Entering, we found it to be almost empty of people. Everyone had left for a religious convocation in another city. Even the head swami himself would be leaving two days hence. Save for the swami, a lone caretaker, and us, the place was unoccupied. We were given permission to stay, but the decision about going to the cave would be made the next morning. The swami added it would probably not be possible to grant us permission seeing as there were no guides to take us there and it was most difficult to find. It was not their policy to allow total strangers to hike up to the cave alone.

So, when we went to bed, after meditating in the ashram's very cold temple, we had no assurance we'd be allowed access. Still, I was optimistic; not ready to give up my dream.

The next morning, after sleeping on the hard-wooden beds in our chilly rooms, we took an ice-cold water bath using metal buckets. We then ventured down to the ashram's temple to meditate. Afterwards, we had a simple breakfast of potatoes, along with some hot tea, then met with the swami in his office. I explained that I had waited my whole life for this opportunity to see the cave and might never be able to return. It would be a huge spiritual disappointment to have come so far and fail to visit the cave.

He asked me about my meditation techniques and my affiliation with Yogananda's organization, *The Self-Realization Fellowship*. We looked directly into each other's eyes for a few moments. My gaze included a tearful stare of pleading. Suddenly, he threw up his arms and granted my request. He then took out a scrap of paper and began drawing a map of the trail system—little more than chicken scratch—then said, "Do you think you can you follow this map? If so, then you can go." I trusted somehow, I'd be able to find the cave, even though the map made no sense to me. I nodded an eager 'yes.'

Before departing, the swami told our driver to drive us about an hour away to a place where the road simply ended. This would put us on the trailhead to begin the ascent of a mountain. The old swami smiled and gave me the keys to both the cave and to a temple located there, a place to meditate and rest. He concluded by telling us that he locked the gates to the ashram at 5:30 in the evening. We thanked him, then set out for the cave.

Our driver found the "end of the road" as instructed, and Dave and I got out and began walking down a dirt road blocked to all vehicular traffic. At the end were dozens of trailheads. We looked for clues on the map, but it was of little help. Finally, we chose a route, based on an old arrow sign lying on the ground near it, and began the upward trek in search of Babaji's Cave.

To further complicate matters, I was suffering from a stomach ailment, causing me great pain and a bad case of dysentery. I'd been dealing with it for three weeks and had lost twenty-six pounds in the process. Weak from the weight loss and illness, I had little energy; breathing was a major effort. I experienced dizziness when I walked. But I wasn't going to let health problems stop me. No way, not after traveling halfway around the world to get to this place.

We kept finding intersecting trails; all appearing to be the "right" trail to take. We made best guesses as the map offered us no clues. In our excitement, we hadn't thought to bring any food or water with us. It was hot and the going was tough. On top of all my physical ailments, I was very dehydrated from sweating profusely. My t-shirt was soaked. It seemed like hours had passed, yet we were still going up, and not a cave in sight.

As we began a steep climb, the shape of a temple rose upon the horizon. Amazingly, we had found the right location on a hilltop and reached it. I took the keys and unlocked the temple doors. Inside, I sat on the floor, completely exhausted and having trouble breathing. At the far end of the temple hung a huge painting of Babaji. I tried meditating, but my concentration was off.

Somewhat rested, we left the temple and headed to the cave, a further hundred yards up and beyond the temple. My legs were weak, but the cave was near. I pushed myself to the end of the trail.

And there it was: a small opening in a rock face with a jail-like door of iron bars. My heart's desire manifested. I fumbled through the set of keys and found the right one.

Dave allowed me to enter first.

We said nothing.

The cave wasn't as big as I had imagined it to be, yet it resonated with a very subtle peace as we sat on the rock floor and meditated.

When our meditation session was over, I took out a prayer list compiled before leaving for the trip. The list included several hundred names of family and friends, even those who might be considered enemies who needed Divine intervention in their lives. I had symbolically brought these people to all the sacred places I'd visited on my trip. If they couldn't physically experience this journey with me, then they could at least be present in spirit. I silently read all the names, then folded it, and put it back into my pocket.

For some time, we remained in the cave, then I remembered the old swami had warned us he locked the gates to the ashram at 5:30. We reluctantly rose and stepped outside the cave. I gave it one last loving look and locked the barred door behind us. I might as well have been leaving another world. Such was the impression I had as I slowly began the downhill trek.

Dave, for whatever reasons, trusted me to lead us back to the car, unaware I was dizzy and disorientated as I led us down what I presumed to be the correct path. Unbeknownst to me, I was having not only a heart attack, but also a partial brain seizure. I had no clue as to where I was walking and was absorbed in my own thoughts, or more accurately, lack of them. I did not know it but I was headed the wrong way—*several miles* in the wrong direction.

When Dave began to doubt my leadership, he pointed out we were in big trouble. The late afternoon shadows from those lofty Himalayan Mountains in the distance caused the temperature to plunge. As it became darker, I experienced the inability to concentrate, so Dave took over navigation. I stumbled along, having managed to develop a rash from one of the plants along the trail, affecting me much like good old American poison oak: itchy welts and bumps all over my arms, legs, and chest, and unfortunately, around my crotch. I was truly miserable, tired, thirsty, uncomfortable, and in more medical danger than I was willing to accept.

We stopped near the edge of a cliff; a thirty foot drop below. I desperately needed to rest and catch my breath. And as I did, I heard my heart pounding inside my chest. For a few minutes, I labored to breathe and had difficulty focusing my thoughts. I started getting more light-headed, then dizzier and dizzier.

Suddenly, I lost my balance and fell off the ledge. I began bouncing and rolling quickly down the steep slope. My descent wrenched to an abrupt stop thanks to a large boulder. As I lay face-up, it felt like an elephant was sitting on my chest. Breathing was almost impossible. The pain in my chest was unbearable. I was in big trouble! Yet, I found myself totally at peace. I was in the process of dying on that rock, but with no fears or concerns. After all, I'd already visited Babaji's Cave.

Inch by inch, I surveyed my body. The arms and legs were in working order, but I could not find the energy to move any part of me. I remained in a daze, staring at the blue sky and white clouds. It was as if I could surrender my body and leave. My physical self, began ebbing away. As I looked at the clouds, I could tell I was no longer breathing, nor was I mentally attached to my physical body. I was passing into death and quietly accepting it.

I found myself staring down at my lifeless form on the rock. I endured no remorse or regrets. The experience was of total peace, great love, and serenity. Though ready to leave, there was a nagging sense of duty to family and friends, and to my 'life mission,' whatever that was. I hovered between life and death, hesitant to take the final step.

Then I had an inner-awareness of something moving near my feet. From above looking down at my lifeless form, I saw the hooded head of a large cobra! I watched as its head crossed the open space in front of me to a grassy area on one side of a path. His long body slithered slowly past me.

But I was not afraid.

In fact, I was joyous about seeing the snake. I swiftly jumped up from the rock, got to my feet, lunged forward, trying my best to grab the cobra in the middle of its body, with my bare hands. Alive with excitement, I forgot all about my heart and brain problems as I attempted to capture this wonderful snake. Even now, I wonder why in the world I insanely chased a cobra. God only knows.

Dave watched me from above on the edge of the cliff, yelling about the dangers of what I was trying to do. Ignorant, or just blissed out I paid no attention to his warnings. I was unable to catch the cobra. It slithered behind a small waterfall next to the path, fed by an ice-cold stream, reminding me of the description in Yogananda's book where he describes the place Lahiri Mahasaya bathed when he was at the cave.

All was harmonious with me physically and mentally once again.

The snake had, in some strange and mystical way, functioned as a lifesaving defibrillator. It was like someone had put a couple of those electrical paddles on my chest and had yelled "Clear!" The event had jump-started my heart and cleared my brain. I went from having no breath and pulse and a fading physical consciousness to being fully alert and alive.

Dave finally joined me on the lower trail and took charge of finding our way off the mountain by following the flowing creek to a farmer's home. We found several children there who were more than helpful in showing us the way back to our car. The driver was asleep and had not missed us at all. As we scrambled into the car, we asked him to hurry back before we got locked out of the ashram.

Our driver exhibited no urgency what-so-ever on the return trip. Yet, in the near darkness of late afternoon, we arrived at 5:29, right when the swami was preparing to lock the gate. Exhausted and chilled by the dropping temperatures, and the fact we were only wearing sweat-soaked T-shirts, I physically trembled as I spoke to the swami.

I related all we had been through to find the cave and to get back. I spoke of all my health issues, getting lost on the way back, falling off the hillside, and the encounter with the cobra—that got his attention—sparing no details.

When I finished my tale, I heard a woman's voice next to me. She uttered, "Don't you know what they say?" I turned and stared, not fully understanding what she meant. She spoke again. "It is said those who go to Babaji's Cave, and have the hardest and most difficult of journeys, have the greatest of blessings."

I processed her words.

The swami smiled as he took the keys from me. The woman turned and left the ashram, retreating to her hotel room in the village. I stood alone in the darkness of the ashram's courtyard, wondering about all that had happened that day. *What did it all really mean?*

I'd certainly had a most arduous journey to Babaji's Cave and, as I would learn several months later, I had almost lost my life. A chill traveled up my spine as I walked with Dave to the ashram's temple for the evening meditation. I had fulfilled a lifetime desire by going to the cave. I was joyous and truly alive for the first time in my life.

# The Choice

On our journey, back down from the Himalayas, we rushed to return to Delhi and came to the Ganges River. As we approached, traffic in our lane came to a near standstill. The impasse was created by people double parking their cars on each side of the asphalt paved road to get out and collect water from the sacred river. It made moving past them almost impossible.

From my front row passenger seat, as we sat waiting for our lane to move, I saw trailer in front of us loaded with farm produce being pulled by an old tractor. An older man, dirty and worn out by life, perched on top, along with many others who had hitched a ride. Although his face showed no emotion, I became fixated on it, particularly his eyes. We began staring at each other, as though there was a bond. I registered an emotional connection. For a few moments, we were as one. Such a presence of nobility in him!

In the opposite traffic lane, a few vehicles moved and several trucks pulled out from behind our line of stopped traffic and then sped past us. They were weaving back and forth into and out of both lanes as oncoming traffic would divert them. Soon, an over-crowded bus with people on the roof top sped by to pass, but there was an oncoming truck coming straight at it, so the driver veered abruptly back into our lane directly in front of us.

The bus slammed into the tractor, creating a jack-knife effect between tractor and trailer. The people riding on the tractor and the trailer were thrown off, some landing several yards away. The man whom I'd been watching flew way high into the air before landing with a loud slap on the hot asphalt road. His head took the brunt of the impact. He did not move. The bus driver instantly pulled into the wrong lane and sped off in a hasty getaway. I opened my car door and ran to the man lying there. His eyes still wide open, he did not blink or make any sounds, nor could I detect any pulse or breath. He was motionless and limp. It felt like he was all broken-up inside. I wanted to help him in some way, anyway. Training from my old lifeguard days flooded back, reminding me I might be able to get his breath going again by administering mouth-to-mouth. His chest looked caved in, so I did not want to go banging on it to get his heart going.

I gently cradled him in my arms. Lifeless. My love for the man played with my heart and mind. I wanted to do something to help him, but recalled the last time, when I'd saved a drowning victim. The teen had vomited in my mouth and down my throat when he'd come to. I'd taken my chances back then with a seventeen-year-old boy, but now I was looking at the body of an aged man who did not look healthy, even before the accident. The thought of AIDS and other major diseases prevented me from doing it. I held him with great love as I fought an inner struggle over attempting to save him versus possibly making myself ill. Then there was my wife, children, grandchildren, and all the people I had been helping in various ways. If I saved him at the cost of my own life, how would that affect all those in my life who needed me? Furthermore, there was still a mission I had to do in this lifetime and it depended on me being alive and well.

As much as I loved this man, there was a higher obligation. I silently prayed to Babaji for an answer.

The old man sighed and gasped for air. His eyes blinked and his pulse and breath were restored. I laid his head gently down on a jacket someone had donated for his comfort, then opened a bottle of water and wiped his face of all the blood and dirt. He never spoke a word, but he kept looking at my face. We were connected once again.

Just about then, I heard raucous sounds coming from the crowd around us. Four men dragged the bus driver through a jeering mob who kicked and hit the man. He had been captured down the road when his bus stopped. Now he was getting beaten and spit on by dozens of people who had earlier witnessed the accident. The poor driver looked terrified. He was bleeding from the nose and had several cuts on his face. He was getting worse by the second as the assault continued.

I gently returned the old man to his makeshift pillow and jumped up, rushing toward the small mob, pushing my way through to the driver. I tried to stand between him and those who were beating him. I didn't want him to be killed.

All at once, two strong arms wrapped around me from the back. With my arms pinned I could not move, and was dragged away. Then I heard the voice of my driver telling me to get back to the car, saying this was "community justice" and it was unwise for me to be involved, dangerous, in fact.

When I looked back at the mob, a police officer with an automatic weapon had moved into the group and freed the bus driver, leading him away in handcuffs. The bus driver looked very willing to be arrested, and went willingly with the officer. His life had been saved.

I breathed a sigh of relief.

I sat there on the front bumper of our car emotionally absorbing everything that transpired; contemplating the contrast of choices I'd made. One: not to expose myself to any possible illness with the old man. The other, to risk physical injury or worse by stepping in to protect the bus driver. It was a lot to take in, but I couldn't just stand by and watch someone get beaten to death no matter what he has done, even in this case when I had started out by helping his victim. Who knows? Perhaps I had karmic connection with one of the two men. At the time, there was no fear, only love flowing from me to those two men. I had made the right choices, but I was grateful for my protective driver who may have saved me from a beating of my own. Still, in the back of my mind, there was this little thought that perhaps it was Babaji who had been protecting me again. I smiled and made a mental note to myself not to give Babaji so much of a workload in the future.

## Welcome Home Brother

One morning, Dave and I decided to travel to a city five or six hours away. Dave took out all his road maps of India and spent half-an-hour going over the directions with our driver. He emphasized the exact route he wanted to take to get us there. He even used a yellow marker to highlight the way. Dave and I didn't want to be driving late into the night, due to the dangers of traveling on the back roads. Our driver affirmed he understood Dave's instructions. We all got into the car and headed out on our adventure.

It wasn't long before Dave noticed our driver wasn't following his selected route. He leaned forward from the back seat and asked the driver for clarification and was ignored. Dave pulled out the maps and began yelling at our driver, telling him to follow the yellow highlighted route. But Dave's complaints made no impact on our silent driver who simply drove onward in a direction that made no sense to us.

Dave's anger was all-encompassing. He reminded the driver *we* had hired him to take us where *we* wanted to go. The driver's response was to turn to me and say, "I am taking you to where *you need to go*, Mr. Bill." The reply made Dave even angrier, but I decided to sit back and see where we were being taken. This was so strange. Perhaps I was being led somewhere important. So, I relaxed and let the universe navigate while Dave continued to berate our mysterious chauffer, with no effect.

Soon after, we came up over a hill, and before us stood an 800-year-old Jain temple made entirely of marble. It was a structure of magnificence, grace, and sacredness. The parking area was alive with dozens of monkeys. A tourist bus, carrying Westerners, dominated one area. Beyond the parking lot, the temple sat framed by the glorious sunshine. Many steps lead to the temple itself. We saw some Americans and Europeans remove their shoes and ascend, then enter the temple, so we did also.

I stood inside, captivated by the carved marble columns. About 250 of them! As I leaned on my walking stick, I sensed movement at the back of the temple. A robed monk rushed across the floor of the temple and zeroed in on me. He swiftly bypassed many others in his haste to reach me, and when he did, he wrapped his arms around me in a firm embrace, then whispered into my ear, "Welcome home brother, I missed you."

When I looked into his face, he was smiling in true happiness. He took me by the hand and asked me to follow him, with Dave trailing right beside. We ended up at the altar and he requested us to kneel, to do as he did.

For about twenty minutes, Dave and I followed his instructions and chanted whatever he said. A crowd of inquisitive and perplexed tourists gathered around us in silence to observe and to listen. The chanting echoed throughout the temple, sounding powerful, even coming from the likes of Dave and me.

When we were finished, he summoned someone to come and take Dave around to see the temple and take photos.

The monk escorted me to a secreted part of the building, showing me several hidden rooms and places tourists were not allowed.

I asked him if he could pray for my grandchildren, Spencer and Daylana. His response was to reach into his robe and pull out a velvet pouch containing all kinds of precious gemstones—diamonds, rubies, and other colored stones—some of which he squeezed in his fist, then placed his fist on his forehead right between the eyebrows and began chanting.

My imagination went wild! The very air in the temple was wavy, much like the air one can see on a hot day over the surface of an asphalt road or in the desert.

When he finished chanting, we sat. He began asking me all sorts of spiritual questions. I was totally confused. I assumed he was the head of the temple and I was just an American on my own spiritual quest who had come to India with questions, not answers. Our conversation went on for almost an hour, with me talking about Kriya Yoga and other spiritual topics.

As this blessed experience concluded, he took me to a secret stairway that led to the temple's roof, accessed by pushing a moving wall, revealing the staircase. Motioning forward, he invited me to meditate. With much reverence, I asked him to find Dave so he could join me. Soon, we were both on the roof; Dave taking photos while I attempted to absorb the sacredness of the temple. It was dreamlike; something exceptional was taking place.

In due course, we came back down the stairs and found the monk again. I was never sure of his official title, but gathered he oversaw other temples as well. When I told him we had to leave, he was saddened to see me go.

He embraced me again and spoke in my ear, "This is your home. This is your temple. You are welcome to stay as long as you desire. You never have to leave. I will miss you. We will not meet again in this lifetime, but I will see you again."

I could see genuine love and sadness in his eyes over my impending departure. For some time, we gazed at one another, seeing the purity of our spirits; a soft penetrating exchange between true brothers. I did feel like I was home. At some level, a part of me recognized the place. For a moment, I hesitated. I did not want to leave. This was, after all, my temple. The pull of a past life was drawing me back. It was an odd farewell to a strange kind of day.

Dave was ready to roll, so we left the temple and went back to the car. I was still floating high over the chance encounter, even though Dave was still mad about the driver not following his directions. He went on and on chastising the driver, who was taking us to a place to eat.

Even during our meal, he continued to complain, as I sat there in my own world, still wondering how our driver knew *this* was the place I needed to be on *this* day. *Had I somehow met a real brother, or better yet, a friend from my past?* I tried explaining to Dave what had taken place, but his mind was consumed in a different way, negatively. Both Dave and I had physically gone to the very same place, yet had totally different journeys and experiences.

## Baby Owl

After almost four weeks in India, I found myself looking for the perfect gift for my daughter. Since owls serve as a sacred and spiritual symbol, as well as having always come to me as messengers, I decided to get her one. A wood or metal owl might look good in her home. I had casually looked for owl art pieces from the moment I'd arrived. But on this day, the search was more urgent. I was somehow more connected with her for some reason. I wandered from market to market viewing many fine examples of artwork depicting various owls, but none awoke my inner knowing. Then at one open-air market, I spotted the 'one.' When I picked it up to examine it, I discovered it had been carved from a single piece of wood. The artist had hollowed a stomach on the owl and carved a baby owl inside the open space—a carving within a carving—amazing work by a talented craftsman. It fascinated me, so I bought it and carried it around the city.

Later, I saw a holy man standing near the road. Wearing colorful attire, I assumed he was a guru. His intense focus was on the owl, so I walked over and asked if he'd bless the carving for me. He nodded once slowly, then took the owl carefully in his hands, stating something in Hindi. A great wave of love surrounded us, as well as the need to save an image of the man, so

I asked Dave to take a photo of the guru and me. Though I gave him an offering of money for his services, he was disinterested. I believe he accepted it so as not to offend.

In the afternoon, when I pulled-up my emails at a local internet café, one of the messages was one from my daughter Daya. She had written to announce she was expecting a baby in seven months. (My youngest grandson, Gianni, was born on June 11th 2005.) The significance of the gift I'd purchased earlier was uncanny and, I decided, a good omen about my unborn grandchild. Over the next few years, I was not surprised to witness his profound spiritual gifts.

When I arrived home, I gave Daya the gift of not just the owl, but the story of how I was inspired to find it, along with a photo of the guru who had blessed it. Daya fully understood the significance in the way all had unfolded. Once again, my daughter and I connected on another level.

A few years later, the owl fell and the mother owl broke. Daya was upset, but I pointed out the symbolism: it had totally freed the baby owl.

## Sunrise over the Ganges River

We arrived in the city of Varanasi during a major holiday. Diwali (Festival of Lights) is like a combination of the USA's Fourth of July and Christmas rolled into one week.

Dave and I walked down a main road toward the river to watch some holy men who would be performing religious rites. All around us, the streets were filled with people looking up at fireworks bursting in the air. Others were tossing firecrackers about to add to the sparks and flashes.

We came across a friendly young man who was not making the most sensible decisions. He was throwing large firecrackers; bigger and more explosive than any American cherry bombs I'd ever encountered. Compared to the other celebrators we'd seen, he was a little on the reckless side. I had a gut feeling there was going to be trouble.

He threw a huge firecracker, which bounced and rolled under a very expensive sports car parked on the street...and the driver was still inside. The force of the explosion rocked the car. It must have sounded extremely loud inside his vehicle. Milliseconds following the blast, the driver—who looked to be well over six feet tall and in great shape—jumped out, ran across the street, and grabbed this fool by the throat, lifting him about a foot off the ground. The young guy with 'poor judgement' was seriously skinny and maybe all about five-and-a-half feet tall.

I stepped forward, without thinking about the possible repercussions, following my heart, and stepped in to stop a fight. I figured my short, old, fat body was not going to impress him, so tried a soft approach and spoke calmly to the angry man. "Have some mercy on this very stupid young man." Seeing as it was a religious holiday, I appealed to his sense of the sacred as well. The driver stood there, perhaps wondering who this fat, old, bearded American was; maybe wanting me to mind my own business. Moments later—in my mind forever—he released his grip on the young man and dropped him on the sidewalk. The driver mumbled something about me being a crazy old baba then left, totally disgusted with the both of us.

Dave had been watching my not so wise actions from a safe distance. He shook his head in disbelief. The young man got up, more than a little thankful for my assistance, figuring he'd been saved from a savage beating. He chose to follow us around for a bit, but luckily, we managed to lose him in the crowd on our way to the river.

We rose early the next morning and headed out to rent a boat and a man to handle the oars. We arrived well before daybreak and negotiated a price for a sunrise on the Ganges.

Our guide maneuvered the large rowboat downstream past magnificent scenery. We saw people bathing out on the Ghats at that early hour, even an occasional yogi sitting near the water's edge.

The sun first began to make its appearance on the horizon in a painted sky of orange and rose. As we drifted lazily downstream, the dawn's early light danced off small waves. The morning haze provided shading to the sky and smoke-softened red and pink tones from the big ball of light we could not yet see, but was surely beyond the curve of the earth, under lighted all we could see. Then there it was! A fiery red-orange line on the horizon, materializing into a rising fire-ball. Awe inspiring. Despite my tingling spine, I experienced inner silence and became one with all.

In my mind's eye, I could see Yogananda himself sailing on this very same stretch of water lifetimes ago. What divine grace to float on the very same river. I had waited my whole life to perform this sacred passage.

I took out the prayer list I'd been carrying with me all over India and silently read each name on the list, asking God to bless each.

In the next moment, I struck a match and set the list on fire, holding a corner where there were no names. The flames consumed the entire list and transformed the paper to ash. I dropped it into the water and let it all float away. My prayers for those on the list were consumed by the gentle ripples of the sacred Ganges.

Still entwined in the spiritual moment, I noticed our oarsman was heading toward shore where there was a beach that held a religious statue. *How fitting he might be stopping to offer a gift or flowers or prayer.* On the contrary, what he did destroyed my sacred silence. The oarsman got out of the boat, walked up the beach, stopped near the religious statue, pulled down his pants and defecated. It totally blew my mind. Dave and I looked at each other and had to laugh. The absurdity of it all!

When he returned, without any visible shame or embarrassment, he rowed past several funeral fires where corpses were being cremated. Afterwards, they are dumped into the river; a river already loaded with floating trash.

There was a part of me that wanted to cry for the maltreatment of this historic waterway and its sacred past. Despite all the desecration, my focus was held by the spectacular orange and pink horizon and the prayers I'd offered to the Ganges at sunrise. All those on my long prayer list were somehow blessed that morning. It was my hope, at some level of consciousness, each of them would feel the cosmic ripples.

## River of Cosmic Dreams

Sunrise on the Ganges River
My heart has waited patiently
For this sacred morning.
I have come
To add my humble prayers
And my heart songs
Which flow like small rivers
Down my cheeks

Somewhere, where there are no constraints
Of time, or space, or emotions,
A divine being beholds my simple offerings
And blesses all those named
On my long prayer list

I burn and consecrate that petition
And scatter their names
Onto the holy waters.
May all those whose names
Were uttered in silent prayer
Feel the cosmic ripples
From Lord Shiva Himself
Flowing within their soul.

## Funeral Fires - Past and Present

One of the first places we visited on our journey to the Himalayan Mountains was one of the most sacred of locations along the Ganges River, a city called Haridwar. Home to a spiritual festival held every twelve years, the city can draw as many as thirty-million people over the month-long celebration; the largest crowds in the world.

The city was built as a holy site. Pilgrims from all over India and many western countries come to bathe in the river. It's a place of mingling, where sadhus, gurus, and various holy men come down from the high mountains and mingle with the large crowds of spiritual seekers.

Dave and I found ourselves as part of a smaller group of seekers and waded out into the river where Indians were submerging their entire bodies. We chose to be more conservative and splashed ourselves with the not-so-clean-water. There was some hesitation on my part due to the potential health risks. (I based my decision on all I'd heard about raw sewage being dumped into the river from villages and cities along its path.)

We spent the day exploring the area along the river and eventually found ourselves driving to an isolated beach area across from the city, on the opposite shore. At the time we arrived, several bodies were being cremated. The corpses had been placed on top of sticks, old lumber, and large branches of trees. Smoke from several fires filled the air and whirled around us when the wind changed direction. It was kind of strange to realize human bodies were being burnt up and thrown away so casually. Several crowds of people, all of them male—boys and men—were present. I saw no women participating in the services.

Some men were having all their hair shaved except for a small patch on the top of their heads. As we watched, but did not intrude, we were invited to join one of the groups. The offer came from an elderly, bearded man, a famous mathematician, who told us he'd lectured in California and other places in the USA. The old academician enlightened us on local customs, the reasons why no women attended, and the significance of husbands and some older sons having their heads shaved.

Then he told us why he was there.

He was attending the funeral for a young man of about twenty who was electrocuted at his workplace that very morning in a bizarre accident. Soon after his death, his body had been wrapped in a rug and tied to the hood of the company bus. The people involved loaded firewood on the roof of the bus, then coworkers and some of the young man's relatives were brought to the river. Although not all his relatives had been notified, the cremation was going on anyway. It struck me as rather odd someone could be alive in the morning, then just a few hours later have his body burnt to ashes.

I sat a short distance away from the smoke and fires, just observing as several bodies were consumed in flames. One group took the ashes from an earlier cremation and smashed the skull to bits.

I began to reflect on the funeral and cremation of my mother...

My mother's funeral had been like a bad dream. She had grown negative and unhappy those last few decades of her life, so a chasm of sorts had developed between us. I was too righteous and judgmental to see her as a flawed human who needed my love and approval as much as I needed hers. It was sad to think of all those years wasted when we could have enjoyed one another. One of us should have reached out and made a better effort to connect. Time is so unforgiving once it is spent and gone. I lamented my mother's sad and lonely existence. She missed out on expressing her own love, and experiencing so much more love that was available to her. As I sat on the beach, my heart shattered. I'd loved my mother more than I had ever realized before.

The saddest memory about my mother's memorial service was my inability to cry. I handled her passing as I had all the deaths I'd witnessed in Vietnam. I had erected unemotional walls around my heart. Yet, here I was in India, sitting on the sacred banks of the Ganges River, getting emotional about my mother's death. Such great love and forgiveness for her and our lost relationship! She was present, right there with me, at that moment.

There I was, fourteen years after her death, at the cremation of those that I never knew, sitting quietly, sobbing unashamed, in front of total strangers. It was as if a huge emotional dam had broken loose. Divine love and understanding poured into my heart. My mother had done the best she was ever capable of doing. More importantly, she had introduced me to meditation and encouraged my personal search for God. What greater gift could she ever have given to me in any lifetime? And she was *still* teaching me about the importance of compassion and true forgiveness.

A part of my past life was being cleansed in all those blazing infernos of death I was witnessing. I was being reborn emotionally as I released all the old hurts and wounds to the flames. In my mind's eye, I saw my mother, within the glow and smoking mist of the funeral fires, standing at the river's edge smiling at me. True peace and love enveloped me. Now I could go forward with the rest of my spiritual journey. My soul rejoiced. I loved my mother, but more importantly, my mother *truly* loved me.

## The Sun Guru and the Cobras

There was something amazing about riding on top of a massive, seemingly awkward, camel. I could have traveled all over India on one. I considered myself in heaven up there in the saddle. I am still not quite sure why I loved them because the one I rode really smelled terrible. He would even wipe his nose on my pants leg spreading mucus and slime on my clothing. But being part of a small camping group, spending several days in the desert, traveling on camels was an absolute pleasure and I savored every moment.

When Dave and I returned from camping, we ended up sitting around the hotel's pool chatting with a couple of Germans. With an enthusiastic demeanor, they told us about a place they had recently visited they thought would be of interest to us. Although they could not remember the real name of it, they called it *"The Valley of the Sacred Monkeys."* We took their general directions and set off later to discover why they thought it was so special.

It was surprisingly easy to find the place, considering we did not know its name and had only basic directions. We parked the car just outside the entrance area and began a short trek up through a narrow canyon. Each side of us, old, abandoned, or perhaps seldom-used, temples had been erected. These buildings provided a hallowed atmosphere and were steeped in history. The distance between the rock walls of the canyons was no more than a hundred yards, the perfect Indiana Jones movie set. I was right at home wearing my old hat and using my walking stick to trek through the opening.

Near the end of the valley, we climbed a series of steps leading to another set of smaller temples. There we discovered a pool of water where dozens of monkeys gathered around and begged the few visitors for food.

It was not a crowded place by Indian standards; only three or four small family groups. These spiritual seekers splashed "holy water" from the pond all over their bodies in hope to cure whatever diseases they had. I did not give much credence to the health and healing claims of the pond, but I scooped a handful of water and splashed it only on my right shoulder, which had been bothering me throughout the trip.

One of the older men there told us about a guru who had a temple dedicated to the sun god, only about a mile up this mountain. Though I wasn't keen on hiking a steep grade, Dave said it might make for some good photos, so we decided to continue up.

When we sighted the small, open-air temple, we stopped and compared notes. We didn't want to meet another "spiritual person" seeking money from gullible Americans, nor did we need to pay for a colored string, complete with blessing, to be placed on our wrists. With that in mind, we decided not to walk the last few yards to see the small shrine to the sun.

However, the guru was intently focused on us. His eyes became locked totally on me, calling out, "Come, American Babaji!" He waved for us to join him at the temple.

As we approached, I told him we were not going to give him any money for blessing us. He smiled and shook his head indicating he wanted nothing *from* us. In fact, he related, he wanted to *give* us something.

We strolled over and stood next to him inside the temple. He was shorter than me, had a white beard, and two dark, penetrating eyes. His gray, wavy hair flowed to the bottom of his neck, and his pierced ears held two large earrings. He resembled a "Moses" type; an old, spiritual looking man.

I am almost totally sure this is not what he looked like, but as I write this description, this is the only image that pops up. In fact, I would bet lots of real money he did not look anything at all like this, except for the eyes!

He then blessed us and placed a flower garland around each of our necks crafted from local flowers. He asked for nothing in return, only smiled. We thanked him, turned, and headed down the small mountain. But as I took one look back, his stare penetrated through me with a powerful energy. He had me in his sight, even when I was not looking back.

A few hundred yards down the path, I noticed an Indian man, perhaps in his forties, wearing material wrapped around his waist and a T-shirt, was following me. He began calling me "American Babaji." This made me uncomfortable. There is only *one* real Babaji. I had to remind myself, in India, the term has a common meaning of 'revered father.'

Though mesmerized by my Indiana Jones hat, he said he wanted to ask me some spiritual questions and spend some time with me. He then tried to touch my feet, something I would not entertain. Finally, I stopped and talked to him.

I took off my flower garland, given by the sun god guru, to put it over his head, but he pulled back saying he was not worthy and would not allow me to do this. So, I told him, "The God in me gives this to the God in you."

I knew he'd *have* to take it, and he did. We spoke for a time, and I taught him a simple meditation to use for his own spiritual evolution. As we parted ways, I gave him a bottle of water.

As Dave and I descended the stone steps near the pond, we saw an old woman sitting beside a large basket. She used a small branch from a tree to beat the sides of the basket in front of her. Next, we witnessed a whole bunch of hooded heads of cobras rise out of the basket. She had angered them. They hissed and moved around within the basket.

I took exception to her treatment of the snakes, so I walked over to her and stood right next to the basket filled with angry snakes, my legs touching the basket itself. I reached into her basket and pulled a cobra out by the middle of its body. The cobra wriggled and struck out in fear, but did not bite me as its strikes went wide of my head. I began giving this woman a real chewing out, telling her what she was doing was cruel and mean to these beautiful creatures.

While I was giving her a lecture, the snake was right in front of my face. I could feel its tongue licking away at my right eyelash; kind of 'butterfly kisses.' I stopped talking and stared at the snake. I could see through past its large fangs and open mouth to its throat. (Most snakes used to entertain tourists are defanged, but this one had its full set.)

Looking down inside the throat of the snake incited a deep meditation. It drew my total focus and attention, like traveling into a sacred cave. My consciousness flowed within the snake's body. We were one. I was mesmerized and in a trance-like state for several minutes, staring at the inside of this snake. But it was more than just a snake, it had become a sacred being. There was such peace and bliss radiating within me. Surely, this snake and I were dancing in some other dimension. Not of this world.

I could not help but consider how gifted I was to receive this opportunity. After all, how many times do you ever get to look down the throat of a cobra? I finally stopped moving my hands and allowed the snake to move onto my body and out of my hands. The snake circled around my neck a few times and then rested its head back in my hand.

I loved this snake so much I really did not wish to return it to the woman. At her insistence, I gave back her snake and paid her for the pleasure of its company.

I was euphoric from the experience. Dave, who'd stepped back more than twenty feet when I'd picked up the snake, expressed his bewilderment by this strange episode.

I was disappointed he had not taken any photos until the hood of the cobra was almost fully down. His excuse was they could have been 'spitting cobras', and so kept himself a safe distance away.

It was rather an odd experience, even for me. In looking back, I must wonder what made me act so fearlessly, or foolishly. The answer is most likely love; a deep love for all those snakes. And knowing the absence of fear is love, I will accept it as such.

## Paying for Blessings

I had grown tired of so-called priests, gurus, and holy men blessing us and then expecting money in return. Being an American meant they expected a larger sum of cash for their "services." Perhaps God wanted more money from westerners to be blessed than locals.

Seemingly everywhere we went there was a lively trade in blessings. On one such occasion, heading to a desert city called Pushkar, we were given some free flowers and told it was good luck to throw them on the lake within the city. Indeed, great blessings would come of the gesture. It was quite odd to have finally received a freebie; no payment for a potential blessing from God himself.

We found our lodging, parked the car, and walked into the center of the city. Everywhere we walked, carrying those 'free flowers', we were advised by strangers how to find the lake. Everyone went on about the great blessings to be received from this act.

We finally found an entrance to the lake in the city center, surrounded by buildings concealing it from public view, unless you accessed one of several openings from the street.

We passed several bathing Ghats on our way to the water, then entered and headed to the shore to toss our flowers and receive our "instant" blessings. We were met by a couple of local "priests" who said they would help us with the ceremony and would offer us blessings. I told the guy closest to me (the other one had ensnared Dave and was pitching his script). I did not want nor needed his services. I also told him I do not pay someone for God's abundant and free blessings. The "priest" assured me this was in service to me; there'd be no 'charge' for this blessing.

Once I got his full guarantee he was not 'selling' me his blessings, that it was, in fact, just a service of love from him, only then did I allow him to assist me. He took my hands and wrapped several strands of red colored string around my wrist. He said something I did not understand and instructed me to repeat his words of the prayer. I told him I would not repeat words in a language I did not understand; that being a Christian, I was not sure of his words.

He became physically rough with me, grabbing my hands and demanding I do as he said. Disgusted with the whole process, I tossed the flowers out myself. He then demanded I pay him 500 rupees, over ten US dollars, for his services. I refused. He got angry and combative with me, saying I had received the blessing from him; told me it would be bad for me not to pay him; told me this would be very harmful karma. I laughed at him, then took his "blessed red string" off my wrist. Continuing in anger, he said I owed him the money and alluded to threats of getting the police or using his friends to collect on the debt. I, of course, stood firm and laughed at him.

I noticed Dave had paid off the other guy, and now my "priest" was saying my friend had paid and I should do so as well. It got ugly. I told Dave we were going to leave. There was no way I was going to get sucked into the scam.

We left the lake with the two priests still yelling bloody murder about getting ripped off, and wandered back onto the streets of the city. I found a market stand where merchants were selling prayer beads and I bought a couple dozen as gifts for my friends. Soon after, I took all the beads to two sacred locations on the Ganges and dunked them into the water to bless them…and I didn't have to pay any priest to do it for me.

We roamed the streets and alleys for a while, just taking it all in. But the entire time, someone was watching me. When I turned, I saw a person, a holy man, perhaps a yogi guru. It was becoming a familiar occurrence; men with penetrating eyes fixed on me. This man's gaze followed me down the street. And though my memory may be totally incorrect, the image of him was being short with a white beard and long white hair. *Familiar to me, but from where?* I could sense his divine love—immense and limitless. I checked several times and, on each occasion, met his penetrating eyes. A chill ran up my spine.

His countenance suggested I should recognize him. And strangely enough, I did on some level. Yet, in my conscious mind, I couldn't pinpoint why. Although, I did recall the story Yogananda tells of his first meeting on the street with his own guru, Shri Yukteswar.

When I stopped walking, and we were physically separated by only a few yards, not a single word passing between us, my mind went blank and all thoughts ceased. Finally, I managed to turn away, and found myself smiling. Silent joy filled my every cell as I realized I'd received a special blessing from this city.

## We Travel by Train

Dave and I finally reached a point in our journey when we were ready to say goodbye to our driver, and began using public transportation. Not only did our driver make sure we got to the train station early, he arranged our tickets, provided information for the exact train to catch, and insisted on staying with us so we'd board the right one. He'd seen lots of the country with us in his car and we'd thoroughly enjoyed his company. Homesick for his wife and daughter in Delhi—he'd not seen his family since he'd started driving us five weeks earlier—we'd covered over 10,000 kilometers together.

The train station was crowded with people, some sleeping right on the dirty cement station platform, and the whole place reeked of urine. Surrounded by dogs and garbage—not a clean bench in site—we chose to stand and wait next to the tracks. We then told our driver he could leave us there; we could figure out the correct train car to get on without him. We tipped him and wished him well. It was a sad farewell, even though we'd only known him for a short time.

When our train pulled into the station, it had a long string of passenger cars attached. Regretting not having taken the former offer of help, there was a lot of confusion as to which of the cars to board. The crowd around us surged and pushed us toward the train. Meanwhile, other mobs were in the process of getting off sections of the train we wanted to board.

Men, women, and children, regardless of age, engaged in a physical battle to beat each other onto the train. I was fearful, having heard stories about several people getting stomped to death in a train station in India that very month. On high alert, my heart pumped hard. I almost got pushed down, but was lucky enough to fall against someone else's backside and avoided hitting the ground and possibly being trampled. I just focused on hanging onto my bags and staying upright.

As I was searching for train car numbers, Dave and I became separated in the moving hoard. It turned out he got on about four cars further down than I did. It wouldn't have mattered which car I *needed* to be on. I could not move in any direction but toward the car in front of me, same as everyone else; essentially pushed and manhandled into one of the cars.

The wrong car.

There was no room inside. All the seats were filled, and bags and people occupied the middle of the passageway. I had to step over and around people, seeing as no one was willing to move aside nor make any kind of room for my bag and me to pass through the car.

It was a horrible experience, taking about fifteen minutes to traverse the length of the first train car. Battered and exhausted from the effort, I stood between the former car and the next, looking down the passageway ahead to the same hellish scene. In all, I would repeat the ordeal four times, and go through the kitchen car with all the cooking and workers going about preparing meals.

What made this even more of an issue for me were some emotional flashbacks to the Vietnam War; to one day's event in the spring of 1967. We had just landed in an open field where there were 300 South Vietnamese Army troops trying to hold and maintain a defensive position. They were running around dodging explosions from falling mortar rounds. Our task was to quickly drop in with our helicopter and pick-up about eight of their wounded soldiers.

The rounds were falling inside the small opening between the trees where we set down our Huey, like a large stationary target on the ground. The longer we sat on the ground the more time there was for the enemy to zero in on our position.

But it was our allies who mobbed us. Surrounded by half the panicked troops rushing to get on the helicopter, their fear overrode common sense—we couldn't take them all; we'd come to pick up the wounded—and they had abandoned discipline and order. They fought each other to climb on board. Some of the wounded were being stepped on and re-injured, perhaps even killed.

The pilots were yelling at me to shoot them all, but I was engaged in physically fighting them to get them off. I was never going to shoot anyone. As I threw them off, as fast as I could, the pilots pulled the helicopter up about three feet, trying to get some transitional lift. We had troops hanging onto the landing skids and stuffed inside with us. The pilots turned the aircraft around and around in fast spinning circles; the tail rotor was chasing them away with what amounted to a giant buzz saw. Finally, we managed to get enough forward speed and lifted our helicopter just slightly above the tree line. We found a safe place to land and dumped those remaining cowardly men off the helicopter.

One effect of that experience was, when I returned from the Vietnam War, I totally avoided crowds. The train car was a real emotional test for me. It brought up the very same panicked feelings I'd tried so hard to overcome.

When I reached the right car with our compartment, I slid open the door and found Dave sitting with about nine oversized Indian men. I looked at the seat numbers and at our own tickets. It was clear there was only room for four passengers in that car, and those men did not have tickets for this first-class compartment. I told them they were in our seats and showed them my ticket. A couple of the men made a gesture of moving to the other side to give me room to sit down. But I was not happy about the situation and pursued it, asking if they had tickets for this compartment.

The biggest one of the group told me they needed these seats so they could all study together for a state examination. They were part of the government security forces and were preparing for a promotion exam. The man insisted they 'needed to study,' but they were willing to share the space with us.

I then decided to make them feel a little less welcome by asking, "In this country, isn't it true a guest is always to be treated as if he is God Himself?"

They looked at me bewildered, then some began to show expressions of uneasiness. I went on to explain we were guests in their country and we were not being treated with any kind of respect. I pointed out there were only four seats in the compartment, we had tickets for two, and none of *them* had a ticket to be in there with us.

Several of the men left the compartment, yet the 'leader' of the group remained with a couple of his friends. I decided three extra people were better than nine. Only a four-hour train ride, we could all endure a little over-crowding. A partial victory. I didn't want to make any more of it. We sat back and enjoyed the rest of the train ride.

I took a real deep breath and relaxed, realizing I had handled it all OK; that I had faced one of those inner-demons about mobs of people. Maybe the whole affair was just a divine set-up to toughen me, even to awaken me to possibilities of change.

## In the Shadow of Buddha

Bodhgaya is the place where Buddha became enlightened after meditating under a tree for forty-nine days. It is considered one of, if not *the* most holy place for Buddhists around the world. Dave and I were really looking forward to going to the town housing dozens of temples built and occupied by other nations. The entire place is reported to evoke sacred feelings to visitors; the kind one doesn't get from any other town or city in India.

We arrived in the early afternoon, checked into our hotel room, then embarked on a quick walking tour of the town. We wanted to look at the temples and perhaps mingle with the monks there and on the streets.

Thousands of monks clad in different colored robes walked around the town. We'd only just started our trek when I saw a large group of monks walking away from us, about 100 feet ahead. I told Dave I recognized one. He looked at me like I was nuts, saying something about how I could only see the backs of their heads, and that they were all dressed the same, so how would I recognize anyone. I insisted I did, but Dave wasn't having any of it, and so wandered off in the opposite direction. I followed him.

About an hour later, as we were walking across a cobblestone courtyard, I felt I was being watched. Stopping, I turned, setting my eyes on an orange-robed monk, accompanied by one other, staring at me, waving his hand to join him. When I got closer, I recognized him as one of the monks from The Self-Realization Fellowship, Brother Devananda. He opened his arms and we embraced.

Seven months previous, I'd heard Brother Devananda give a public talk in Sacramento. Afterwards, we'd had a long conversation and he'd stated he might possibly go to India near the end of the summer. I jokingly told him, if he went, I'd meet him there. At that time, I had no plans for any kind of trip to India. The fact we both found each other in this small, isolated town, within the huge country of India, was amazing to say the least. Dave stood nearby, taking it all in.

There was a small annoying issue between Dave and I that had brewed over the previous couple of years: his refusal to read my first book, *A Spiritual Warrior's Journey*, an autobiography including my childhood, my tour of duty in Vietnam, and stories relating to many spiritual experiences. The funny thing about it was there were four chapters in the book relating to common experiences from our trip in 2002, when we returned to Vietnam. He'd told me, after I gave him a signed free copy of the book, "If you've read one autobiography, then you've pretty much read them all. What's to be gained by reading yours?

That comment had left a thorn in my paw, so what Brother Devananda said next really made my day. "You know, Bill, I found your book to be absolutely inspiring and uplifting. I have shared it with the other monks and they all loved it, too."

Dave shook his head in disbelief. Not only had we traveled halfway around the world and run into a monk I knew, but that very monk had read my book and found it inspiring.

Our conversation was brief. Devananda and the YSS Swami who was with him were getting ready to leave town. We'd run into them when they had less than half an hour left on their trip. Fantastic timing!

We all said our goodbyes, then Dave and I walked to the centerpiece of the town, the very place where Buddha awoke from this dream of life and became enlightened.

Dave and I wandered into an area where monks were performing a spiritual practice we did not fully understand. We watched them fold their hands in prayer and prostrate their bodies forward onto the ground. After this, they'd get up again, doing it repeatedly for hours.

We wanted to better understand the practice, deciding to make a point, at some time while we were there, to ask about this and what it meant.

*My unknown Tibetan monk friend with me.*

The problem was we did not speak Tibetan, and none of the monks spoke English. As we discussed our dilemma, we noticed one of the older monks had stopped, totally focused on me. He indicated with his arms he wanted us to come to him. Given we were fifty feet away, he could not have heard our conversation, even if he understood English.

He grabbed my arms and hands, forming them into the same position the other monks had. He pushed and pulled my body through all the physical motions. Soon Dave and I were doing what the others were doing.

Not a single word was spoken as he instructed us in various spiritual exercises he showed us over the period of one hour. He'd answered all our unasked questions; ones never vocalized. It was an interesting experience to learn so much without exchanging any words. He even showed me a Yoga technique where one breathes through one's navel. (I have now come to know it as *Nabho Kriya*. A Nath Yogi technique, it is generally not something a Tibetan monk would practice.)

It was a wonderful afternoon. We thanked him graciously for his attention.

The next morning, Dave and I began wondering about this monk as we went to the Om Café at the Tibetan refugee camp; a very simple place, with wooden tables and white plastic chairs; typical of any international watering hole for spiritual adventurers.

Around us were small groups of young people from Europe and Russia, but we were the only Americans.

At *The Om Café*, each menu item (all in English) had a number, so all you had to do was write the number(s) for the server, who spoke not a word of English. She would then take the paper and pass it to the cooks. The system worked perfectly; each person got exactly what he or she ordered without having to say a word.

I ordered a bowl of cooked oats and barley with honey, and a warm piece of bread that must have weighed about a quarter of a pound; a truly stick-to-your-ribs meal. We chatted with some Germans, I made some notes in my journal, and came up with a few ideas for some new poems. And then Dave and I continued to contemplate about our newly found monk friend. We had been so touched by the experience. What a special gift.

When we left the café, and stepped out onto the courtyard, who should be waiting there to greet us, none other than 'our' monk. He greeted us and laid a white silk scarf over Dave's shoulders, then another over mine. He silently blessed us and then we went on our way. We wore those scarves all around the town and made note of seeing no one else with any. Blessings.

On our last morning in town, we wondered if we might be lucky enough to run into our old friend. As we walked around checking out the stalls, I mentioned to Dave I wanted some chai tea. This is *so* unusual coming from me. I'd not had any so far, nor did I want any, but was *compelled* to order some.

Across the large cobblestone courtyard, near the sacred monument, was a tea vendor. When I looked across, 'our' monk friend was sitting in a white plastic chair with an empty one on either side of him…as if he was expecting us. He waved for us to join him.

I ordered tea for everyone and we sat down. I noticed 'our' monk's prayer beads were all worn out; some were cracked and ready to fall off the string holding them together.

I managed to find a young man nearby who could speak Tibetan and English. I had him tell our monk friend I wanted to buy him new prayer beads of his choice. Once the monk was told this, he smiled.

After tea, we walked together to a shop. Inside, he picked out some wonderful looking prayer beads. When I began to barter, the monk stopped me, telling me through our interpreter he wanted me to have the same kind for myself; wanted to gift me the same beads, even if he did not have the money to purchase them. I bought two: one for me, one for him. He was very pleased.

Then our monk friend walked with us to the place where Buddha had sat and had become enlightened. He took us inside a small, cave-like temple.

There was a huge statue of Buddha we all prayed and bowed to. He gave us each another white scarf to place on the Buddha. We became still and quiet. Candles burned and incense caused clouds of smoke; a most holy moment.

The monk then took us to another temple where several monks and nuns were at the altar. He brushed them aside and brought us up front to pray and to take a photo. The other monks had high respect for him, though we had no idea of his status. His robes were threadbare, but extremely clean. His hair was closely cut to his scalp, but not shaven. His most outstanding feature was his eyes, otherworldly and mesmerizing.

We spent the rest of the day with him and the young interpreter who remained with us. Even though we could now communicate, we found out very little about him other than he was from Tibet. His age was a real guessing game. It could have been anywhere from fifty to seventy. But one thing was certain: his abundance of spiritual energy and power was uplifting. His presence took over any room or place he entered. He had a magnetic pull that vibrated the heart of those he met.

When we had to leave, and say good-bye, I took some photos so I could always have his face as a memory. He blessed us as we left. My heart leapt with joy then, and even now when I type these words and remember him. He was a gift to me on my personal journey to find God.

DESTINATION: INDIA 2004

# Reflections on Leaving India - 2004

*"Where Ganges, woods, Himalayan caves and men who dream God.
I am hallowed; my body touched that sod."*
— From the poem *"My India"* by Paramahansa Yogananda;
also, the last words of his life.

My first trip to India was an epic spiritual journey. A lifetime in the making, it certainly did not disappoint me, even though it wasn't what I had envisioned from the 'comfort' of the USA.

India managed to push all my emotional buttons; every possible emotion a human being could feel was felt, then tested, retested, and reviewed to draw upon for future experiences. The greatest of joys and happiness, and sadness, anger, and frustration. I was challenged physically, emotionally, and spiritually.

Physically, I almost died when I fell off the cliff near Babaji's Cave. I endangered my health by contracting a major stomach bacterium, and took risks with cobras, and encountered and challenged individuals, as well as crazy mobs of people. One night I was almost run over by an elephant in a narrow alley in Hardwar. And God only knows how we avoided being killed or injured in numerous 'possible' car crashes.

We traveled over 10,000 kilometers in India and saw so much of everything. The real disappointment was I never found that "guru on the mountain top" to whom I could ask my spiritual questions. All the gurus I found had asked *me* questions. They were more interested in my knowledge than sharing anything new. The only holy man who taught me something new was my nameless Tibetan monk friend.

But the trip was not a spiritual failure. Far from it. I discovered more of God's blessings than I could ever have imagined, and I learned a great deal about myself. It was a voyage of true self-discovery.

My dream of traveling to India had been absolutely satisfied, but my dream of "being" in India might have only just begun. I vowed if I ever returned, I wanted to spend all my time in one place, at the feet of a true Self-Realized Master. It was true, a part of me was still searching for a 'living master' experience; time with a Satguru who could answer questions from my soul.

Innocently, I did not fully understand all of this at the time I returned.

When I arrived back in the USA, I had to face and resolve some major life and death health issues, and deal with family problems, but I no longer desired nor had any burning need to go anywhere again. If I never went back to India again, I felt blessed for having walked on holy soil.

*Part Two*

# LESSONS FROM THE HEART

## The Heart

Upon my return from India, it hit me just how physically and emotionally exhausted I was. Thirty pounds lighter, my stomach was in a continual state of discomfort. Dizziness was an everyday symptom, and I experienced severe chest pain. Over all, I had been physically, mentally, and even spiritually beaten-up. I was also *changed* in every possible way.

The first medical issue I had to deal with was a cancerous tumor located directly on my face, right between the eyebrows where the spiritual eye is located. Surgery was immediate. Closed with nine stitches, it was a small wound, but it got me thinking symbolically, as if I'd had my spiritual eye cleansed and purified.

Stomach issues came next, with a thorough series of medical tests at the hospital where nothing was overlooked or left to chance. The results showed toxic bacteria, originating in the GI tract, had spread to my entire body; obviously attributable to my trek across India.

I was given a two-week course of antibiotics and, though I did as the doctor advised, my symptoms never completely went away. I became much weaker. The dizziness persisted and my chest continued to bother me, as if there was a huge weight sitting on it.

Having been home since just before Thanksgiving 2004, by the end of January 2005, my health had further deteriorated. The light-headed feelings continued and I found it extremely difficult to breathe, even to the point of once collapsing on my garage floor.

I continued to ignore the warning signs, even though I'd had the exact issue in October when I'd fallen off the cliff near Babaji's Cave. It was much the same, symptom-wise, when I'd hiked in the Andes in Peru and Bolivia a couple of years before going to India. At those times, I'd put the symptoms down to being out of shape and at high altitudes. But now I was at home, not trekking in the mountains, and I was turning a deaf ear to the symptoms screaming at me.

On January 31, as I sat on the sofa reading, my chest pains became intense and sharp. Though I was sitting, I could hardly breathe. I became light headed and felt myself leaving my body. I kept coming and going in and out of my physical self.

After about an hour, I figured it was time to go to the hospital. I told Carol I wasn't feeling well; that I would drive myself. "Don't worry," I said. "Back shortly."

I climbed into my old pick-up and drove six miles to the Hospital, then took ten minutes to find a parking spot. Mission accomplished. I got out of the truck and walked several hundred feet to the emergency room. I then joined a long line of ill and injured people waiting to get checked in. I stood patiently, waiting for my turn to talk to the admitting nurse.

Fifteen minutes later, the nurse handed me a clipboard with several official forms and a questionnaire. I took a seat and proceeded to complete the forms, answering everything, then returned to another line and waited to turn in my papers. When I finally got to see the nurse, she asked me to sit while she went over the forms. She raised her eyebrows and asked me if what I wrote down was correct. The rest went something like this:

"Well, Mr. McDonald, according to what you wrote down, you *really* believe you are having a heart attack," she stated. Her look was of disbelief mixed with annoyance.

I looked at her and said, "Yes, exactly."

The nurse paused and looked at me and said, "Well, I will be the judge of that. Let me listen to your heart."

She did not act with any urgency; assumed all my symptoms and chest pains could not be that bad due to my calm and controlled demeanor. She took a quick listen to my heart and then became very serious. She said, "Sir, you *are* having a heart attack!"

I replied, smiling, "Yes, I know. That is why I came in."

Within minutes, I was inside a treatment room, on a bed, waiting for a doctor. It had been a couple of hours since the onset of chest pains and difficult breathing issues. By now, I looked, and felt, almost normal.

The doctor proceeded to ask a lot of questions, beginning with my diet and lifestyle. I told him I did not eat meat, sugar, drink soft drinks or caffeine, nor did I add any salt to my food, and I normally avoided eating cakes, pies, candy, and chocolate. I also mentioned I'd never smoked and was into yoga meditation.

He shook his head and made the quick assumption I was probably *not* having any kind of a serious heart attack, then proceeded to tell me he would recommend that I begin taking baby aspirin every day as a preventive. He believed it would help whatever minor ailments I had. I decided he was readying himself to dismiss me; just another over-reactive, over-weight, middle-aged man.

Yet, there was more to this issue. You see, I had experienced several years of these same kinds of symptoms. I wanted a more definitive check-up to determine the nature and depth of my health concerns.

He did not agree with my self-diagnosis.

Then I related several stories about my treatment at that very same hospital in the past, where they had ignored what I had told them and even misdiagnosed me. This included my experience in the emergency room several years before. I had been having bouts where I had vomited for six to eight hours, non-stop, after eating. At the time, I had told the doctor in the ER it was my gall bladder, but the doctor had insisted I had an ulcer caused by my high-stress management job.

I was certain he was wrong, and after a further six months—suffering and following a treatment for ulcers—a test was performed based on my original suggestion, followed by immediate surgery to remove my gall bladder.

I demanded a little respect and requested he look further into my heart situation. He relented and decided to send me for tests, that week, at Mercy Hospital in Sacramento. I believed he did this simply to appease me as I'd been firm in my demands for a deeper evaluation.

I drove myself home and told Carol they did not think too much about my heart situation, but I had insisted on more tests to make sure they had not missed anything. Intuitively I could tell there was much more wrong with me, but I did not wish to worry her until I had all the facts.

On the appointment day, I had a friend drop me off at the hospital where I signed in for an angioplasty procedure. A local anesthetic was injected where an incision would be made to insert a small fiber optic camera called an arthroscope. The camera would travel from my upper thigh into my arteries to look for blockages. The doctor who performed the procedure was from India, having been in the US for three years. We chatted a little while he made the incision and inserted all the wires and cables with the tiny camera. Then we watched the monitor's screen as he added a fluid dye into the blood vessels. It was very fascinating.

Then he shouted out, "Oh my God, there really is a problem there!"

Those are not the kind of words that bring comfort to a patient lying naked and helpless on a cold metal medical table, nor are facts containing percentages of blockage. The blood flow to the back of the heart was blocked by over 90%, while the rest of the areas of the heart were about 80% obstructed. Serious and life-threatening, I was no longer an over-sensitive complainant of chest pains. The doctor continued to speak, but it all faded due to the shots and pills they had given me.

I was wheeled into a recovery room where the attending nurse read the doctor's report and explained I would be ambulanced to another hospital for open-heart surgery that very afternoon.

The nurse called Carol and began to describe all my medical problems in detail; stressing that within the hour I'd be transported to another hospital and what open-heart surgery entailed; about how they would open my chest, cut the arteries, and put me on a heart lung machine while they stopped my heart and packed me in ice. Then she went on about harvesting replacement arteries from my arms and legs. It was more information than my wife needed to hear. I was seriously upset.

Though I was still drugged and hooked up to some tubes in my arms, I told the nurse to get me the phone and unhook me from all medical equipment. I was going to call my friend and go home. There was no way I was going to allow anyone to decide about my health treatment without me having time to think it over. More importantly, I wanted to be able to make that choice when my mind was not doped on pain meds. I was finally able to call my good friend, Fred, who drove to the hospital, picked me up, and took me home so I could consider my options.

I happened to be responsible for several events that weekend. Whatever health decisions were made would need to wait until the following week. I gave a lecture at the Lutheran Church in Elk Grove that Saturday to a full audience of senior citizens. I talked about some of my personal spiritual experiences mentioned in my book, *A Spiritual Warrior's Journey*. It was one of my better presentations. I stayed to meet and greet people and to sign my books. On Sunday, I conducted a funeral service in Sacramento, and spent a few hours helping the family of the deceased. That night, I was very tired from what I'd done all weekend, but I called my heart doctor to confer on what we would do the next week for my heart situation.

The doctor told me the best option, the one he recommended, was heart bypass surgery. He told me he wanted to do it no later than Tuesday afternoon. I asked about less invasive procedures, to consider them as potential options.

He mentioned having stents inserted. But from his perspective, there was so much blockage it would take more than five. And even then, because of the locations of the blockages, five was all they would probably be able to get in there. With the stents, there were no guarantees it would help. He really wanted me to have the surgery, and get it done right away.

Surgery was a bad idea. I just did not see how cutting up my body would make things any better than stents. I told him I would come in Tuesday for stents and take my chances. I trusted my own feelings and went against his medical advice.

I had consulted my old high school friend, Karen, who is a nurse and had been acting as my unofficial family medical advisor for almost twenty-five years. She was adamant about listening to my doctors on this issue. She did not agree with my decision, but respected me enough to support my choice. This was really a difficult decision for her. She, of all people, fully understood the risks.

I was still having chest pains on Tuesday morning, but my daughter, wife, and I got into the car and headed to Sacramento. I was confident about my decision, but found no support for it among my family, friends, or anyone in the medical field. Daya and Carol were truly worried about me.

## The Operation

We registered Tuesday morning. Our son, Josh, was working up in Truckee, but available for updates. We went upstairs to the pre-surgery room and, although it was a procedure and not an operation, I'd still be drugged and there would be an incision near my groin.

I was given a handful of pills that made me goofy—quite good in a strange way—so we all joked around. I tried to be funny to help my family relax. I was more concerned about everyone else worrying about me than the procedure itself.

The doctor who came to my room—all business and zero bedside manner—was not the same one I'd dealt with before. He spent ten minutes telling my family and me why I was making the wrong choice. He told Carol he only guaranteed the stents for thirty days and expressed concern I would eventually need the full open-heart surgery, putting a damper on our little gathering.

After what felt like forever, someone wheeled me to the operating room. My daughter and wife were frantic, having heard what the doctor said. I'd made the right decision. I was betting *my* life on *my* choice.

The cold metal table had only a thin sheet over it. A male nurse put a heated blanket on me—a gift from the gods—easing my anxiety and relaxing me. I got another round of shots and pills in preparation for the doctor to make an opening in my left groin, this time. There was already a hole on the right side from the previous week.

I wondered how long it might take. It was slow-going for the surgeon, much longer than he'd indicated. I heard him complaining about the time it was taking and all the troubles he was having. He was still pushing and pulling wires inside my body when I told him the drugs had worn off; that I could feel what he was doing.

The surgeon continued working and told me not to worry, he'd be done shortly so to tough it out a few more minutes. I watched the wall clock tick off thirty more minutes before he finished. The last half hour which droned on forever, was excruciating without any pain relief.

Out in the recovery room, I wondered how many stents he'd inserted. I also hoped I'd made the right choice. A little later, I was taken to a room where Carol and Daya were waiting. I saw them for a few moments before the unfriendly surgeon came by to repeat what a horrible decision I'd made. He said the blockages were too many and in "hard to get to" locations. He'd only been able to insert five, and was unsure if the procedure would help much with the chest pain.

After he left the room, everyone was staring at me, wondering if I'd done the right thing. I certainly had the same concern. In time, I was left to rest and went right off to sleep.

When I opened my eyes, I saw my best friend Mike Domich sitting on my bed, also dressed in a hospital gown. He was dragging around several IV bottles on a rolling metal stand. I smiled at him. It was bizarre. We were in the hospital at the same time, a few rooms apart.

He'd been admitted to the emergency room a couple of days before. His spleen had burst due to a huge cancerous tumor inside it. He, too, had been directed from another hospital to this one.

It was a wonderful surprise seeing him, even under those circumstances. We sat in the dark and talked well past midnight; me about my trip to India, him about his life, some issues with his wife, his worries about his children. We got into some deep spiritual stuff and discussed the possibility we might not make it out of the year alive. I told him I had a feeling only one of us would be around come the holidays. He told me he wasn't worried. He'd had the Catholic priest come visit him in his room to pray for him. He was confident about skiing on the mountains around Lake Tahoe before the snow melted.

Soon, a nurse came by and asked us to get some rest. We'd been so into our conversation, sleep had never entered our thoughts. Nevertheless, as soon as Mike had walked down the hall, I rolled over and fell into a deep sleep. In the morning, I had severe chest pains and rang for the nurse. She came and gave me a few nitro pills to stop the pain. Not even twenty-four hours after the stents and I was dealing with pain. Maybe I *had* made the wrong choice.

The nurse came back again and told me I'd be checking out of the hospital before lunchtime. Now they were pushing me out the door! Thank goodness! I would be more comfortable at home with my family. Yet there was an urgent need to go down the hallway and see Mike again. I found his room. His mother was in there visiting with him. He was still in grand spirits. We talked for about an hour, then I had to go and take a mandatory information class for all heart patients.

Afterwards, Carol came for me. I got dressed and went back to say goodbye to Mike. I just had this awful feeling about him. I wasn't sure about my own health issues either, but I had too much to do to die at this point in my life.

The very next day, having been home less than twenty-four hours, I packed my bags and headed to the airport. I was on my way to Michigan to film and work on a documentary for PBS TV called *The Art of Healing*. It was an important project I'd been working on the previous six months, and the airline ticket had already been purchased for me a month before. All the production people were ready to roll. I felt an obligation to be there regardless of how little energy I had. The film was our attempt to build public support and awareness for the treatment of PTSD veterans. I had worked on a new treatment program as well, with the VA. One day out of hospital, exhausted from the procedure, I willed myself to get on the plane.

I managed to put in twelve hours of work on the production the first day there; some narration and some on-camera work. I made my body and mind function with great deception. We completed filming and prepped everything for editing, then I packed up and was taken to the airport, only to discover we were snowed in. A storm had closed in on the Great Lakes area. I spent half the day waiting at Kalamazoo Airport before getting a seat on another flight to Detroit, then I was fortunate to board an airplane to Minnesota. I got stuck *there* when we landed. But as luck would have it, the airline decided to put me up in a Five Star Hotel and gave me certificates for meals. I had a great room where I could rest. Something I really needed! If it had not been for the accommodations, I believe I'd have been in medical trouble; that's how physically exhausted I was.

The day after I arrived home, I saw the doctor. He went over a basic physical rehabilitation program to get me functioning back in the world again. He was going on about making sure I got plenty of rest and sleep, and gradually and slowly working a little activity back into my life over the coming six weeks. I then told him about my trip across the country to work on a PBS TV project and added my tale of getting snowed in at three different airports; i.e. taking the last two days to get back to California. He looked at me, shook his head, and tossed my personal rehab plan in the trash.

The big, brave, tough-guy persona was just for public show, as I really was *not* feeling well, even after the procedure was done. My heart doctor gave me all kinds of pills to take, as did my regular physician, the side effects of which caused additional problems. The good news was I was still alive. The bad news was, at times, the doctors did not fully understand how to heal me without making me sicker in the process. Determined, I continued to do what they recommended and they, in turn, kept increasing my doses of drugs. At this point, I still trusted them and was listening to their advice.

## My Continued Health Issues

Following the cardiac procedures, my health continued to deteriorate. One evening, I rose to walk down the hall and found the entire room spinning out of control. I reached out to brace myself against the walls and collapsed on the floor. Unable to get up, I'd briefly blacked out. Coming to, I was not able to cognitively evaluate my own physical state and called out for Carol. She found me crumpled on the floor, disoriented, and called the paramedics.

A short time later, I was in the back of an ambulance with an IV in my arm. They kept me in the hospital all evening and into the early morning hours. Unsure as to what had caused it all, recommendations were to return to see my heart doctor, but also a neurosurgeon since the issues appeared to be brain related.

One week later, while watching television and dealing with chest pain, I began to feel as if I was drifting out of my body. I thought my heart stopped beating. I sat looking at the picture of Paramahansa Yogananda on the wall in my family room, thinking maybe it was my time to go. But at the same time, I pleaded for more time. There were things I needed to do for my grandchildren and others. I had a vague sensation of some mission and purpose.

I took three nitro pills for the chest pain, as instructed by my heart doctor, yet it continued. I had Carol drive me to the ER where they gave me seven more doses of nitro, plus a nitro patch. Totally ineffective, so the doctor injected a large dose of morphine. That did it, thank God.

This went on for more than the next year-and-a-half. My heart was just one of those issues. Later, it was the brain. The doctors had me taking so many pharmaceuticals, the side effects were killing me. I mean that, in retrospect, literally.

At times, when I could not fathom how to move through it all, I would call my old high school buddy, Bob Amick, to discuss what I was going through. He'd been there, done that, and truly put my mind at ease. A true friend, he was there when I needed someone to help me deal with these issues.

In the meantime, every muscle in my entire body ached, especially huge pains in my joints, causing me to lose more energy each day. Other problems also arose, festered, and persisted: my urine turned dark brown, my memory failed, concentrating on anything was shot, and all I wanted to do was sleep. Most days I slept fifteen to eighteen hours, and then still needed to take a two-hour nap in the afternoon.

Physically, I could barely drag myself off the sofa. If seated on the carpet, I could not get up without herculean effort. I would have to roll over onto my stomach, then grab a chair or a coffee table to pull myself upright. I suspected all the drugs I was taking were doing me much more harm than good. When I complained to my regular doctor, she would increase the dosage. The same thing happened with my heart doctor. My neurosurgeon wanted me to take some additional medicine for my brain seizures. I refused. I couldn't handle all the side effects from the *current* drugs, much less more.

One morning, I said no more. I'd had enough. I was a mess. I couldn't function physically, let alone think or talk. I drove myself to the Emergency Room where, by now, they should have known me on a first name basis.

I decided to see a new doctor to consider what was going on, since all my complaints to my other doctors were being ignored. They had been treating me as a whiner and a wimp, discounting all my pain and symptoms. My request for another doctor to look at my situation with a new pair of eyes paid off.

The female doctor pulled up my computer medical files and looked at all the drugs and doses I had been getting from all the specialists, then stated flatly this *was* the problem. She told me I was having major side effects from taking two of those drugs together. These drugs were in effect killing and destroying my muscles, joints, liver, and kidneys. She told me to stop taking those two drugs and ordered a series of blood tests to determine the extent of the damage.

When I arrived home, I went into my medicine cabinet, pulled out all the prescription drugs I was taking, and emptied them into the trash; wiped out my entire warehouse of drugs. I decided then and there I could not trust any of them; not necessarily a great medical decision, but I was determined to take control. I figured I knew my own body better than the doctors did, related to what was working and what was not.

I went cold turkey, slam-dunking my body hard for the first three months. My condition regressed at first, but I stayed the course and committed to following my own medical and healing program. Not confident in what I would do—the best advice from my doctors had almost killed me—I figured I could do no worse.

(Note: Please do not even think of following my personal example. Work with your physician before doing something as dangerous and radical as what I did. It may not have been so wise on my part.)

When I went for my follow-up appointments, the doctors were visibly upset with what I'd done. Yet, I vowed to improve, was determined to convince them I could get healthier on my own. If I did not, I would, at that time, consider their future recommendations.

I was out to prove to them and to myself, intuitively, I could manage my own health better.

Of course, throughout this whole health issue, all my friends gave me huge amounts of their loving expert advice. Everyone wanted to help me over the course of my illnesses. Each had at least one suggestion to offer; a 'sure-fire' solution. I got advice on using herbs, spices, oils, massage, colored lights, drinking lots of water, positive thinking techniques, yoga mantras, vitamins, fruit juices, a daily dose of sunshine, new age devices, and pills of every sort. I received over a hundred different recommended courses of action. Several people even said their solution had come to mind to pass on to me, so it could not be just an accident. It might be God Himself letting me know what to do through them.

I did not see anything but good friends wanting to help me, even if they were clueless about the medical world or even what my problem was. They all became "experts" and could give me cases where treatments worked, or they'd read it in a book, or had seen the solution on the internet. They all trusted their words of wisdom. Finally, I put my foot down and told everyone I had my own program and was not looking for any more medical advice. Thanks, but no thanks.

It was during this period of healing I decided to change my diet for a while from a simple vegetarian one, where I included eggs and cheese, to a vegan one. I stopped eating eggs and all dairy. I gave up eating pasta and pizza, and cut back on all processed foods. I wanted to clean out my system and lose some weight. The diet alone allowed me to lose over forty pounds, without increasing my physical workouts. The result: all my blood numbers came in at safer levels and I began to feel *much* better after several months. My blood pressure stabilized to a consistent 109/65, and my blood sugar levels improved as well.

I was also getting weekly treatments from a female, Korean doctor, who gave me acupuncture treatments for my brain issues and stomach problems, as well as for my heart circulation. I had taken complete control over my medical care and, for me, it worked.

## Wine and Prayers

One night, I woke up in the early hours of the morning, wide-eyed and fully alert, compelled to check my email. Not a normal occurrence, but the urge was so strong I left my warm, comfortable bed, went into the computer room, and turned it on.

There were about a hundred messages mixed in with junk email, so I scanned the list, looking for something to catch my attention. One, sent within the last few minutes, I did not recognize. The subject line appeared to be an inquiry about my book, a letter from a young woman, the daughter of an acquaintance from the meditation center in Sacramento. She began by telling me how she'd been up late one night and accidentally spilled a glass of wine all over her mother's copy of my book, *A Spiritual Warrior's Journey*. Very upset, she wanted to know if she could buy another signed copy. A part of her message shot right through me. *What was she doing up so late drinking wine?*

From the brief details she continued to provide, I gathered she was an unemployed single mother with a preschool son. My senses told me she was also an alcoholic, or at least had a problem with her drinking. My soul ached for her. I paused, sent her a silent prayer, as well as some of my love, and then read her simple but profound question. "Do you believe God answers our prayers?"

I began typing, clueless of what to say. I just let it flow out of me as my fingers hit the keys on the computer keyboard; meaning one finger on each hand moving as quickly as possible.

I wrote something that, when I read it back before sending it, sounded a little casual and superficial. "Sometimes God answers our prayers through a movie we are watching on TV."

I really did not know how she would receive it, but I do not second-guess myself. I trusted it might mean something to her; that perhaps it would relate to the answer she sought.

The next day, I received a reply from her saying, when she got my message, she'd checked the time I'd sent it. She had been, at that very moment, watching a movie on TV called *Bruce Almighty*. She went on to say she had received her answer from the movie's dialogue.

She went on to describe how she'd received my message; that this was how to get an answer to her prayers, a sure sign. She said she was amazed by my answer and wanted to talk more about spiritual matters with me.

We exchanged some more emails about the spiritual aspects of her life, as well as "real world" problems. Then, in one of her emails, she claimed I'd been in her bedroom one night giving her spiritual advice; that my image had comforted her.

This is not the first time I've had someone say this to me. Every time I hear the claim, I never really know what to say. Sometimes I use silence, to not encourage anyone to 'have visions.' I certainly have no memory of visiting any of these people, yet I've gotten this same kind of story from a Catholic priest, Father Jack. Such comments always make me wonder about the imagination and sanity of the reporters, because there is no way I can confirm their experiences.

In due course, the "emailer who'd spilled the wine" went with her mother and me to learn yoga meditation techniques through *The Self-Realization Fellowship* in Sacramento. I continue to keep her in my daily prayers. I trust she will find her path and soar heavenward, as one special angel and soul, and add light to this world before she leaves it.

## Chicago Radio Show Host

One morning I went to my computer and decided to dig through some old emails I'd saved. There were many, but I was struck by one from Holly Campbell, a woman in Chicago, who'd sent me a message about eighteen months earlier.

In the message, she'd asked to interview me on her radio show. I was not sure why it never happened, but I had to contact her right away. I sent her an email and then left to take one of my grandchildren out for a walk. While I was out, she called and left a message for me; one clearly indicating she'd not seen that morning's emails.

In Holly's message, she said something like this, "Bill, you may not remember me, but I contacted you about eighteen months ago to be on my radio show. Well, I am asking you again if you would like to do it now." Then she went on with further information.

I called her back and asked her to check the email I'd sent, including the time. I wanted her to see we were 'tuned-in' to each other. I was excited and thankful for the opportunity to be on her program. She wanted me to talk about some of the stories in my book, *A Spiritual Warrior's Journey;* particularly one she loved called "Amazing Grace." We set up the interview.

She had wanted to play the song "Amazing Grace" right after I told my story, as a closing. Though she didn't have the music available before the interview, one was found and she did what she intended.

She called me back afterwards to confirm it had been played, then she said she was in a hurry, just getting in her car, and began to close our conversation. Without knowing why, I kept talking, even though she reminded me a few times she really had to go. Finally, when it was the right time to end the conversation, I abruptly said good-bye. She muttered something about me having delayed her about five minutes.

She called me back fifteen minutes later to tell me she'd missed a huge multi-car pileup on the freeway. If she had left when she'd planned, she might have been right there in the thick of it. She truly believed my long phone conversation, one she'd tried to hurry up, might have been the difference between being alive and safe, or injured, or worse, in an accident.

The next time I went on her show was about a month later. In between, we became good friends, chatting on the phone and exchanging emails regularly.

On her next show, I asked her to open the program for people to call in and ask questions. Before we went on the air, I mentioned to her another crazy person said I'd come to offer advice in their dreams or a vision. In this case, I was referring to the young woman who had said I was right there in her bedroom talking to her.

When I laughed about this situation, she stopped me. She told me there was nothing crazy about such a claim at all. In fact, she said I'd visited her just that week, and claimed to have seen me in a dream/vision as well. I was dumbfounded.

I muttered I did not understand how everyone could be saying this to me. I had no memories of ever doing anything in my sleep. In fact, on the night involved I was in one of my death-like sleeps, unconscious to the world. I had no clue why all these people, over many decades, claimed I'd been present. Most were total strangers who'd not known me before having these experiences.

When we went on the air, I gave a talk about some spiritual experiences and the importance of love and forgiveness. Then I took a phone call on the air. It was from a woman who sounded about my own age. I began to relay some information about her relationship with her daughter. Within the conversation, I spoke of lots of personal issues I had no prior knowledge of. When she became very quiet, I gathered I'd opened some old wounds. The woman, named Jean, I would later learn, was the radio show host's own mother.

When the radio show ended, I received a call from the host who was upset. Her mother had blamed her for setting up the call with me; insinuated I'd been supplied various pieces of information to use. But she hadn't, nor did I.

I was emotionally distraught; wondered if I had done the compassionate thing by telling her all I had on the phone. I normally never filter any of my words, they just roll out. This way, I do not allow my mind to judge them or even create them. It may sound strange, but I do not think before I speak.

I asked Holly to give me her mother's phone number so I could personally call her. When I did, her mother went from very defensive and cold to loving and receptive of my words. We spoke for over an hour. I let her know her daughter had not set up anything, nor did I have any prior information about the troubles they were having. All that came out on the radio show was what flowed through me. It was all meant to be healing for them both.

Over the next few months, we spoke a lot. In one conversation I bluntly, but confidently, stated she was being protected and in God's hands. Twenty-four hours later, she sent an email saying how wrong I was; a massive windstorm had blown through their section of Chicago. A huge tree had fallen between her home and her car missing everything.

I laughed and sent her a reply, asking her what part of being protected did she not see or understand: the tree missing the house, or the tree missing her car? I got an instant email back with a different response; she saw the light and recognized her sacred protection.

In one of my further conversations with Holly, I asked how the health of her son was; that I was concerned. She informed me he'd had a skateboard accident and injured himself. I'd had a nagging feeling he was hurt.

As for Holly's mother, we have become best friends. Years later, she even came to visit me, to hear me introduce Gurunath in Los Angeles. In fact, she is truly one of the more spiritual souls I know. And her grandson, who happens to have the same birth date as me—March 16th—has the potential energy of an angel. It is truly a most wonderful family.

## Do You Have An Owl?

On Mother's Day 2006, I received a phone call I will never forget. It was from a New York Times Best Selling Author, whom I had not met before, named Gayle Lynds. She and I began a conversation around noon; one we both assumed would be brief. That telephone call lasted over five hours and heralded the beginning of a wonderful lifetime friendship.

Gayle had been emotionally moved to call me after reading my autobiography, *A Spiritual Warrior's Journey*. Once she'd introduced herself, she proceeded to go on about how my life story had inspired her; that she'd laughed and cried. A serious tone came into her voice when she told me the messages in the book had re-awakened something spiritual in her own being. She said she'd like to help me get my book to a traditional publishing house, and offered to rewrite and promote the book. What a gesture of valuable influence and assistance!

I listened, and then totally interrupted her flow of conversation by asking her what, at that time, she may have felt was a rather odd and perhaps a little crazy question. "Do you have an owl at the entrance or back door of your house; perhaps a work of art of some kind?"

"No," she replied.

The conversation continued without even inquiring why I'd asked the question. But I interrupted her again a few minutes later. "Do you have a metal sculptured owl by one of the doors of your house?"

A moment of silence followed, then with a hint of aggravation in her voice she replied with a strong "No."

Before she could get back on her train of thought and resume talking, I asked again, quite firmly, adding some specific details to the original question. "Do you have a metal sculpture of an owl by the back-sliding glass door of your house?"

It was odd, my asking questions of her about her house, never having been there, and never having spoken to her before. Yet, I insisted on asking a rather stupid question, which had no logical place in the conversation. Not only that, I was interrupting someone who had taken time out of her own personal and busy schedule to call me and offer me help. She wanted to help me market my book.

Basically, I was badgering a famous, New York Times Best Selling Author with an insane line of questioning about an owl sculpture. If I had been thinking about my delivery and responses it might have been different, but I naturally let my words flow and do not censor them. My approach in speaking is to let the words come through intuitively instead of arranging and analyzing my thoughts in logical patterns. Yet again, I am saying I do not think before I speak. This often produces some interesting results; as much a surprise to me as they are to the person I am talking to. In any case, I took a huge risk in giving this wonderful woman my impression of a total nut case.

My detailed question about the owl prompted silence. Then I heard an excited scream. Gayle told me there *was* an old metal sculpture of an owl hanging outside her back-sliding glass door.

She was amazed I could know such information. Even she had totally forgotten about it. There was a personal story behind her having that owl, but along with the story, the owl had simply faded into the details of a busy life.

She'd read my book and understood interesting things happened in my life that could only be called supernatural, and now she was experiencing what she had been willing to believe from those written accounts.

The tone of conversation changed. She asked me if I could interpret dreams. I asked her to recount her dream and we would see what it meant. She went on to describe a recurring dream where three whirling dervishes visited her. They would dance around her room and reach out to her. She was perplexed. Did it mean anything?

It was not about dancing itself, but about engaging in the dance of life. The message was for her to fully engage in the dance of life again.

She had recently become a widow and was dealing with being alone, and with many other issues. I picked up a copy of one of my poetry books and read her a poem on dancing, as it related to this very theme. My words failed to give me the fullest meaning of what I wanted to say about the dream experience, so I suggested we set this aside and let the universe to provide the answers, then let all thoughts on the dance fade into the background of my mind.

So, we continued to converse about her personal life and I began to reveal some things I felt she needed to hear. The whole time I was speaking, the image of an opening rosebud kept coming to mind. Metaphorically, her life was very much like the rosebud I saw around her. Living her life to the fullest would allow it to blossom and become fragrant, a gift to the world, so others could smell the spirituality of her soul.

She listened without interruption, then whispered she could smell roses everywhere around her home. Even *I* was surprised by such a blatant connectivity. She later told me the scent lingered for three days; truly a powerful message for both of us.

When we'd finished our conversation, I scrolled through my email and found an odd message from a friend who is a former Army MP and Vietnam veteran; not the kind of person who would send me anything mushy or sentimental. Yet his message contained the lyrics to a country-western song he thought I'd appreciate.

The words of the song spoke about getting back on the dance floor of life and mirrored my attempted explanation to Gayle. The time did not go unnoticed. It was sent exactly when I'd turned it over to the universe for a better explanation. I cut and pasted the lyrics from the song and forwarded them on to her in an email.

That long telephone conversation did not end because we had nothing left to say. In fact, it was an interesting and strange way to begin a new relationship. But was it new? A part of me could see clearly this was a reawakening of an old friendship. There is no doubt in my mind Gayle and I have been friends and comrades over many lifetimes; spiritual warriors from way back. She truly is a blessed spiritual soul. I was glad to have rediscovered her love and friendship in this lifetime.

## My Friend Mike

Mike Domich and I became great friends from the first time we met each other in Sacramento. We belonged to the SRF Meditation Center there, and had many wonderful experiences together, including several long stays at the SRF's Hidden Valley Men's Ashram near San Diego. We used to go there to work and meditate in the peaceful surroundings. Mike had helped build several of the buildings at Hidden Valley.

We'd had many personal talks about our lives, was privy to each other's secrets; a valued and trusted relationship. When his father died, I gave a eulogy and made sure I was present for Mike and his family. His personal life was filled with all sorts of odd drama and old karma. He suffered from events and relationships that did not appear related to his present actions, or deeds from this current lifetime. His marriages and relationships with women were one of those areas of his life where he came out on the short-end time after time. He did not complain or get angry, but always approached situations with compassion and forgiveness; a part of him that resonated well with me. Never thinking himself a victim, he simply faced what needed to be done and dealt with it.

Mike was truly an all-around Renaissance man; could do almost anything he put his mind to. A master chef, he'd once owned a successful restaurant. His talents included being a contractor, plumber, electrician, carpenter, brick layer, roofer, draftsman, designer, mechanic, pilot of twin-engine airplanes, composer of music, player of several instruments, artist, writer, actor, singer, and public speaker. But the most important thing about Mike, he was completely loyal to his friends, his guru, and his family. A man of his word, he could always be counted on to get things done, especially when no one else was available.

One painful memory I have is the time he jumped off a one-story roof onto the ground instead of using a ladder. The force shattered dozens of small bones in each foot. When I visited him in the hospital, I was uneasy looking at all the tubes used in the process of draining blood to mend him. It took him ages to walk again, with the aid of a cane. But after a while, it was like nothing had ever happened to his feet. He was strong willed, a survivor. That was why I wasn't too worried when he told me he was fighting cancer.

You recall, in the former chapter, he'd visited, sat on my hospital bed after my heart procedures, giving me comfort, while wheeling around an IV pole with bags and lines attached to him. He was so optimistic and positive about his chances to regain his full health.

Well, I'd had an inner sense one of us was not going to make it to the end of the year. I even had doubts about *my own* situation! The heart procedure had not fixed my problem and there were many other health issues, including brain seizures.

I had this old vision from my childhood days when I was in the San Jose County Hospital. I was confined to a bed for almost a full year of my young life. While lying there every day without TV, radio, toys, books, or even visitors, I had lots of time for my mind to internalize and dream. In that state, I saw the future, and all came true, but none revealed anything beyond age fifty-nine. Everything from that point forward was a blank.

I'd seen a moving image of two numbers, twenty-nine and fifty-nine, so I always wondered if I was going to die at either of those ages. When I turned thirty, I felt like I had avoided a fatal number. When I had the heart procedures, I was forty-three days shy of my fifty-ninth birthday.

To make matters worse, I learned my childhood friend, Paul O'Bryan, had just passed away. We'd been born in the same hospital in San Francisco, on the same day, almost the same hour. His age at passing did not go unnoticed by a fearful me.

Mike and I went over our concerns about dying. He was positive he and I would be okay.

When I went to see my heart doctor for a check-up, I complained to him about how unfair it was for someone like me to have such huge blockages to the heart. After all, I told him, I do not eat meat, use any sugar or salt, and do not drink alcohol, coffee, tea, milk, or soda. I never smoked, did not do drugs of any kind, and I even avoided chocolate and candy. My life was centered on a healthy diet and lifestyle. I continued whining about the injustice, and he did listen for a bit, then said something profound, "If you had not taken all those early health precautions, and had not lead the pure and clean lifestyle you chose, I have no doubt you would have been dead at twenty-nine, given your genetic make-up. And, you would not be sitting here right now, at almost fifty-nine, complaining to me!"

The doctor's words stunned me. Twenty-nine and fifty-nine. He was trying to get me past the age of fifty-nine and helping me regain my health. Regardless, neither he nor my other doctors were optimistic. All they recommended was surgery and drugs.

Although my health continued to tank, my old friend, Mike, called me on his cell from the ski slopes of Lake Tahoe, reporting he felt wonderful and energized. I was happy for him. He acted determined to kill off the cancer, and it looked like he was succeeding. I, on the other hand, was weaker and still ill.

One evening, after officiating a wedding ceremony in Sacramento, not too far from Mike's house, I called to check on him. It'd been a couple of weeks since we'd last spoken. He told me he thought he had the flu; that he was losing energy. He told me if he didn't feel better by the following week he'd call his doctor. He invited me to come over to visit, but I declined as I was tired myself and wanted to go home. I came to regret not going to see him that night. His next call to me came from his hospital bed. The cancer would be fatal, he said. He'd not leave the hospital alive.

I was hoping his words were an over-reaction. I rushed to his bedside and found him lying there, pale and thin. The high-energy level I was so used to seeing in him was gone. I wondered how he could have been doing so great, and then, BANG, the cancer could return with such vengeance.

He was surrounded by his family, even his ex-wives showed up. There was mutual forgiveness; a gift to witness all the love in the room. I spoke to him, but he kept drifting in and out of sleep. My heart ached to watch him fade. I returned the next day, expecting it would not be long. When I arrived the next morning, his family was present, surrounding his body.

The odd and sad part for me was I did not realize he was dead. I walked into the room and talked to him for perhaps twenty minutes, thinking he was listening to me. Then it finally dawned on me he was no longer alive. I was embarrassed it took me so long to see it, but no one noticed. I assumed they thought I was talking to Mike's spirit. I stayed and offered consolation to the family.

The following day, I had an interview with *Senior Magazine* for a featured story on my life. I asked the reporter, Nan, to meet me at a local coffee house I'd never been to. I arrived a half-hour early and found a spot on a sofa in the back corner of the café. When I looked up, I saw Mike's brother-in-law buying coffee, so I called him over for a chat.

Neither of us had ever been there before, yet here we were, chatting away about Mike and how ironic it was we'd both decided to come to the same place at the same time.

I recalled the last time I saw Mike, in Elk Grove, when I went to the local sandwich shop to buy lunch. It had been a random choice for me, but Mike had been there getting food for his workers to take back to the construction site, someplace out of town. Mike and I had marveled at the chance meeting. Now we were just down the street from the very same shop talking about him.

I gave an extended eulogy for Mike at our meditation center; the crowd was massive, so many people in his life. I could almost feel Mike's presence there. It was a sad ending to a long friendship. Unfortunately, my prediction of only one of us making it to the end of the year alive had been correct. I had months to go to my sixtieth birthday, and was more than a little concerned about my own future.

## Who Was That Stranger?

I met a Vietnam Veteran online to whom I took an instant liking. A darn good singer, song writer, and musician, he'd experienced some heavy combat during his tour of duty. His tale of survival was harrowing. I admired the man's courage and his ability to deal with life. He did suffer from Post-Traumatic Stress Disorder (PTSD), and worked hard on dealing with the past. We ended up becoming good friends. He went on graciously to offer his music for a DVD I was making. The project, about four veterans returning to Vietnam, was one I wanted to finish, but due to my health issues, had taken a back seat. Another unfinished creative dream.

I invited him to come to my home and take part in a lecture on yoga; a grand opportunity to learn several techniques of meditation. The talk was held in Sacramento, and afterwards, we all went out to eat, joining a group from my meditation center. I began having some major chest pains at the dinner table, so we left early. It was just another typical day for me, but my new friend was obviously worried. Yep, my recovery was going to take much longer than I thought.

A few months later he invited me to come down to his house in Southern California to work on editing the DVD with his music. I spent the weekend at his home, but the DVD wasn't the only reason for my visit. Something else was pulling me to be there with him. Of course, if we made progress on the movie, great, but I just intuitively knew this was not the reason I had to be there.

That night I slept in his extra bedroom, in a king-sized bed, facing an open sliding glass door to the backyard, letting in some of the cooler, ocean air. I was dead tired and dropped off into one of my coma-like sleeps where I do not even dream. I awoke abruptly at three in the morning and sat straight up. On the other side of the sliding glass door, that lead to the backyard, I could make out a silhouette of a man, who was staring at me. Though it was rather odd, I was not afraid or even concerned. His face and body were shadowed and did not allow me to determine his physical features, other than he was about my height and weight.

The man began to walk towards the bed (He seemed to just walk through the glass door) where I was lying. He briefly stopped, just short of the bed. Subconsciously, I went to identifying him as my friend; maybe he'd had a spat with his wife and had been kicked out of the bedroom. The *"shadow man"* certainly had an air of benevolence about him. I could not think of any other logical explanation for someone coming into the room. As he reached the edge of the bed, I rolled back the blanket and threw a pillow on the other side of me so he could lie down. He sat down and swung his body into bed. I had moved way over to my side and turned my back toward him.

Then the mattress moved. He was getting closer to my back. All at once, there was a powerful bolt of energy, like something moved directly into my spine. Chills and tingling traveled up and down my backbone. I turned over and discovered the man had vanished. I was confused, but for some reason it felt natural; that perhaps he'd moved right into my spine. I rolled back over and went directly to sleep. Odd, but that's the way my mind worked at night. Who and what this guy was never occurred to me again until the next morning.

As we sat having breakfast, I relayed the dream to my friend. It must have really sounded crazy to him, but for whatever reasons, he listened with an open mind. Then I got into a discussion with him about his relationship with his family and his father. I gave him what I considered good advice at the time, and he was open to it.

Later in the morning, we went to the Self-Realization Fellowship Temple at Lake Shrine in Pacific Palisades. To our amazement, the lecturing monk hit on every single point I'd made earlier; some of the wording almost identical to those I'd used. It was like the universe had wanted my friend to hear the advice twice. It was something he needed to heed or seriously consider.

On my drive back to Northern California, I mulled over what had happened. I kept thinking how "the figure" had merged into my spine. Then it struck me! After all these years of having been told by total strangers I visited them in their dreams or visions in the night—apparently giving them life advice, inspiring, even preventing suicide—perhaps I had been visiting them. Those stories had always been flawed for me, having had no memory of leaving and visiting them. The best I'd figured was those were the nights I'd had one of those death-like sleeps.

Is it possible "my visits" were related to this stranger who melted back into my spine? The logical answer was beyond my own belief system or understanding. Perhaps I was leaving my body—not in an astral out-of-body experience, like I have experienced through meditation—but leaving and returning in a body both separate and a part of me. Was I, in fact, manifesting another body to go off into the darkness of night to minister and visit others? The possibility blew my mind, but it was the only logical answer; one that creates many more questions.

## Kidney Disease and Surrender

As a small child, I was hospitalized for almost a full year with a rare form of kidney disease. It took many years of treatments and medical appointments to get me healthy. I believe a change in diet and lifestyle early on in life helped.

Almost six decades later, I awoke one morning to some of those old symptoms, causing me to revisit those childhood memories, jolting me to action. My stomach was full and bloated, my back hurt, and my urine was dark brown. I was losing my life energy. I felt like I was dying.

I went to see my acupuncturist in Sacramento who examined me, poking and prodding. It hurt like mad. She advised me to see my doctor. There were kidney issues.

I returned home in so much discomfort, I went right back out to the hospital. I wanted to see if it was my kidneys, as both the acupuncturist and I had thought.

The hospital staff drew blood for some tests and sent me home. Later, I received an email message to check my results online; no comments, only a bunch of numbers that did not so look good. One number represented a measurement of blood filtration rate. According to their chart, a healthy number should read greater than sixty on the scale. My test a couple of months prior was above sixty and considered normal, but today's results showed twenty-six.

I went to the Kidney Foundation web page and studied their information on Glomerular Filtration Rate (GFR). Estimated Glomerular Filtration Rate or (eGFR) is a number resulting from a blood test for creatinine. Basically, it tells how well your kidneys are working. Dropping below fifty-nine indicated kidney disease. I scanned the chart and saw a twenty-six put me in stage four kidney disease.

I was stunned. You see, when one reaches fifteen, it means permanent rotation for dialysis. The immediate question that occurred to me was how fast my number was dropping. Two months previous, I'd been over sixty, now it was critical. Had it dropped over the two months or bottomed over a week or even a few days? Obviously, I required medical intervention.

Imminent death hung over me as I disclosed my test results and internet findings to Carol. After our discussion, I went back to research more information on what this might mean to me. I did the math: I'd gone down thirty-four points in two months or less, just nine more points and I'd be in huge trouble.

I read articles about people dealing with the three-day-a-week ritual of hooking up to a dialysis machine. On average, patients spent four- to eight hours sitting there with lines going in and out of their bodies cleaning and filtering their blood. It was a life-saving procedure, but a massive impact on one's social life. Dialysis patients could not travel far from home, needing to be hooked up almost every other day.

There were all kinds of stories on the internet about people not electing to go through this ordeal; choosing to die rather than live on a machine. It was a larger number of people than I would have guessed, with accounts of serious depression suffered by some of those on regular dialysis, as well as a great physical toll on the body.

I sat fixated on my monitor's screen. Reading all the negative accounts only added more serious weight to the issue. To go on the machines meant my traveling days were over—no Nepal or Tibet, no cross-country lectures, book signings or out-of-town events. I'd be forever leashed to a machine. And at what costs emotionally, physically and spiritually?

I read that once a GFR number had reached the level mine was at, improving it was not possible. Recovery from stage four kidney disease would take Divine intervention.

I refused to entertain that.

After a period of quiet, I began to think about all the people in my life who needed me to be around. Images of my wife, daughter, son, and grandchildren; faces of those I'd been praying for; those I did not know followed. There was an ever-present sense my life mission was still ahead. I needed to do everything I could to remain alive so I could carry that out, whatever 'that' might be.

I decided if my future was to be on those damn machines, then I would look at all the positive things I could do in those circumstances. I would have uninterrupted time to read, to write more books, even to meditate while sitting there three days a week. I would be surrounded by others on machines who might need some spiritual cheerleading and inspiration. I figured I could use all that time to pray for others as well as those there with me. I began to see dozens of ways to use dialysis as an opportunity; a way to serve others. I spent a whole hour just going through all the good things I could do.

By the time, I went to bed that night, I was feeling positive. I had totally surrendered to the situation. Now I looked at what good I could make from it.

I read more information on kidney disease so I had a greater understanding of what others were going through. Then I made an appointment with a doctor for two days later. Strange, two days before, when I felt like I was dying, I'd gained about eight pounds in a week's time, yet I was eating less than half of what I normally did.

But when I went to his office, I was rather healthy. My energy had returned and the back pain had subsided. I was not the same person I had been when I went in for the blood tests. The doctor took note of how I looked and concluded the test results had to be wrong. He said anyone with the GFR number I had would be very ill indeed. I did not appear to be physically ill at all.

The doctor scheduled me for another round of testing, after which I went home to wait for the results. When I walked in the door, I got a phone call from my good friend Gayle who declared the word "impossible" did not mean anything to me. She challenged me by asking, "Bill, don't you believe you can move the GFR number up even though they say you cannot?"

I took it as a question from the universe and a challenge to my own personal faith. I did not hesitate, "Absolutely! I *know* I can!" In a moment, I fully accepted the numbers would not only improve, but also soar upwards. I was fully confident.

A few minutes later, I got a phone call from the doctor. He said there must have been a mistake on the blood test. The GFR number was now well over sixty on and there was no indication of any problem with the kidneys. I then asked him which test was wrong: the first one or the one I'd taken that morning. He paused and said someone would contact me.

True to his word, I got a call from the hospital. *That* doctor told me my case was the subject of an early morning staff meeting. They had been discussing my situation and concluded it was 'impossible' for anyone to move those numbers in two days—forty-eight hours—from the levels they had been to where they now were. They decided I should be fully tested to ensure the last test results were correct.

I pointed out the possibility that perhaps both tests were correct.

He quickly contested the theory saying, for that to be true, it would take a miracle, and this hospital does not endorse nor officially believes in such things. He was adamant about the 'impossibility' to turn around the numbers as I had done. Then he asked me if I would mind going back to the lab and undergoing another series of tests at no charge.

I agreed.

The series turned out to be more than forty tests; screening of my entire body's health. All those tests came back showing me to be the healthiest I had been for some time. For me, it was a huge turn-around from four days before.

I got to thinking about what had happened and what the doctors had said. It had to be a test error. It was 'impossible' to change those numbers as I did. Even so, they could never figure out why I was feeling as if I was at death's door with all the pain and symptoms when they did the first blood test. It had reflected how I was physically feeling at that time. When I surrendered to the disease and to the will of the universe, I began to feel better. When I finally got to see the doctor, I was feeling healthy, and the new tests proved it. So, was there an error in the testing? And if so, why did it reflect and mirror my actual physical conditions?

Was this nothing but a spiritual test; a lesson learned? Perhaps the need to endure the karma was already met. I will never be able to prove this to anyone else, but I believe with all my heart it was my ultimate surrender to the will of the universe that had changed the disease and my future, once again.

## Jim's Kidney Disease

One day, Carol, an old friend from my Sacramento meditation group, asked me if I'd pray for her brother, Jim. He was terminally ill; hanging on by going to dialysis three days a week. Other than "he was a really nice man, several years younger than me" I knew nothing about him. I affirmed I'd add him to my prayer list and send out my loving energy to him as often as I could.

After a few months, my friend mentioned Jim was worse. I offered to visit him, and she welcomed my suggestion. When I called him, and discovered much of his time was spent undergoing dialysis, I decided to meet him at the center and spend time with him while he was hooked to the machine. I figured he'd be a captive audience, and it might serve to break up some of the boredom of that procedure.

The next morning, before I went off to see Jim, I had spoken to Jerry, a friend and fellow author. He also does something called "angel readings," a service for which he usually charges. But when I told him about Jim, he spontaneously decided to do one. He proceeded to provide a lot of information that didn't mean much to me; adding he saw a red heart of some kind playing a role in Jim's life. He wasn't sure if it was a red candy heart, perhaps something from Jim's past, but Jerry figured it would confirm a spiritual message.

I met Jim at the dialysis center and watched him get hooked up with the needles to the machine. It was not a quiet process with all the machines running, serving other people who were hooked up. I was given a chair and sat as close as I could to him so we could talk without shouting and still be heard.

I opened the conversation by relaying the information Jerry had provided. Jim said it all made sense to him, so I figured all was cool, but neither of us could figure out the message about the red heart.

One of the things that had been bothering Jim was guilt about being a burden on his sister. She'd been taking care of him at her home for some time; cooking for him and cleaning up after him, basically taking care of anything he needed.

I went on about how much his sister loved him; that by allowing her to be kind, he was giving her an opportunity to earn some good karma. And if no one was willing to receive the good others could give them, then they were not helping to fully connect the circle. By that I meant, to have heroes in the world, we need others to become willing receivers of those gifts of love. So, he was, in a way, helping her as well, by permitting her love to shine and grow.

I believe this was one of the things holding up his dying process. We went on about death, dying, and angels; even what our life mission may be. He said he didn't have a mission any more. I pointed something special out to him: by smiling and praying for others in the dialysis unit, he was carrying out his mission. Even though he physically could not serve, he could use the power of his love to help others. His continued mission was to cheer and inspire others in the dialysis unit, as well as to return all the love he received from his sister, through his prayers and thoughts.

Well over an hour later, after a deep dissertation on all sorts of spiritual things, it finally dawned on the both of us: I had forgotten I'd given him a copy of my book, *A Spiritual Warrior's Journey*. On the cover of the original, unrevised book there is, in fact, a red heart symbol. We both looked at it and had a wow moment. It symbolized our previous conversations were being confirmed. His smile grew even wider.

I spent a good part of the day with Jim, and some of the nurses and other patients had been close enough to hear us. I was not told until later, they usually did not allow visitors. Strange, no one there enforced that rule. On the contrary, someone had provided a chair for my comfort.

I received a call about a week later. Jim was fading and would be going into the hospital soon. I showed up at his sister's home that afternoon, right after delivering a speech on veteran's issues at the state capitol. I went inside and found several other close meditation friends there. We sang to him, spoke to him, and prayed. He was his normal smiling self, except this time his skin was a vivid shade of yellow; the liver code for big trouble, an unspoken given.

The next week, I visited him at his hospital bed. He was dying, yet hanging on for all his family and friends who had come to visit him. His sister subtly whispered to him it was alright to go home. She said goodbye, and he passed away shortly after.

At his memorial service, one filled with more friendliness than sadness, I spoke of him as a friend. One person after another, after another, opened-up to their appreciation of Jim and his role in their lives. Such love. I believe he'd won over more hearts with his smile than many preachers ever do with their Sunday sermons. He would be greatly missed.

## My Youngest Sister

When I was an infant, my mother and father got divorced. From all I had been told over the years from relatives, it was certainly not his fault. The details of what had happened were never made clear to me, nor why my father never came back to see me.

In my life, there was always this giant hole inside of me when it came to questions about my father; like where he was, and why he had abandoned me. I did not know if he was alive, well, or even where he lived. Absolutely nothing.

Though a few attempts were made over time to locate him, the results were disappointing. I reasoned, due to my age, this was one mystery that would remain unsolved. I cherished the stories I'd heard about how he was a great person.

One day in 2005, I received a phone call from my half-sister, Marsha. She'd been calling on me occasionally, so I expected nothing more than an inquiry about my health. But this call was one where she might as well have dropped a bomb on me. Her hobby of searching the internet for family information had been long-known to me, but since we had different fathers, I hadn't much interest in her clan. Neither did I give much attention to my mother's family tree either. I'd never met any of them.

But that afternoon, Marsha caught my full attention when she said she'd found a listing for someone with the same name and date of birth as my father and was going to follow up. A few days later, she called and told me she had located my father's death record. He had died in 1973 at fifty-two. She went on to about how she'd located him and verified it by cross-referencing records and social security numbers.

My heart began to hurt. I managed to thank her for her efforts and hurried off the phone. I then went to my bedroom and sat alone. I wasn't sure how to react to the news of losing my dad, some thirty-two years after his actual death. Nonetheless, warm tears streamed down my cheeks. I found a tissue and wiped my nose and face, glad to be alone so no one could see me sob. I wanted to cry out loud, but held back. The hope of finding my father had ended for me with that short phone conversation. I had been abandoned once again.

I got myself together and went downstairs to tell Carol what I had learned, passing it off rather casually. It did not fool her for a second. She knows my fake, brave exterior.

Over the next few days, I had dreams about my dad and imaginary conversations within those dreams. Though it hurt to know he was gone, I had some closure.

Everything changed a few days later when Marsha called me again with more news; she'd found records showing my father had married again, and his widowed wife had just recently died. Then she dropped a bomb, "You have a little sister."

Curious as to what other research she'd done, I inquired. She told me she had found the address and phone number of my sister. I was thrilled and wanted to connect. I figured I should be cautious, so I let Marsha contact her first. In my mind, I was already planning this huge reunion with her, sharing photo albums of our father and her family.

Though excited, I didn't want to call someone up and say, "Hello, I am your brother," which might be an awkward situation for the other person. I wanted to be sensitive. She might not even be aware of her father ever having had another child.

As agreed, Marsha would call my sister for me. I lay awake all night wondering how great this would turn out for all of us. I just could not imagine a better gift in life than to discover you have a sibling.

Marsha called her and had a long conversation, finding out some personal history. My little sister was married and had children, and lived in the state of Washington. She told Marsha she'd first learned about me at the reading of my father's Will, where I was mentioned. How I was mentioned or why, she did not say, although she did ask her mother about me after the funeral and was told who I was. So, she had known about me for over thirty years, yet no attempts were ever made to connect.

Although I had not spoken to her—she'd declined an invitation to do so—she did send a few emails to me. I sent her a huge package of my books, some photos, and a long letter, hoping it would give her a better idea of who I was. She, on the other hand, stopped short of giving me much information, except things she felt I should know, like why my dad had passed away and, more importantly, why he never came to see me after he left.

I discovered he'd paid child support for years; news to me. If only someone had told me, I could have found an address and a way to contact him. I also learned he'd tried to visit me on more than one occasion, but was told by my step-dad never to come around. He had been given the impression, should he do so, my stepfather would physically harm him. In the end, my dad stopped making child support payments and never came back to see me.

Sadly, she refused to send a photo of herself or her family. She mailed only one of my dad, from before he'd remarried, wearing his military uniform dated 1948.

Her final email stated she was happy being an only child and had no room in her life for an older brother; that she never wanted me to visit her, nor phone or write. She ended by saying she hoped I would understand.

No, I really didn't understand at all. It was like a knife to my heart. Being the kind of person I am, I replied with a long email, wishing her well with her life. I wrote I harbored no ill feelings at all.

But I did.

What I had wanted to say was not so nice. It would not have been a kind or compassionate response. I chose to close this chapter with some class. One cannot, after all, force someone to love another. I tried to downplay my anger and hurt feelings about being rejected. I was more concerned about her state of mind and how she may experience great remorse in the future.

That night, I must have been grinding my teeth, because the next morning I found I had completely broken one of my back teeth. The shards were forced into my gum. It hurt terribly and I was bleeding profusely, inciting an emergency visit to the dentist for a *major* repair job. Incredibly, the physical pain was not as great as the emptiness and hurt still inside me. I could not believe I had been rejected so off-handedly by my little sister. I was her only living relative and she didn't want me to be a part of her life.

I wondered if she was concerned about me being entitled to some of her inheritance. She never stated why my name was mentioned in my father's Will. This had to be the only logical reason. The sad part is, there never was, nor ever will be, any intention to take anything from her. It was a shame she chose not to become a part of my life.

The good that came from all of this was I finally understood my father did not make the choice to leave me; that decision had been sealed by my mother and step-father. I was also made aware of some things about his health, and of the family, providing well-needed insights. I also could truly forgive my father for the first time in my life. I'd gained and lost a sister, but I learned much about myself as a person in the process.

An odd twist to this tale is when some of my women friends from my old high school days, heard about the situation, they all volunteered to become one of my sisters. Now I have these wonderful "spiritual sisters" who love me for who I am. I feel graced by these women in my life and blessed they have chosen to be there for me when I needed them. Thank you, Linda, Mahaila and Karen!

*Part Three*

# THE GURU FINDS ME

### The Far-away Grandfather Dies

My grandchildren always called their father's dad "The Far-Away Grandfather," because he lived about fifty miles from them. They didn't see him a lot, mostly only on special occasions like holidays and birthdays. When he died, Daya, called me up to let me know. She was sad to lose her father-in-law, and had heartfelt sorrow for her husband's loss.

When Daya and her family drove to the funeral, something caught her attention. They were on Highway 80, just past the campus of UC Davis, heading west. Sitting in the full sunshine on a tree branch was a stunning white owl. She managed to say a quick something about it. Gianni, saw it as well.

My son-in-law's adoptive dad was part Native American, and although Daya was unsure of the tribal nation he was descended from, she understood the owl was a symbolic communication from her father-in-law. In addition, for many years the owl, our spiritual messenger, had deep meaning to Daya and me.

After the funeral, she'd shared the experience of her and Gianni having seen the owl with her widowed mother-in-law; bringing some additional consoling, spiritual healing.

The funeral was dignified and very well attended. My son-in-law, Mark, delivered a moving and powerful eulogy, speaking eloquently and emotionally about his dad. The grandchildren, being two- and four-years-of-age at the time, did not seem to be too concerned about death. They did not see it as adults do.

Two weeks after the funeral, while I was playing with Gianni, something unusual happened. In the middle of my talking to him, he raised his little arms and hushed me, saying Grandpa was talking.

I said, "Yes, of course, I am talking."
He quickly replied, "No, not you, Far-Away Grandpa!"
I asked him what his other Grandpa was telling him.
Gianni replied innocently, "He says he loves me!"

I was speechless. This toddler was communicating with his dead grandfather. I sat back in awe, then suggested Gianni tell his Grandpa he loved him, too.

I called Daya's mother-in-law, who was crying when she answered. She had been sorting through her husband's belongings for Goodwill. This had made it hit home that he was truly dead and no longer going to be a part of her life.

I imparted what little Gianni had experienced and ended by reassuring her the "I love you" message was meant for her as well. She sobbed some more, a good emotional release, then her spirits lifted a little. The message was specifically intended for Gianni and his grandmother to hear.

There was more to my grandson than meets the eye. My suspicions had been confirmed several times in conversations where he not only told me he used to fly helicopters, but described these flying machines in detail. On other occasions, he knew what others were thinking. A wise little owl I love very much!

## The Power of Visualizations

One night, after a long meditation, I began a series of visualizations for various people on my prayer list. I attempted to picture them in certain ways, to aid their healing or to give them strength and protection.

I started on visualization for Daya, who was experiencing some heavy harassment at her workplace. She had brought serious charges against some of her bosses. In response, they were making her life a living hell. She'd felt physically threatened after her new car was vandalized in the parking lot. In addition, one of her bosses was seen carrying a gun in his car.

I began picturing Paramahansa Yogananda standing slightly behind her on her left side in a protective stance. I visualized him in an orange robe, his long hair flowing over his shoulders. I gave this my fullest attention and energy, and prayed for Yogananda to remain alongside her for protection.

Next, I created an image of two of my friends standing under a shower of electrical bolts of wisdom; energy to awaken them. I saw lightning bolts hitting them in the head and surrounding them with an electrical aura of wisdom and understanding. I saw little lightning strikes in my mind during this visualization, while I prayed. I wanted them to gain understanding and wisdom so they could handle all future problems.

I finished my two visualizations and all my prayers, then sat back to think about things. I had become a little exhausted from the growing list of people to pray for, and over the email and phone calls I received from those in need of spiritual and emotional support.

There was a little part of me that thought maybe life would be much easier if I had a short break from all the responsibility. The prospect of getting hit on the head and resting unconscious for a few days sounded like a good idea. I'd finally get some rest, yet not feel guilty about not being there for others. It was no more than a fleeting thought.

I went to the bedroom and pulled back the covers and hopped into bed much like I did every other night, except I hit my head on the wall. I saw stars and almost passed out from the impact. As I rolled over, it dawned on me, I had, through my own visualizations and concentration, created this situation. I had a good laugh at my own expense, but at the same time I found out how important it is to guard random, negative thoughts. Then I wondered if that same energy would be there for my daughter and my friends for whom I'd performed visualizations.

Daya called and told me about what had happened the night before with her daughter Daylana. When Daya was tucking Daylana into bed, she looked up at her mom and said, "Mommy, who is that woman standing next to you?"

Daya had no idea who she was talking about, so replied in the parental way of, "Sweetheart, no one's there."

Daylana was insistent. She looked directly into her mother's eyes and asked, "Are you telling me I am seeing a ghost, Mommy?"

She went on to describe the woman in an orange robe and long black hair; but my daughter did not connect the significance at the time. Later in the day, Daylana saw a photo of Yogananda in her mother's walk-in closet she also uses for a meditation room, and called out, "That was the woman I saw!"

I told Daya about my nightly visualizations, where Yogananda was standing exactly where Daylana had seen him. I recognized, as she did, he was looking after her. We could trust she would be okay.

A day or so later, I talked to my friend whom I was trying to help with my visualizations. She went on about the strange accident she'd had at the public library the night before; even said she was thinking about filing a lawsuit against the library because of their computers. She stated it was like 'lightning bolts' had hit her on her head when she was touching the keyboard. She was literally shocked, wondering what could have caused it. Then I told her about the visualizations I'd been doing that same night. She asked me what time I had done them, and I said it would have been about 9:30, the same time she'd been zapped by the computers, or by something from the air.

She'd been puzzled by the event, but now had some insight. She told me it was nice to be prayed for, but it might be better to visualize love around her next time.

Those visualizations taught me something about the power of our thoughts when focused with visual images and prayer, *and* the power of meditation. It might serve us all well to carefully watch what we think about: positive and negative.

## The Owls and the Postmaster

When I went to my local post office to pick up my mail, the window clerk informed me the person who would soon be the new postmaster had asked about me.

With a few minutes of spare time, I decided to go into the postmaster's office. The new postmaster was someone with whom I'd worked indirectly with before I retired from the USPS. She was one of those managers who looked after what was good for the company's bottom line *and* focused on others in a caring and compassionate way. She had stepped down from her previous position for reasons I totally endorsed.

We'd never had any personal conversations since she was a simple workplace acquaintance. At the time of my visit, she'd not officially stepped into the position of postmaster.

I was led into her office for what we both presumed would be a brief conversation. She wanted to chat, but said she had only a few minutes. I opened the conversation by saying there are no accidents in life and began to speak about some things she might need to hear.

I wanted to tell her the story of my first meeting, on the phone, with my friend Gayle. Before I began the story, I said she'd find this story related to her. When I finished the story of the owl sculpture hanging at Gayle's back door, she smiled.

I said, "And now you know why the story relates to you."

She told me she had two owls at her house, one out front and the other at the back door. They were plastic owls she'd put there herself. She looked at me, waiting for me to say a little more about their significance.

So, I said, "People who are in some way connected to me, or who need my help, always have an owl connection in their life." It is symbolic to me. I continued to expand on many personal things about her life—even though I had no knowledge of her personal life—and mentioned she might want to be attentive to her relationship with her father, whom I was sensing was not going to be around very long. (He died several months after our conversation).

The conversation went on for almost two hours in her office. We touched on several spiritual matters in the process, then I had to leave.

A week later, she called to ask if I would consider being the official chaplain for her postmaster swearing-in ceremony. She wanted me to deliver a benediction for her. I told her, of course, I would be there.

All sorts of present and former USPS managers and postmasters attended the swearing-in. I had suggested she invite one of my old bosses for whom I had worked eighteen years ago. Susan confirmed she'd already extended the invitation.

The interesting point was this former postal manager had, for years, made deliberate efforts to discredit me. She had tried her best to make my working life difficult. Holding no grudges, I had put this woman on my prayer list and been actively praying for her for over eighteen years. No matter how badly she had treated me, I'd kept sending her my loving prayers.

Of course, this former boss never knew I was doing this for her each day. I had always made it a point never to talk badly about her to anyone. I was always loving and compassionate in both thoughts and words regarding her. In my heart and mind I always saw the wonderful person she could be.

When I saw my old boss at the ceremony I greeted her like an old friend. She responded kindly and with so much love. She embraced me and told me of her concerns for my health she'd heard about from others.

She truly *was* a compassionate and caring person; one I always knew she could be. The time spent with her was a wonderful reward for all those years of praying for her. It proved no loving gesture or prayer is ever wasted. God has his own timetable and schedule. I also found, by praying for her, I was also healing myself as well.

I was truly blessed to have been asked to be a part of the ceremony. If I had not stepped into the new postmaster's office that day and talked about owls and spiritual things, then I would not have been officiating. More importantly, I would have missed out on seeing the results of my prayers. Like I'd said to the postmaster, there are no accidents, and everything is as it is supposed to be in its own 'time'.

## Night Visitors

Daya kept telling me Gianni wasn't getting any sleep at night. When she'd asked him about being up all night, he said he was spending time with his friend and some of his friend's friends.

He described them as men with robes; that they talked to him and taught him things. I suggested, when he got up from the afternoon nap he was taking at my house, we should ask him about "his friends" without any leading questions.

When Gianni woke up, Daya brought him to see me in my computer room. Gianni was still half-asleep, rubbing his eyes and hugging his mommy. I had been watching a YouTube video and left its frozen image in the upper corner of the monitor's screen. I asked him to tell me about his new friends and what they looked like.

He looked at the monitor and smiled, pointing to the upper part of the screen. "That's my friend!" he announced, identifying the man in the video. I looked over my shoulder and saw he was referring to Yogiraj Satgurunath Siddhanath. This was an advanced yogi whom I had viewed on YouTube and obtained a copy of his book to review.

I was amazed he'd pointed out this yogi, whom I'd never mentioned to anyone in my family, nor had I shown him the book or any of the videos I had watched.

I picked up the book, *Wings to Freedom,* and showed it to Gianni. He held it like it was his favorite teddy bear. He touched the photo image on the book cover and continued to say this was his friend. I opened the book and had him look at all the photos of the other yogis in the book.

Gianni studied each photo, saying all those yogis came with their friends to visit him each night. He pointed to Babaji, then to others, and then looked over at my personal altar at a photo of Paramahansa Yogananda, and said, "She was there, too." The little guy thought Yogananda looked like a woman. This was not the first time someone I'd counseled had received a vision or image of Paramahansa Yogananda as a 'she' instead of 'he.'

Next, he focused on the photo in the book of a stern-faced yogi named Shri Yukteswar, an Avatar and the guru of Yogananda; a no nonsense spiritual teacher. Gianni put his little hand on the face in the photo and reached out with his other hand and touched my forehead just between the eyes. He then, with all the seriousness a three-year-old could possibly muster, said, "And this one will really wake you up, Papa!"

Daya and I were left speechless as Gianni leapt off my lap and ran downstairs to his grandmother.

Certain we had not filled his head with this information, it left us wondering what kind of little boy had Himalayan gurus and yogis in his room each night to talk to him. This was beyond our scope of understanding.

A few nights later, I dreamed of yogi master, Gurunath. He stood in front of me and, with an Indian accent, said, "Bill, hurry up and finish your books!"

In the dream, I replied, "Yes, and I understand why." But when I awoke, I really had no idea why I needed to finish my books. It worried me a little. Could it have something to do with my health? Cause I did have some *serious* health issues.

Earlier that month, I'd collapsed at the Lodi Zoo. A neurosurgeon at Kaiser Hospital confirmed my brain seizures, and other issues, were worsening. They also discovered my spinal cord was dangerously worn in the neck; that all it would take to kill or incapacitate me would be a neck adjustment or a nasty case of whiplash. The protective shield around the cord had been actually thinning each time I looked up or down or moved my neck.

The original injury was from being thrown forward by the force of a rocket— blasted about eight feet in the air, landing on my head on a cement floor—in Vietnam in July of 1967. Those neck and head injuries were not diagnosed nor treated back then.

For years, this old injury has taken its toll on me and was the cause of my brain seizures. On occasion, the damage has numbed my arms, face, and even my legs.

It was also the reason I passed out at the zoo, cutting off my lower nervous system. The diagnosis was quite complicated. Doctors recommended I should have a CAT SCAN several times a year to see the progression. I chose not to. Doing so would not make me any better nor lead to any improvement, but only cause more anxiety and cost a fortune.

I was told, after decades of trouble, that almost any future seizure could possibly could be fatal; my brain simply couldn't take any more.

I had almost stopped driving, simply limited myself to one-mile trips to the post office and grocery store around town. When I felt a seizure coming on, I'd get myself home or park the truck and wait it out.

The first eight months of 2008, I had about 250 seizures; almost daily, and sometimes more than once a day. Thank God most of them only affected my vision and memory.

While these things were going on with my health, I still managed to review Gurunath's book, and nominate it for a national book award from *The American Authors Association*. Later, I received an email from Doug, a follower of Gurunath, who informed me I could come hear Gurunath lecture at a public satsang the following week in Berkley, but I would most likely not be permitted to speak to him directly.

I decided to experience this with some friends, and so I called a couple from my meditation group with whom I had a close relationship. They said they'd love to go and would even drive me there. This solved yet another dilemma. Driving, for me so far and at night, would not be wise. I also let an old buddy, TJ, know, who replied he'd meet us at Berkley after he finished work.

We arrived early at the temple in Berkeley and hooked up with some of the people there. Again, I was told not to expect to meet with Gurunath as he would be unavailable. As soon as the program began, with a screening of his documentary, *Wings to Freedom*, I was tapped on the shoulder and told Gurunath wanted to see me. I was led out of the main temple area to a back room where he sat alone on a couch.

It was a little awkward coming into the room; not knowing the protocol for meeting a living Master. He, on the other hand, was not concerned with my feeble attempts to second guess my gestures of respect. As I approached him, I bowed slightly while holding my hands in a prayer-like fashion.

So, genuine, warm, and friendly was his greeting, I felt like God Himself had come to earth to give me a spiritual hug.

I then blurted out he'd been visiting my three-year-old grandson, Gianni, for several weeks and it had been keeping him awake at nights.

He looked at me and humbly nodded his head.

Then I told him about my own dream, and his telling me to finish my book. I ended it by telling him, even though in that dream I had *said* I understood why I needed to do it, in my waking life, I did not. I shrugged my shoulders and looked at him with a puzzled look, saying something like, "Is it because I am going to die soon?"

He burst out laughing at my words, and then said, "It is because you will be helping me to write my book about Babaji and writing other spiritual books." Much more was left unsaid about what other books he might be 'referring' to. In the dream, he said to finish "my books." (You see, I had just begun *this* book.)

Of course, I was flattered, but he might have been just showing kindness. He went on about how he loved my writing; mentioned he was serious about me helping him.

I asked, "Why me?"

Then he did something for me I had waited all my life for. He told me things I had longed to know; that I'd ached to hear someone confirm. What made it even more significant was it came from someone I believed was a

Self-Realized Master, who proclaimed I was a very spiritual person; someone compassionate and loving. *He said I was his friend.* As he spoke, old hurts dissolved in the energy and love of his words.

In my unfiltered conversation style, I said I already had a guru, Paramahansa Yogananda, and I was not looking for a new one. He said that was okay, I could be his BFF! We both laughed. But honestly, he was offering much more than Divine Friendship. He presented the opportunity of a lifetime; an invitation I could not pass up.

He asked me to come to his ashram in India, as his guest, to stay as long as I wished; told me not to worry about paying for anything because I was family. It amazed me, at the time of meeting him—in about ten minutes—I'd been invited to India, asked to help write his books, and told things I'd hungered to be told my whole life.

The conversation went on, but I clung to his words and ideas. I was beginning to wonder if he was one of those love-and-compassion-for-everyone kinds of gurus. *Does he treat everyone this way?* That question remained in the back of my mind.

Not needing to tell him about my health problems or ask him for anything, I was satisfied with what he gave me. After half an hour, we ended our talk and I returned to my place in the temple, sitting next to my friends on the floor.

Gurunath came into the temple, changing the atmosphere instantaneously. Charged with his energy, there was complete harmony. He sat on a platform slightly elevated from the attendees. Dressed in white, complete with his white beard and flowing hair, he radiated in the soft lighting around him. His image resembled a Moses or Zeus; a living image of an ancient god-like person. A Hollywood casting director would choose this image for the role of God! Gurunath had an aura of spiritual magnetism. I totally focused on his face.

He fielded questions, and went into deep explanations. He saw the universe in ways few, if any, ever could. Those present were enthralled and hung on his every word. This lecture was something much different than I had ever heard before. Near the end of his talk, between questions, he stopped, placed his right hand on his forehead, and announced he was sending healing vibrations for the brain. He looked out in my direction where I sat stiff and uncomfortable on the floor. He stopped abruptly and then took another question.

I remember at the time how odd it was, and so out of rhythm with the questions he'd been receiving. The healing wasn't for cancer, or world peace, but for the brain.

Near the end of the lecture, he exposed everyone to a unique experience, his 'no-mind state', and transmitted his energy and love to their heart chakras.

NOTE: There is a much deeper meaning and explanation for this, but I wanted you to understand what I observed from my own limited perspective at this first meeting. Gurunath was transmitting his love, energy, and no-mind state, and we were to focus on him the whole time.

When it was over, he asked if everyone had seen the aura around him. Of course, every hand went up except for possibly one or two. I had seen a bright-white glow around him, but believed all of us there at the temple *wanted* to see it, and questioned myself as to what else I'd seen.

Maybe it was a product of suggestion and our own desire to see it that created the image for us. I wanted to remain open, but I approached some of it with a little skepticism to keep what happened as an honest experience, not just an emotional voyage.

Then he asked if anyone had seen anything else.

The guy sitting directly in front of me raised his hand, then said he'd witnessed Gurunath change into someone else.

Gurunath asked who that might be.

The man said he saw Gurunath transform into the living image of Shri Yukteswar, the very yogi my grandson said would really wake me up.

*Gianni put his little hand on the face in the photo and reached out with his other hand and touched my forehead just between the eyes. He then, with all the seriousness a three-year-old could possibly muster, said, "And this one will really wake you up, Papa!"*

I was floored! It was the very same image I had seen as well, and I'd thought it was just my over active imagination. Then Gurunath asked if others had seen the same image, and over three-quarters of the group raised their hands. A couple of others said they saw Moses or another old sage.

I figured this was more evidence than I needed to tell me something most unusual was taking place that night.

When the lecture ended and the place was serenely quiet, Gurunath stood, as did all us who were there, and walked through the crowd, without speaking.

I was pleased to have had my time with him, the one who fed my soul life-giving manna.

My head buzzed as if charged with a small current of electricity, but I did not feel as if I was having a seizure. We were collecting our belongings and shoes when someone came and told us Gurunath wanted to meet my friends.

We followed him inside the temple, to the same room where we'd previously spoken.

Gurunath greeted all of us warmly and asked about every one of us. One of my friends then asked a question of Gurunath. When he tried to answer, she interrupted him three times. Gurunath stopped talking. He folded his arms across his chest, then lit into her with a brief lecture about treating gurus with respect. He became cold and hard in his conversation with her; totally the opposite of what I had experienced. I was hurting inside for her as I watched her exchange words with this man of God.

He told her, "A guru cannot lie. He must always tell the truth."

Finally, she changed the direction and energy of the conversation by asking me if I had informed the guru about all my serious health issues and my brain problems.

I waved her question off and said, "I do not need to tell the guru. He already knows and has taken care of it."

Gurunath sat smiling and nodding.

*Why am I so positive? How is it I am so sure those words are truth?* I firmly believed what I had said was fact. I had just stated something directly from my heart.

That was August 16, 2008. I have not had a brain seizure since.

Later, on the way home, there was more. The woman, whom I'd traveled with and had sat next to, said she'd seen Gurunath turn into an image of me. It really kind of spooked me; sent chills up my spine.

Still, I went home with my brain floating in a deep well of loving energy. Over the next few weeks, I found I only required a couple of hours sleep each night. I was fully charged with energy. Something profound had happened and my life was forever changed.

## Car Crash – Computer Crash

Shortly after meeting Gurunath in person for the first time, I received a phone call providing a cellphone number and a request to call him. We eventually hooked up and had a wonderful conversation. He wanted me to come and spend a week meeting and working with him at his son's apartment, so we could spend several hours each day on his book.

The following week I traveled to the San Francisco Bay Area, stopping in to see my nephew, Todd, in Sunnyvale, as I was a little early to go directly to Foster City where Gurunath was staying with his son, Rudra.

When I phoned Gurunath and asked what time we should meet, he said he was with Rudra and not near his apartment, but visiting a friend in Sunnyvale. When I informed him, I was in fact, calling from Sunnyvale, he gave me the address where he was. It turned out we were not much more than a block away from each other.

He said he'd come by to say hello. Arriving across the street, as I stood out front speaking to him on the phone, he got out of the car and said he could only stay a few minutes.

During the visit, Rudra left and Gurunath stayed with me at Todd's house. We had a long conversation—a couple of hours—then we climbed into my pickup and set off for Foster City. After a few minutes, he went off into some higher altered state. The truck, our moving temple, rolled comfortably down the highway of life.

We spent the week working on his book, but it was more like Gurunath was working on me. Our relationship was like an old one rekindled. Even moments of silence were not awkward. Everything about being in each other's presence was sublimely natural. Conversations were of the lighthearted and serious variety. He mentioned he considered me more Indian than a Westerner, but did not go into any more detail, although he'd hinted we'd had many lives together, and we were family.

At the end of the week, I prepared to leave. I finished up late Friday night and returned to my nephew's house to sleep for a few hours before heading home where I was expected to babysit my grandchildren at six the next morning.

At two-thirty in the morning, when Todd rose to go his UPS job, I joined him and we had breakfast. Then I headed toward Elk Grove, two hours away.

The good thing about driving in the early morning hours is there is little-to-no traffic. Being Saturday, I was able to make *really* good time, and zipped along at times going ninety miles an hour on the highway. I pictured arriving home, showering, and unwinding before spending the day with my grandchildren. Then, twenty minutes from home, around Lodi, I heard a voice inside my head telling me to slow down.

I did.

Just as soon as I did, I caught the outline of an overturned truck in the blackness ahead—no lights, just a shadow of solid metal waiting for impact. I jerked the steering wheel to the right and barely missed the upturned truck. I could not see the lane next to me, but prior to slowing I'd noticed several cars in the lane alongside me. As I swerved into the right there were no other cars. Nothing in either lane. I was all alone on the highway.

I pulled out my cell phone and called 911. I was advised the Highway Patrol would be there in minutes, and I should move along; that it was dangerous to attempt to get to the jackknifed truck and trailer.

I drove home cautiously, pulling into my driveway, feeling blessed I had listened to my inner voice. Strange, that was the exit to the Lodi Zoo.

I announced my arrival, then checked my email, seeing as I had some extra time. When I turned on my computer it began to make sounds, like metal clicking. I could not pull up any programs or files. All I could see was a white image before me. My computer had crashed and I had lost all my files; everything was wiped out!

Two years of work were stored on that computer, including all the early work on this book. Over 5,000 photos and all my music, as well as two years' work of poetry. Even worse, if it could get any worse, every email address—gone.

I sat staring at the blank screen. Then I began to laugh. A wide smile cut through my misery. No one had been killed or injured. Yes, it was a massive inconvenience, and it would create more work in restoring the book, but it was a computer. In the real world of life, this crash was small stuff. After my close-call that morning, I figured a computer crash was better than having a car crash. Certainly, good CAR-MA!

It soon dawned on me I needed to change the way I went about writing this book. This story was not going to be just about me, but about the living master who'd found me. Losing all my data helped me refocus on the whole way I saw my life and viewed the creation of this book.

## The Ashram 2009

The end of December 2008 had finally arrived. I'd been waiting a lifetime for the calendar to catch up with my heart's destiny.

Soon another lifelong dream would be fulfilled and I would return to India to spend time with a living Master, one who had invited me to visit and stay at his ashram. This opportunity did not come to everyone, and I was both grateful and humbled by it. I had no idea of what to expect. I was totally open to whatever happened and whatever gifts and lessons the universe gave me.

When Carol and Daya took me to the Sacramento Airport, I picked up on their discomfort, their feelings for my safety, and the unfortunate fact that each time I've left for an extended period, "stuff" in their lives began to fall apart. But this was something I had to do.

I had hoped and prayed things might be different this time. Once I got on the plane, things would happen I could not directly help them with. No matter the feelings, I could do more for them at the ashram, being at the feet of Gurunath, than if I stayed with them.

Daya also needed to learn to handle these 'life things' on her own, without my ever-present help. After all, I would not be around forever. She needed to build those spiritual and emotional skills and empower herself. From an emotional point of view, I was concerned about being gone for nine weeks. It was a long time to be away from Carol, my children, and my grandchildren; a terribly long time in the life of preschoolers.

The flight went smoothly, but it took *forever* to get to India. I left on December 31, 2008 and arrived in Mumbai on January 2, 2009. Even with a thirteen-and-a-half-hour time difference, it was a long, hard journey.

Whenever I changed planes, I always got a seat next to an empty one, no matter if all the other seats on each of the flights were occupied. I thanked God I had lots of room to rest. What a blessing!

On the final flight from Frankfurt, Germany, an elderly Indian man sat on the other side of the empty seat. He leaned over to me and began to talk in an Indian dialect as if I fully understood him. He smiled and I smiled back. He later said he believed I was Indian.

When we landed in Mumbai, security was intense, a direct result of the terrorist attacks a month previous. It took a long time to leave the airport and get a taxi. The driver, a knowledgeable native, recognized the location of the ashram and headed straight there, or so we assumed. I was exhausted, but still fully awake. There really was nothing to see at night, but I was so excited to be back in India, I looked anyway. I was also eager to see Gurunath. It was going to be a most interesting stay.

Our driver saw all the red lights as mere suggestions to look both ways and zip through. Having gotten lost several times, he had to make at least a dozen phone calls to various people for directions. We drove from two in the morning until almost sunrise. So, hidden was the ashram—tucked away from main roads—when we did finally arrive, I was amazed he'd found it at all.

The final ten minutes were on a rutted road with a lot of large rocks. The road, if it could be called one, did not look like it was going to take us anywhere but to the deepest of jungles. We pulled onto an even narrower dirt road with more potholes; the driver honking his horn the entire stretch. I'm sure he managed to wake everyone at the ashram.

When we reached a creek bed, with a trickle of water flowing over some rocks, he stopped and refused to cross.

I got out of the taxi, not knowing if the ashram was fifty feet or ten miles ahead in the darkness. I had all my bags on the ground and was ready to begin walking when a couple of young guys from the ashram hiked toward me. Jay Ponti, a thirty-one-year-old from California grabbed the largest bag and advised me to follow him. I paid the driver, then walked a few hundred feet, over a stream, up a slight slope, and into the ashram, where we came to a bungalow they said was mine. I dropped the bags I was carrying and asked to see the temple.

We walked up a rise to what I could see, in the semi-darkness, was the temple. I noticed two shining eyes of an animal crouched in the trees to the side of our path. Though the size of a large dog, it moved like a cat.

It scampered off into the mango grove. At some point, I would have several run-ins with what turned out to be a panther. They prowled around the ashram on their nocturnal visits throughout my stay, including holding a vigil directly outside my door one night.

When we reached the top of the long stairway, leading straight up to the temple, Jay opened the doors. I stood in awe at the magnificent structure. Overcome by the power inside the place, I simply allowed my jaw to drop and my heart to open. The temple houses the world's largest, solid mercury stone—set inside a marble setting above a marble tank filled with water; basically, surrounded by a moat—called The Philosopher's Stone. It is said this mercury stone emits massive bursts of energy and aids in meditation. My first impressions of its energy had been overwhelming. I was more than satisfied.

I meditated until sunrise. When I left the temple, I saw the ashram in the valley below. I walked down the stairs, found my bags, and put them inside my room. My initial impression was that Gurunath had given me the best room available—did *not* have to share it with anyone—with a desk, so I could use my computer and write.

Though I was extremely tired when I'd arrived, the time in the temple had recharged me sufficiently to continue until well after midnight on my first day.

As I wandered about the ashram, Gurunath spotted me, and walked briskly my way. He threw open his arms and wrapped me in both of them. His loving energy melted my heart, and the warm embrace and words of welcome made me feel like the most important person in the whole universe. He introduced me to everyone, then made sure I was comfortable physically, emotionally, and more importantly, spiritually.

I had finally come home. It had taken sixty-two years of this present lifetime, but I had finally returned to the feet of my guru. Heavenly.

## The Mercury Shivalinga: A Spiritual Wonder of the World

People at the ashram began to share their personal stories about the place. Without fail, almost everyone claimed to have experienced an increased level of synergy and spirituality. Many told me about seeing things while meditating at the temple.

The ashram temple was no ordinary place of worship. Filled with enormous energy, it simply radiates with power generated from The Philosopher's Stone. To most of the world, they think it originated in Europe and not India. Its creation remains a closely guarded secret. The stone is egg-shaped, weighs over a ton, and rests directly in the middle of the temple where it is surrounded by a pool of clear water.

Upon arrival, as I meditated in front of the stone, my jet lag vanished, even after traveling for about forty hours. The 'recharge' was more than I expected, but I learned this 'little blast' was nothing compared to what others had experienced.

Many supernatural tales were related to me of what others witnessed, such as visions of various saints and sages coming to life, animated, inside the shivalinga when they were the subject of focus. Some people had even spoken of the stone disappearing and being replaced by images of a spiritual being.

One morning, a long-time devotee of Gurunath from California came to breakfast with his face shining. He said he'd seen Jesus in the stone itself.

One other phenomenon I discovered was whatever was "thought about" would manifest in some way, and very quickly. The key was to watch one's thoughts while near this stone. With such discovered knowledge, I could only assume prayers for others would also be given more power and energy. So, at the end of my meditations, I made sure to include all those in need of loving energy in my prayers.

Every day, while Gurunath is at the ashram, he transmits great energy and love to this stone when he goes into his own personal meditation cave under the smaller temple below the hill. The key is to be inside the main temple when he is meditating, to receive the full force of energy. This stone is truly one of the wonders of the spiritual world. There is an energy vortex inside the temple caused by this mercury shivalinga. Any person who is psychically sensitive, or even slightly spiritually conscious, can feel the power. For me, my 'head' felt different, as if it was filled with static electrical charges.

The stone works as powerfully as it does because it is continually bombarded with new and loving energy from Gurunath. I like to assume the stone becomes more powerful each day. Over the seven weeks I spent there, I noticed the stone often sweated; small droplets of mercury, all around the stone, trailing to the base. When I asked about it, Gurunath stated he'd stepped up the energy he sent, causing this to occur.

I do not fully understand why mercury works as it does, but I do know what I have experienced in its presence. I use the term "presence" since it feels like the stone has a living consciousness. There are, in fact, many stories about the stone coming to life and moving. One thing is for sure, Gurunath is the channeling force behind all the energy. How and why he uses this stone is another ashram mystery. Truly serious spiritual seekers are advised to make the journey to this energy center of Kundalini Kriya Yoga in the hidden valley of Sita Mai, near Pune, India.

## Ancient Sages in the Temple

In the temple, during a morning group-talk, Gurunath had us focus our attention on the mercury shivalinga. He suggested we work on keeping our physical eyes open for part, or all, of the Kriya meditations; to absorb this vast energy. He went on to say he would be sending a strong transmission that morning, so we should be in the temple.

I headed to the temple feeling rather tired from some long nights of working on the book projects with Gurunath and a couple of other devotees. We had been attempting to wrap up the editing and revisions of his first book, *Wings to Freedom*, as well as laying the groundwork for a new book on Babaji. Another work in progress, a book on dealing with children, would have to wait. We'd never run out of work! At the time, I was also penning the beginnings of *this* book.

I climbed the steps to the temple on the hill and, once I reached the top, turned to take in the peaceful valley shimmering in the morning sunlight. I removed my shoes and entered the temple barefoot, then approached the shivalinga and mentally bowed. My body was never limber enough in my ashram stay to physically prostrate myself in front of it. Too many hours sitting on cold, marble floors made my body stiff and sore. I was far from agile; my history of back and neck injuries catching up with me.

I found a place on the west wall of the temple and slid my old body against it to support my back and balance myself. Others in the temple—young people not even half my age—held the classic yogic posture no walls required. I then began my meditation techniques, working to shut out, as best I could, my thoughts of home, family, and worldly desires.

The morning's meditation was a little easier than normal; the time passing comfortably, almost effortlessly. I opened my eyes and concentrated on the mercury stone, breathing up and down my spine, my mind locked onto the stone.

I noticed something rather odd-shaped inside the stone surface. It was more than a reflection of light and had three-dimensional qualities—a face! Then the image shifted to show me several more faces; all staring out at me from within the stone itself. Not human face types, they rather resembled those like carved statues one sees on Easter Island or in other South Pacific locations. The faces varied, but each possessed the look of an ancient sage; otherworldly features containing spiritual, non-threatening energy. They moved very much alive. No fear, only great peace.

I observed the rotation of faces for well over twenty minutes, then closed my eyes and returned to a deeper meditation. Afterwards, I left the temple, not willing to disclose what I'd experienced. I didn't know if it was my delusional mind at play or not.

I stopped in at the bungalow of three men with whom I'd become friends. One was from Hawaii and only a few years younger than me. The other two guys were from California. I sat at the foot of one of the beds and we had a great conversation. It was more like me telling spiritual stories and tales, but I was having a hard time talking. My spine felt as if it was moving and jumping around inside me and my head was light.

I mentioned this to the guys, who agreed they also experienced something powerful inside them. The energy was the strongest where I was sitting, so I had the guys rotate around so everyone sat on that same spot. Amazing! This great energy and power flowed up and down each of our spines. No matter where we sat, we were getting blasted.

When I left, the men were sitting in their bungalow totally zoned out; spiritual children high on life. I wandered to the courtyard near the dining hall to wait for lunch. I saw Gurunath come out and ask Jay, and another young man, and me to eat quickly so we could go with him to the printing office to make sure our book and the cover were being set up correctly.

We left the ashram for Pune with us three men crowded into the back seat and Gurunath in the passenger seat. When we were almost there, Jay and I noticed a large statue of a horse with a warrior on its back. The warrior held a sword in his upraised hand. We reflected on all of our conversations we'd had with Gurunath on this subject. When we were almost at the printing office, Gurunath motioned for us to look to the side of the road at four differently colored horses inside a corral on the city street. Gurunath just pointed them out very casually by saying something like, "Look at those horses."

We spent about eight hours working with the printer. On break, Gurunath bought us treats. I had a strawberry milkshake and he had a coke-and-ice-cream float. I was deeply touched to be sharing this time with him.

As we waited for the printing to be finalized, Jay talked about what he'd seen in the mercury shivalinga that morning. Identical to what I'd seen myself! Incredible! I had dismissed my vision as a product of delusional thinking and a good old Irish imagination.

When we returned to the ashram, I asked a few others if they had seen something in the temple that morning or afternoon. Several described images similar to what Jay and I had seen. The guy from the islands said when he'd seen 'these people' in his meditations in Hawaii and put it down to an active imagination; joked about having thought he'd lost his mind. My story, along with those of others who experienced the vision of the sages, validated each person's past visions.

The subject was raised that night around the campfire with Gurunath, who said these might have been sages from an ancient race of mankind. I was surprised so many others had seen the same things. When at least six people see the same vision, then it is difficult to write off as anything but a real experience.

In later weeks, I was to discover a host of other people and images in this stone. I saw Jesus, Shri Yukteswar, and Gurunath himself; all inside this stone, alive and real.

One morning, I saw the images of two monks who wore orange robes and were clean shaven, including their heads. Though I did not recognize them when I saw them in the stone, I discovered their identities that very morning shortly after I left the temple. As I entered the office, I saw someone had left a copy of a book* on the desk where I was going to work. The book was about guru and disciple relationships. The cover featured a color photo of the monks I had just seen.

On two separate occasions, I saw a huge owl looking at me. He moved his head and blinked his all-knowing eyes at me. It was the familiar feeling I had when I saw 'my owl' in the stone. These sightings were followed by a long period of embraceable happiness.

I saw other sages and saints, unknown to me, in the stone, but the strongest images were of Gurunath himself. One cannot help but be transformed by seeing one's guru looking into one's eyes from inside a stone.

**Footnote*** *Light on the Guru and Disciple Relationship* **by Swami Satyasangananda Saraswati under the guidance of Swami Satyananda Saraswati.**

## Rat Mind

One night at the ashram, when Gurunath had returned after a couple of day's absence, six of us were sitting in the dining hall eating and listening to one of his discourses. The conversation digressed to the mundane subject of rats. They were, for some reason, very active on this cold night. I did not remember seeing them the first three weeks. But on this night, my mind was not elevated beyond looking for the rat racing around the floor and up to the rafters.

I then listened to an Indian woman, who was there to do artwork in the temple. She went on about how, as a young adult in India, she had a fear of rats nibbling at her feet in the night, making it difficult for her to sleep.

In my ego-centered mind, I could not picture myself ever being worried about rats; certainly, not afraid of them. I was rather brazen with my thoughts, seeing myself as the fearless one able to ignore rats, snakes, and even ghosts.

We talked well past one in the morning. Gurunath retired to his bedroom and I walked back down the darkened path to my isolated bungalow. I removed my shoes, leaving them outside, and entered my private accommodation. It was very cold—the kind of night where you could see your breath, even inside a building. I put on a T-shirt, two sweatshirts, and long pants, and then covered my sleeping bag with three heavy blankets. I took out my flashlight, turned off the lights, and sandwiched myself between all the coverings on my hard bunk.

It was one of those early mornings when you prayed to not have to pee so as not to have to get out of bed. If the call of nature occurred, it meant a walk outside into the cold night; not a choice to make until the sun was fully in the sky.

It was almost two in the morning by the time I propped up my head on several pillows and folded my arms inside my blanket-covered sleeping bag.

As I started to doze off, something fuzzy and warm moved past the nape of my neck and across my pillow. I jolted into a sitting position and watched a large rat scramble down the draped blankets on my bed. Wide awake, my eyes like saucers, I wondered where that "dirty rat" had gone. I decided I wasn't about to get out from under the covers, so I lay there and listened to the rat run around under my bed.

It only took a few minutes before the rat, or a friend of that rat, returned; this time, more brazen, crawling around on my head and under my neck. He was not biting me or hurting me, but he certainly had my fullest attention. I wasn't sure of the rodent's agenda, but didn't trust he had come to just visit with me. I kept moving my body and head, changing positions every few minutes to discourage a return visit. I figured the rat must be cold, and my fat, old body offered warmth, but I discouraged him enough to move away.

Then a rodent's body moved gently across my stomach. I could feel his little rat toenails. But he was not in my sleeping bag, yet. I turned on the flashlight and watched this large lump move across my body under the blanket. I reached down and could feel his hairy body with my bare hand. I gently pushed him down, trying my best not to upset him—a big concern—and have him attack. I didn't want to get bitten, but I didn't want to hurt him. I simply didn't want his company.

I kept pushing his body back down to the bottom of the blanket, then I kicked both of my legs up and down to make it uncomfortable for him. He *did* leave, but I could hear him under my bed planning his next assault. At this point, once again, I was wondering if it was the same rat or if there was more than one ganging up on me.

He came back again, but this time he headed right for my chest, toward my neck, before I could stop him. He was determined to get warm under my blankets. At this point it dawned on me: my thinking had brought this whole rat experience to a physical realization. So, it was time to put it to rest. I stopped thinking about rats; decided just to close my eyes and sleep. I would let the rats go and do whatever rats do at nighttime. I was done with the 'rat-thinking' games.

The rest of the night I slept soundly and worry free. I still had a hard time getting out of bed in the early morning cold, but I had no rat wounds and my rat-mind was cured. No more judging others and letting my ego tell me I was fearless. I hoped I'd learned whatever humble lesson the universe had wanted, as I was not looking for a repeat test.

It just so happened, the rats never returned to bother me.

## Be Careful What You Think About

It did not take me long to figure out the great power of the solid mercury stone created immediate consequences. Basically, any thought I had while in the temple or around the ashram came to be, was reflected, or exampled in a short time frame.

I first noticed the phenomenon after a meditation when I'd thought how great it would be to wash the temple floor.

I let the thought pass.

That very night, at dinner, Gurunath expressed to the group of men there that we should consider it good karma, and service to their guru, if we washed the temple floor. Wow!

While cleaning the temple floor, it was rather odd we three men all hit our heads on the temple someplace. When I mentioned it to Gurunath, he said it was like prasad, a Hindu blessing and a gift.

Another example was when I saw trash outside of the ashram, but in full view. I thought it would be a great idea to clean it up. The trash had been there maybe months prior to my thinking about it, but within hours Gurunath summoned us to clean up the area.

A couple of weeks after this happened, one of the men had mentioned to me he had also had those same thoughts about cleaning up the ashram grounds. We'd both had the same kind of instant connection! I was not the only one!

And again, I was walking through the ashram by the kitchen area and noticed all the holes and ruts in the paved surface around the area and wondered if someone could patch the holes. That same morning, it was already being done by one of the Indian workers.

These occurrences heightened my awareness of the power of thoughts. Either I was picking up Gurunath's thoughts and tuning in with his vision, or he was reading my mind and following up for me. It kind of had me concerned either way. I did not want to have any negative thoughts there because they might materialize.

For several days, I had an idle daydream. I envisioned giving Gurunath a military salute. I debated what kind I should offer, having contemplated a modern salute and the old Roman closed fist across the chest salute. Strange! One may attempt to touch the feet of the guru, or the ground nearby, or bow, as well as other gestures one might do to honor or recognize a guru, but certainly not a military salute.

On one of his daily talks, he mentioned being an old warrior in previous lifetimes; a loose connection about saluting him. I asked if he had picked up on that, and he told me there was a *much* deeper bond between us. Then he fell silent.

One morning, after my meditation in the temple, I had this ego-centered fantasy daydream. In my mind, I saw myself stepping in front of Gurunath in various lifetimes, taking an arrow or a spear into my body to protect him. This daydream of giving up my life to save my guru was rather delusional. As much as I really would, if the opportunity arose, it was a bit self-centered to think such things.

Later in the day, I mentioned my ego-fantasy daydream to Gurumata, Gurunath's wife. She became very serious and stood up from her chair, looked at me, and asked, "What makes you think this did not already happen to you, Bill?" Then she turned and walked away leaving me standing alone, wondering what it all meant.

One night Gurunath joined us in the temple for our meditation. But on this night, it only lasted about an hour and I'd not finished my meditation techniques. When Gurunath left the temple, others left as well; six of us remained. We had been there about an hour when I had this thought about how six of us had chosen to stay, while all the rest had left. It was purely ego-driven, reflecting my pride in how we were more serious than those who left the temple.

No sooner had I finished the thought than a man came to stand in the temple doorway; one of the people who had left earlier. He shouted out a message to all of us from the Gurunath, who was unhappy about us staying after he left the temple, and wanted us to close it up and leave. I was stunned he had, once again, zeroed in on my ego. There I was enjoying this inflated feeling of superiority when, suddenly, the spiritual wind was knocked out of my sails. I was defeated and betrayed by my own thoughts.

We walked humbly from the temple. I was upset with myself, but had to laugh at the whole lesson. Gurunath came back out of his house and joined us in the dining area, where our small group had a long satsang with him. He told us the Indian Army had taken control of the city of Pune due to terrorist threats; a city about forty-five minutes away from us. Rather odd that he would make such a statement. We were insulated from the news of the rest of the world—no TV, radio, newspapers.

We stayed up to about two in the morning, when Gurunath finally left to go to bed. As I walked to my bungalow, talking with several others, I was compelled to turn off the porch light to conserve electrical use as we had been instructed to do. I decided to wait for a few minutes for the rest of the guys to see where they were going, but was getting these urgent thoughts to turn off the lights.

Just then I heard a voice in the darkness, and saw the shadowy figure of Gurunath standing under a mango tree. He shouted in my direction to shut the lights off. I just shrugged it off. I'd been 'had.'

Another afternoon, I was sitting with the guys outside and began to wonder if there was going to be any meal service. Gurunath was gone for a few days, and the schedule is a bit different when he is not there. I was thinking how hungry I was and wanted to eat. At that very moment, one of the ashram's workers stopped in front of us and told us lunch was ready. I was amazed my desire for food had come so quickly to me, seeing as it was not the time of day we'd normally have our meal.

Gurunath walked around the ashram one morning, then headed up the hill to the temple. When he returned, he changed his clothing for the day's outing. We were going by bus to a couple of old temples, almost two hours away from the ashram. While getting ready, he'd lost his set of keys. He asked us all to retrace his steps to look for them. Several of us headed for the temple, but I kept thinking it was a waste of time. I believed they'd be found where he'd changed his clothing. I walked part way up the hill, then stopped and started walking back; convinced of my assumption.

At that moment, someone shouted he'd found the keys. When I saw him, I mentioned I was sure they were where he'd dressed. He smiled and confirmed that's where they were. I should have stated my opinion to ward off much anxiety, but then again, maybe all I had done was to just tune into his thoughts about where to look for them.

Another morning, Gurunath gave a talk, during which I started thinking how I hadn't been showing him full respect, like the younger guys there who bowed down and touch the ground or tried to touch his feet. They also waited on him by getting him food and drinks. I, on the other hand, had been more laid back and casual. Respectful, but compared to the group of devotees around him, I was not of the same cut.

In my mind, I saw myself prostrated on the floor with tears rolling down my face. On the outside, no one saw any emotions as I was only thinking privately. Then Gurunath startled me with the next sentence out of his mouth. He began talking about how one learns more from his guru when he is brought to tears than to laughter. Both served a purpose and taught us something spiritual. *Had he seen my inner image?* The timing was just too good to be a random topic in his morning talk.

One night, around the campfire in the early morning hours, Gurunath noted it was time to wind down the evening. Looking in my direction, as I was getting up, he said something very strong and forceful, directing me to go to bed NOW! As these words blasted out of his mouth, a force of energy knocked me over and I fell onto the person sitting on the grass behind me. Right into his lap!

Gurunath asked me what happened. My first reaction was to blame him for knocking me over; an odd response, but true. He smiled, then spoke on the power of his words; how he had caused this to happen many times before; how he would need to be more careful in the future with the energy and force of his speech.

Gurunath spoke about so many new things to me each day, humbling me with my own ignorance. I thought myself quite intelligent, but now I realized I knew absolutely nothing! The wisdom and depth of his words and spiritual understanding obviously do not come from book reading, but from something much deeper and greater. Listening to him talk was like having a radio station tuned into God.

## The Tarot Card Reading

As I was conversing with one of the men at the ashram, he mentioned an Indian woman had given a Tarot card reading to Gurunath the previous year; and that this woman had impressed Gurunath with her ability. He then informed me she would be coming to the ashram in a few days' time for a seven-day personal retreat. I decided I would ask her to read for me. I wanted to find out about my connections with my family, and with Gurunath himself.

Typically, I'd not have paid much attention to card readings. In childhood, I'd watched my mother, a gifted psychic and card reader, do this for hundreds of people, yet I simply could not pass up the opportunity with someone who'd impressed Gurunath.

Professionally known throughout the world as the psychic Roomela Rai, she spends part of her time in the Arab world and the other in India. I was impressed with her from the moment of our introduction. She came across as strong and insightful without any sign of an inflated ego. She was going to be staying at the ashram for a few days, so I asked her right away if we could set up a reading. She graciously made the time for me, even though she was there for other purposes.

She came to my small bungalow and took out the Tarot cards she carried in a special cloth-like purse. She laid the cards face down on the bed and sat on the opposite side of me. Then she asked me to think of some questions; not an easy task. I really did not care about knowing the future. I was more interested in understanding more about the relationships in my life.

I began asking about my relationship with my youngest grandson, Gianni, who was three years old at the time of the reading. I drew several cards from the deck as instructed. She stated there was a deep connection between the two of us—Gianni and I— and we'd shared at least five lifetimes. She kept referring to him as a "wise old man" who had come into our lives. She went on about how spiritually evolved his soul was. None of this came as much of a surprise. I had already seen him talking to dead people and heard him discussing his past lives, including flying helicopters in a war. He was also the first person in the family Gurunath had visited in dreams and visions. He was carrying heavy spiritual energy with him from the past.

I then asked about my granddaughter, Daylana. Roomela went on about her being a kind of "luxury goddess" with good karma; she would never lack for material things. Daylana would bring wealth and success and joy to others around her. As I listened to Roomela, I agreed. My granddaughter was not only a loving and beautiful person physically, but was also a highly evolved spiritual being.

When I asked about my oldest grandson, Spencer, she said he just needed and wanted my love and support. She described him as a kind person, with a compassionate soul, who would learn a lot in this lifetime. She suggested I not put extra pressure on him and just allow him to grow.

I went on and asked about my connection with Daya, who seems to be the more spiritually attuned with me than anyone else. Roomela began confirming. There was a lot of compatibility between us from many previous lifetimes. I had been a guide to my daughter in previous existences, but it was she who had always managed to lead me to the 'sunshine.' According to Roomela, "Once she is around, you feel her peace." It was true, there had always been a major psychic connection between us. It seems Daya and me are good for each other's spiritual growth.

Next, I asked about my son, Josh. She described him perfectly: a strong and brave soul who, though psychic, was prone to disbelief about his abilities. She pointed out we both had very different communication styles. She advised me to listen to him more, stating he was a practical person, and very intelligent. His opinions and advice would tend to be wise, prudent, and more down to earth in the real material world.

She then talked about my wife and me. In respect for Carol's privacy, I will simply point out that when I first dated Carol in high school, I knew we would get married. The bond between us was deep from the very beginning. She has been most patient and loving all these years. I thank God for her every day. I am blessed to be in her life.

Next, I asked the question about the connection between Gurunath and me. From the very first moments we met in person, he showered me with many blessings, healings, and great love. I could not have asked for any better a reception from anyone, including God! Roomela paused, and then read the cards I had selected for this question. She went on saying this was the closest of relationships. The cards indicated it was a relationship much like family; that we have been connected for many lifetimes and at a very close level. I was here now, in this lifetime, to help him, as much as he was helping me. I found it hard to accept. He was giving me a pathway to God. What could I give to him?

She went on about how our families inter-connect and how my mission was to serve him; perhaps by writing books about him. She said I would help generate greater attention and fame for him, and in so doing, I could not avoid doing the same for myself. There was no way I could help him without helping myself. It was a mutual relationship of serving and honoring. She went on with many more details of this relationship between Gurunath and me, but my mind continued to ponder how I could give him as much as I was getting. Even so, there was a part of me that totally accepted this concept; the idea I was there on this special mission to help. I just wondered if I was truly up to the task.

There were more questions and answers before she finally said she'd lost touch with her source and had nothing more to say in the reading. I thanked her, then sat there thinking over all she'd said. There was much more stated about the connections with Gurunath, but I've discovered almost all those who are close to him have many connections as well. No strangers come to his ashram; he knows them all.

## Blue Lotus Feet

I was totally privileged to be in the company of a true master while staying at Yogiraj's Forest Ashram. I had been hearing some truly biblical stories from some of his long-time devotees, of how Gurunath could walk through walls, be in two bodies, go into breathlessness, and perform a host of other unworldly feats. Then one evening, I got my own taste of what others were talking about.

There were four of us in Gurunath's front room. We were all listening to him expound on subject matters well above my earthly ears and brain. His words were full of serious, spiritual wisdom but he was just as likely, at times, to turn the moment into a stand-up routine that had us all rolling in laughter. He had a way of mixing the very sacred and the lighthearted. Totally spontaneous, he could talk deeply about any subject matter in the cosmos.

On this night, an Indian woman devotee had insisted on washing her guru's feet. This is a huge honor in India and much is said about the energy that can be transferred from the guru to his follower through this act of total devotion. At first, he resisted her desire to carry out this act, but finally relented and allowed his feet to be cleaned. He continued talking while she sat on the floor washing his feet. Each of us listened intently as he continued to deliver deep spiritual principles beyond my full understanding. The longer I spent with Gurunath the more I accepted, as I said before, my ignorance.

At some point, Gurunath asked the woman to allow another devotee, Jay, to finish up the task. She resisted, but stepped back and allowed the young man from California to come forward to massage his feet.

Within minutes, I could see Jay was about to fall over with joy. His whole face was illuminated from the experience; the hair on his arms and head stood up like when someone experiences static electricity. Finally, he pulled back and leaned over on his elbow to rest. His smile was plastered from ear to ear; his heart truly radiating love. Then Jay looked up at Gurunath and asked, "Should I tell them?"

Gurunath nodded his approval. Jay said millions of blue lotus flowers came out of the feet and penetrated him. He said they looked tiny when they came out and then grew as they came at his heart.

We were all in awe. The old Indian tradition always talks about "the blue lotus feet of the Guru." It has been recorded in literature and songs for thousands of years. On this night, we understood it was not poetic expression but also a reality.

I watched the reactions of the others, and could tell the woman was disappointed this had not happened to her while she was washing Gurunath's feet. Inside my own head, I was thinking, *Hey, where is my blue foot experience?*

We left Gurunath's front room shortly after, wanting to finish up the task of painting artwork on the smaller temple's walls. It was already late at night, and the jungle valley became cold that time of year, but we worked barefoot in the temple on cold marble flooring.

I found myself with a few tasks at once: handing a paintbrush to one of the young men, while holding the lid from the paint can in the other hand, to ensure no paint dripped from the brush. Then I walked past the top of a marble stairwell leading down to Gurunath's private meditation chamber. Suddenly, my left foot became snared in an electrical wire strung across the top of the stairs. The wires became wrapped around my toes and I pitched forward, my head on a collision path with the bottom of the stairs.

Due to the super-quick reactions of Jay, I was caught before falling too far down the stairs. The fall could have severely injured or even killed me, due to the spinal cord issues in my neck.

The time it took to tangle and fall was exactly like a slow-motion movie—minutes instead of fractions of seconds. My head was inches from hitting the marble stairs when I was stopped in mid-air and pulled back.

One who witnessed the fall told me he heard the cracking sounds, snapping, like someone stepping on a bag of potato chips. There was tremendous pain shooting through me, as if I had broken all the bones in my foot. I looked down and saw how the electrical wire was wrapped around my toes and cutting the skin. There was a small amount of blood on the marble flooring. Yet funnily enough, I still held the paint can's lid and the wet paint brush. I didn't want to have the marble floors ruined by paint, so I'd not used my hands to stop the fall, and continued to hold them up. When someone tried to help, me get upright all I was concerned about was making sure he got the paintbrush and the lid.

I was unable to stand or walk. The pain was just too great. I pulled myself along on the floor by my hands and slid my body to the entrance of the temple, then pulled my feet in front me and sat on the entrance steps to look at my injured left foot. It was a mess.

One of the men went to fetch Gurunath, who rushed to where I was resting and merely peered at my foot on the cold marble steps—a blue foot, very bruised, swollen, and emanating great pain. It looked like I would need some emergency medical attention; that there were possibly several toes and foot-bones broken.

Gurunath casually stated, "There is nothing wrong with your foot, it will be okay in the morning."

I looked up at him, remembering this same man zapped my brain and stopped my seizures. If he said nothing was wrong with my foot, then who was I not to believe that? I totally accepted what he said.

When his wife, Gurumata, came a couple of minutes later, along with her motherly concerns, I told her what Gurunath had said; that nothing was wrong with me; that the first time I'd met Gurunath, he'd told me a guru can never lie, he could only tell the truth. Upon saying this, I stood up, put on my shoes, and I walked around. The pain was gone. The bleeding had stopped. The color was normal. Moments ago, a twisted foot, it was now straight. I could move my foot and my toes again. Everyone was astonished over what had happened.

The next morning, I approached Gurunath as he walked around the ashram grounds, and touched the ground near his feet. I told him I was grateful for his healing my foot. He looked me in the eye and said, "I did not heal your foot. It was your belief in my words that healed you."

I had totally accepted and believed in the word of Gurunath. He could never lie. He had to tell the truth. Because I believed, I was healed. Instantly. I also laughed privately; a part of me had wanted my own "blue foot experience" with the guru. I just did not expect it to come the way it did. I took it as a blessing, as well as another lesson on watching my thoughts. But the biggest lesson for me, and for those who were there, was to fully trust and listen to the words of Gurunath as the TRUTH.

*Note: A year after this experience, I got a phone call from a woman I had never met, to sort out some of her personal issues. She had 'needed' to talk to me. Before she began to ask her questions and tell me her concerns, I began by telling her all sorts of things about her own life and relationships. Then I told her I wanted to tell her a story. I did not give her much time to say no, and dove right in about the healing of my foot.*

When I finished, she went silent. I wondered if the phone connection had been lost. She then said she had to go and hung up. I had no clue to what any of that was about.

Several days later, she called me back to explain. As she was listening to me tell the story about Gurunath, saying nothing was wrong with my foot, she felt he was talking directly to her. Just a couple of days before, she had broken her foot, went to the ER, and had it X-rayed. They'd set it and put a hard cast on it. But when she heard the story, her faith was such, she hung up the phone, got a knife, and cut off the cast. She had been walking around without any cast, having no pain or issues ever since. She had called to thank me for the story.

Now I must admit, before she told me her news, I had no idea why I was telling her the story. I just trusted I had to do so. After this, there was one more similar experience. Except in this case, I was familiar with this woman's situation. I was with her at the ER, where she was in terrible pain, crying loudly. I told her both stories, and when I finished, her pain went away. She was released a short time later and went directly to a writing conference where she stood for over two hours and delivered a presentation. She says the power of the story took away her pain and allowed her to stand and walk. Though she did receive treatments for her foot when she got back home, it was good enough for her to give her talk at the writer's conference.

## The Yellow Rose

Life was filled with spiritual celebration. I had been invited to go to a royal wedding with Gurunath and his wife; an arranged wedding between royal families.

We left the ashram and headed to Pune to spend the night there before leaving the next afternoon for Kolhapur. The drive was more than four hours through hilly country, reminding me of parts of California's farming areas.

We arrived at a relative's home, then continued to the wedding, taking place at a hotel. Sadly, there were not enough rooms for me to stay with his family at their hotel, so Gurunath arranged for a room for me in a hotel directly across the street.

He escorted me over and asked me to inspect the room to see if I was satisfied. While he remained in the lobby, I trudged on up the stairs, a little disappointed not to be staying with Gurunath's family.

As I put the key in the door lock, my mind continued to fight the disappointment of not being in the same hotel. I had to remind myself this was the room *my guru* had chosen for me. It was then the story of Paramahansa Yogananda giving out roses to a group of people in line who had listened to his talk that day came to mind. He would pick out one from a pile of roses on the table next to him and hand them to the people in line as he blessed those people. When one woman was blessed and given a yellow rose, she requested Yogananda reselect and give her a red one.

Yogananda looked at her sternly and told her, if a guru gives you a yellow rose, you take it. He insisted the guru 'knows what you need.'

That story floated around in my head as I turned the key and entered the room Gurunath had chosen for me. As the curtains caught my attention, I smiled widely. The printed fabric was all yellow roses!

When I came down the stairs and Gurunath asked me how I liked the room, I replied it was absolutely perfect.

## The King of California

After I was invited by Gurumata to the wedding, she purchased a couple of regal outfits for me to wear. I was blessed by the invitation, and overwhelmed by her generous gesture of clothing.

The best part of one week was spent with Gurunath's family at the celebration attended by over two-thousand guests.

When we returned to the ashram, Gurunath had asked me to convey the details of the wedding to the group of devotees who had not attended.

I began talking about the kings and ministers who were in attendance; all kinds of important families, some very wealthy, some famous, many both. I went on sharing details of the weeklong wedding and expressed it was a great experience for me; how well I'd been treated—special attention and everything—providing examples, including the day of the final wedding vows.

There was a trumpet player with an ancient looking horn several feet in length. He wore a traditional costume with funny looking shoes. His job was to blow the horn only when prominent, high-ranking guests entered the wedding tent and walked down the long aisle. I had witnessed him blow it for three people—a minister, and two "king-like" individuals—and when he did, numerous armed guards came to attention, and people turned to see who was entering.

The thing is, when I entered the tent, he ran toward me and stood at full attention. He then placed the horn to his lips and blew the loudest, longest horn blast of those I'd heard so far. He continued in a succession of horn blasts. Suddenly, the place was silent and all eyes turned toward me. The horn blower then proceeded to lay flat on the ground, grab my feet, and laid his head on the floor. All the guards stood briskly at attention with their automatic weapons at the ready. They snapped a full hand salute as I passed them down the aisle, as if I was a king.

People kept coming up to me, welcoming me to the wedding, even though, I assumed, they had no idea who I was. I thought perhaps they didn't want to ask so as not to be seen as being ignorant.

When I was recounting my experience to those at the ashram, my statements contained more than a hint of pride and ego. It was at that point, I heard loud laughter coming from the kitchen area. I stopped talking and asked what was so funny. Out stepped Gurunath's older son, Shivraj. He could not hide his amusement, grinning from ear to ear. He then told everyone there, including Gurunath, I was treated like a king because of what *he,* Shivraj, had told the trumpet player.

"Which was what?" I asked.

He said he'd told the trumpet player, who apparently was not very bright, that I was 'The King of California!"

The whole group burst out laughing. Gurunath, too. The joke was truly on me. From that moment on, I picked up an additional nickname, The King of California!

One must still wonder, what little quirk of karma was at play here. I was truly treated as if I were a king and someone of great importance for several days. It was fun, even if it was a short-lived fantasy. It is not every day someone gets crowned The King of California.

## Road Warrior

I was so comfortable returning to the ashram; so, happy to be back there after the wedding. Upon arrival, I noticed several new people had checked in, so I introduced myself, then made sure they had blankets, mosquito netting, and toilet paper, and confirmed with them the location of basic supplies.

It was about five in the evening when I got word that Gurunath needed help from some of the men at the ashram. He was in the jungle facing a group of thugs. Apparently, half a dozen men had been out drinking; one wielding an axe. When I arrived, I heard loud exchanges of shouting and swearing; a serious confrontation.

These men had been harassing Gurunath and his efforts to build a permanent new road to his ashram property; a road made available and specifically for others to use. The old road was subject to being closed at the whim of the owners of the property. Gurunath had received official government permission to build a new road through to his property three years previous. He had all the court papers giving him the right to build it. Yet each time he began this process, this gang would show up and claim Gurunath was going through their property; stopped him each time by cutting down trees, threatening violence, and intimidation. Though they had no 'legal' authority, they did have the 'support' of local corrupt police and officials.

Apparently, the leader of the hoodlums was a man who had been scamming locals for years with con games. He'd been involved in selling the same properties, illegally, several times to different people, yet no one ever stopped him.

His face bore lots of scars, a history of local retribution by those he'd cheated. For the longest time he'd been doing this, and had acquired immunity from prosecution for reasons only an Indian citizen might understand. The whole concept was beyond my understanding of how a local government should operate.

Gurunath had warned us over the previous weeks there was a possibility of a confrontation. He wanted us on alert; to be there when he needed us to back him up. Gurunath was determined to build his road, and he was not going to let these thugs stop him.

This night these men became extremely aggressive and threatened physical harm to Gurunath. I assume they had mistaken him for some kind of flower-power guru, a peace and love yogi. Well, they did not know this man as we did.

When one man started yelling in the face of Gurunath, Gurunath jumped at the guy and slapped the man on his chest knocking the wind out of him. It surprised the man, but instantly brought him back to his senses. The tone of the conversation began to change. I had been summoned to join the few guys there to support Gurunath, but we reached this spot in the forest just moments after Gurunath had put his hand on the man's chest.

Knowing Gurunath was in total control of his emotions on the inside, his display of apparent anger was an outward drama he manufactured to awaken these men; to assert some control over the situation.

Gurunath had previously had some of us preparing for the road to be built. Much preparation was done cutting back bushes and laying out the path for the road late at night to prevent more confrontations with the thugs, but the real work had to be done in the daytime. Gurunath had hired two big bulldozers to come out early one morning and work from both ends until the road connected. It was a fast process since the road was only about a mile long. I have never seen road construction done so quickly.

One of the leaders of the gang returned and made the mistake of yelling at Gurunath, getting in his face. Gurunath responded by roaring with such a force that the man turned and ran away; a voice like an alpha male lion, full of energy and vibrations felt for a great distance. Gurunath then gave chase, with a devotee following close behind. Everyone assumed Gurunath was angry and getting ready to dismantle the offender. But when he turned toward me, he was all smiles winking at me—all a show with no emotions involved at all. I smiled back in understanding.

Afterwards, when the road was completed and the bad guys had left the area, Gurunath decided to drive his four-wheel-drive van to inspect the full length of it. He got behind the wheel, me in the front passenger seat, and three young guys in the back, then revved up the engine, popped the clutch, and roared down the road. Soon after, we headed for a three-foot dirt embankment directly in front. He put the pedal to the floor and we hit embankment at full speed. The whole vehicle flew skywards, landing some ten yards from where we had lifted off. It reminded me of an American TV show, *The Dukes of Hazard*, when they'd jump their car over a creek.

The young guys in the back seat were hanging on for their lives. Us two old guys, Gurunath and me, laughed and fully enjoyed the entire experience. We then sped down the dirt road and spun out, coming to a stop inches from the edge of a drop. We all had to get out of the vehicle and push it sideways so we would not go off the hillside.

Gurunath and I were flying high and enjoying every minute of it. The energy was explosive. Like being in a bubble of lightning, it truly was a once-in-a-lifetime experience.

It was rather fitting, at the temple that morning, I'd had a vision in the mercury stone of a huge, male lion roaring. It was going to be a part of my day. The 'Lion King' of this jungle had roared, and he was heard across the entire valley.

## An Auspicious Day

The day after almost all the visitors and devotees, who were present for a week of spiritual training, had left the ashram, the valley fell quiet and peaceful again. There were five of us there, all men casually sitting around listening to Gurunath give his insights on everything from time and space to the big bang theory. The conversation was highly charged; the kind that makes one's head swim and one's heart joyful.

That night we sensed Gurunath was taking us on a deeper journey than normal. Most of the things he said were far beyond our common understandings. While many might use intellectual skills to wrestle with the concepts he presented, I simply sat enraptured by the vibrating words of wisdom flowing from his higher consciousness. My heart fully understood what we'd heard was the pure essence of TRUTH.

The morning sun rose ever-so-gently over the horizon as Gurunath brought out a carved piece of jade that had been in his family for hundreds of years. It was the same kind of sculpture holding a sacred shivalinga, which is a much deeper subject for another time. But suffice it to state, this was one of the sacred items from his personal altar. It had great spiritual significance. Gurunath held it up to the sun to allow us see how the thick stone let in the radiant light around the edges. In the sunlight, the solid gem became partially translucent, allowing partial light through some of it.

We then received a rare visit from a large black bird with orange on its wings and long tail feathers trailing out beyond its body. Gurunath silenced, then told us sighting such a bird in the morning was spiritually auspicious.

When I asked him what he meant, he said the bird was signaling immense spiritual growth, changes, and insights. The general message was that things of a spiritual nature were evolving for the betterment of those of us witnessing this morning visitor to the ashram grounds.

Next, two black ravens flew around and behind Gurunath as he spoke to us. One of the men whispered to us, throughout his own life, two of these birds together have always been sacred messengers. When Gurunath paused, he asked about the symbolism of the raven in Indian culture.

I was listening to Gurunath when one of the men interrupted to point out to all of us the sound of an owl's hooting. On this morning, its volume and voice was deeper and louder than normal. Gurunath stated it must be a huge owl. I fell into deep contemplation, as my own spiritual messenger sounded in the background. I began to have the feeling this was truly going to be an extraordinary day. (A little later, as I typed the experience, in my bungalow in the ashram, I heard several hoots from my owl friend.)

As we sat, absorbing not only Gurunath's words but his wisdom and love, he looked at each one of us. His eyes then focused on me and asked why I thought we were so content and at home at the ashram. Then, without waiting for any response, he said because we had spent so many lifetimes in India, it was our home.

His comments applied to all of us, but he locked on me with a magnetic gaze; the power of his physical eyes, as well as his inner eyesight, seeing through to my naked soul.

The morning radiated with a mystical feeling as we began editing Gurunath's book. The printer's deadline neared, and the manuscript required lots of changes. I worked with one of the younger devotees to speed up the project. He was well-educated in the Indian language. After several hours of computer work, Gurunath joined us and began to dictate new information for the book.

The words flowed as if channeled from another dimension, discovering the words much in the same way we were. Every so often he would stop and look at the both of us, truly expressing surprise at what he was saying. We were witnessing something very special and very significant. The book was taking on a whole new profound energy; the creation of a new sacred text. The air was sizzling with a palpable power.

When we took a short break from the book, I went outside to walk around the ashram, where I saw a worker's young children. He was in pain from having one of his rotten baby teeth pulled that day, his face swollen on one side. This little boy and I were special friends, so my heart hurt to see him suffering. I walked over to where he was sitting on a bench, wanting to do something to eliminate his pain. I reached out to gently touch his swollen cheek.

A surge of electrical current shot right through my fingers and hit his cheek with a full force of energy. My fingers tingled like I'd just stuck them in an electrical socket. We were both literally shocked.

This was the only time I'd encountered static electricity at the ashram. Common sense would lead one to assume that this was what it was, but the power of it almost knocked me off my feet. It also made a snapping sound and gave off a faint flash of light. My fingers hurt for several minutes.

Intelligently, I accepted scientific theory. But emotionally, I questioned its source. I wondered if that shock might have had some positive result in the healing process. He was in less pain after that, but it could have been the natural course of healing, so I remained in the dark.

We continued to work on the book for several more hours. At around ten-thirty in the evening, we went off to the kitchen to get something for dinner, just the three of us.

Gurunath radiated joy and love. We were happy to be in his presence, sharing his aura and energy. We began to ask questions about his life mission and who he really was. The conversation got deep into past lives and a future life he was destined to live. He was asked about passages from his book *Wings to Freedom*. After weeks of connecting the dots from the mysterious clues in his book, hinted at from dozens of campfire and public talks, we'd discovered what he had been hiding from others. Now were about to witness the confirmation of our conclusion.

Peering deep into our cores, his humble eyes said he was just a human being, a simple man with a mission.

We went on citing all the connections and why we felt as we did. He offered a humble, but not a very convincing retort to our assertions. He did not attack our belief as to who he was, nor belittle it in any way. He did concede his mission would take someone as advanced as we were suggesting, but he could not comment any deeper on our speculations. Not everything was known, even to him, at that time of his life. Then he looked at us and said his mission, and who he was, would be revealed to him by his next birthday, May 10, 2009—four months away from the time of our conversation.

He had an otherworldly gaze as his eyes stared past and through the both of us. I sat there quietly. Then I spoke up, announcing I knew who he was beyond any doubt. My own intuition, I said, was positive; that what our small group had concluded was the truth.

I half expected him to verbally jump on me for making such a wild and egotistical statement. He became quieter as he reflected on my words. It dawned on me: perhaps the two of us were part of some divine play where we were allowed to be used as messengers. I looked at Gurunath again, knowing I would never again see him in the same limited light. I was in the presence of someone who was beyond our total and fullest understandings.

Sometime thereafter, we went back to working on the book and stayed at it until well past one in the morning. The words flowing from his lips sounded as if they came from far within him. The book was taking on a much more sacred and special energy. We were so blessed to be working with him on it.

I am hesitant to publicly disclose in this book who we think he really is or what his mission will be. Gurunath did not tell me to hide it nor did he censor me in any way in writing this book. However, the impact and importance of what we discovered overwhelms me with a sense of great responsibility.

The next morning, as I went to work on the book, I saw the two ravens again. They were perched either side of his small temple doorway. They did not fly away, but stood there like guardians, watching me, like a pair of angels.

The last twenty-four hours had been auspicious indeed.

## Ghost Stories around the Campfire

With Gurunath away on business, there were only four of us devotees in the ashram. We were sitting around our nightly campfire outside the small temple when one of the Indian women told us the following tale about her grandfather's experience with ghosts:

Her grandfather was a medical doctor, but also practiced an ancient kind of magic. Once, he was contacted by a man who had asked him to come to their home to treat one of the women living there. In fact, he did not want to go, but the man who'd requested his presence had provided a buggy and horse, was willing to pay him cash, and then return him home.

Her grandfather consented to go see the sick woman and headed to her mansion in this carriage. The doctor found the woman, who was a Muslim, all dressed in the traditional coverings, hiding her face and body. He examined her and gave her some medicine. The man then paid the doctor, all in coins, and secured his ride home.

The next night, the same man came again, and the doctor repeated the care. This went on for several nights, each time the doctor being paid in coins.

Soon, he had a bag full of these coins and showed them to a friend, telling him all about the patient. The friend told him the house he was going to each night had burned down many years before. The fire had killed the entire family, including a new bride. This same friend challenged the doctor that the house was not there, betting him the entire bag of coins.

They drove out to the address where the doctor had been going all week to treat the woman and found nothing but an old, burned-out house. The doctor was shocked; adamant he'd been there and treated the woman.

Obviously, her grandfather lost the bet and was spooked as well.

Another person sitting around the campfire had been an up-and-coming rock and roll star who had been on the brink of fame and fortune when he'd developed issues with substance abuse. He told some of his own stories from his experiences fighting 'evil entities' of various kinds. Drugs and alcohol invite these 'entities' into your life. At the time, he told us his stories, he was of pure heart and a young man on a serious spiritual quest. It was difficult for me to see him as his old self. His stories really opened another whole dimension to this campfire conversation.

When it came around to my turn, I offered some stories of things I'd experienced. I ended by confidently declaring—no doubt with lots of ego—nothing ever scares me. I could handle any of those ghostly encounters.

A few minutes later, we heard a growling panther inside the ashram. Close, perhaps less than fifty feet away from us. It was like the sounds one hears in jungle movies, or at the zoo. It was real, and aroused our macho instincts. Instead of taking precautions, we all grabbed our flashlights and went running toward a large, wild cat; not a single ounce of common sense between any of us guys. We just wanted to see it. Fortunately, we ended up chasing it off with all our noise and our flashlights. We were disappointed as well as lucky.

Shortly after, we put out the fire and headed to our bungalows. It was a dark walk to mine, and I had a very small light, but I managed to get to my door and unlocked it. I went inside the room and closed the door, then, in the darkness of the room, I turned my flashlight toward my bed.

My heart leapt into my throat. The light caught the image of a youthful, skinny, semi-naked, long-haired yogi sitting cross-legged on the end of my bed, on top of my blankets. He sat and said nothing, eyes zapping through the darkness like a laser beam.

I became so excited I tossed the flashlight up into the air. It spun around in the air before it banged on the floor and spun some more. By the time, I recovered it and pointed the light at my bed again, the figure had disappeared. I looked under my bed and searched the entire room.

My heart was still beating about three times faster than normal as I sat down on my bed and caught my breath, a little afraid for a few moments. Then I remembered my brazen statement about how no ghosts or demons or even gods could ever frighten me. It looked like God was having a bit of amusement at my expense. I laughed at myself. What an ego! When tested, I'd shown I was just like everyone else. So much for 'Mr. Macho the Ghost Buster.' Thank God no one would know.

The next morning, while I was walking around the ashram, Gurunath returned. He called out to me, smiling, "I thought those things were not supposed to scare you!"

I meekly smiled back. So much for keeping a secret.

## The Four Horsemen

When I was at the ashram, I kept having these dreams about a warrior on a white horse with a weapon. Sometimes it would be a curved sword, and sometimes it resembled a three-pronged trident spear called a Trishool. The man on the horse always had a long white beard and a headful of white flowing hair. At various times, the man on the horse alternated his appearance by resembling either Gurunath or Shri Yukteswar. In fact, in these dreams, it was impossible to determine which image I truly saw; their faces would fade and blend into one another.

From the time of my arrival, a series of non-dream horse sightings took place whenever I left the ashram with Gurunath. We would drive by huge statues in various cities and see white horses on billboards, even on top of a restaurant we stopped at on the way to the wedding. I pointed it out to Gurunath—a rooftop-mounted, large, wooden cutout of a white horse rearing up on its back legs. I told him the only thing it lacked was someone with a weapon. When we arrived at the city where the wedding would take place, we drove right past a huge statue right in the middle of the city—a horse rearing up on its hind legs, with a woman warrior holding a raised sword on its back.

The first night of the wedding visit, I stayed at the home of one of Gurunath's relatives and was given a single bedroom for myself. When I took my bag into the room the dresser had upon it a two-foot tall metal statue of a white horse rearing up. When I told Gurunath, he came and looked at it. An amused smile, along with soft eyes, was his response.

Upon our return, we stopped at his residence in Pune to spend a night before heading off to ashram in the morning. I slept in his upstairs guest bedroom. Once again, I noticed a small statue of another horse with its front feet up in the air. I had to stop thinking about these horses and not get hung up trying to figure it out.

A week or so later, we left the ashram to go to the printer's plant where his book, *Wings to Freedom*, was being printed. When we turned the corner to drive down a city road in a highly-industrialized area of Pune, Gurunath got my attention. He pointed out the window at a small fenced in area where there were four horses of different colors including a white one. He just said, "There are your four horses, Bill."

I still didn't have a clue as to what it all meant, and by this point in time the questions kept building up as to what the significance was if any.

The next morning, I was one of a small group of men sitting around with Gurunath. Suddenly, he broke the silence in the dining room, and blurted out "The question you had, Bill, about the horses is—" He went on about the Bible, 'The Four Horsemen of the Apocalypse.' and how it all fit into revelations of the future. Then he alluded to who and what role he might play in this future drama.

It would take many chapters to explain what he told us that morning. Yet I refuse to steal the thunder of his words nor try to do so without his wisdom and insight.

On my last day at the ashram, when almost everyone else had left, I stood near the driveway by the lower temple, looking out towards the ashram entrance. There, sitting on a big white horse, was Gurunath, holding weapon. But I was more focused on his face. He was grinning at me. I was truly impressed he would take the time and energy and incur such costs to see me off while sitting on a white horse. I spun around, searching for someone to tell, but there was no one. It was then I saw Gurunath talking to his wife near the dining hall. *But wasn't he just on the white horse?* I turned back to where he'd been milliseconds before…only empty space. I *had* actually seen him. It was not like a dream, or a vision. It was real to me. When I told Gurunath in California, he smiled knowingly.

## Part Four

# LEARNING TO SERVE

### I Return Home

Even though I had greatly missed my family, it was difficult to walk away from the ashram, difficult to leave India.

Before the final leg of the journey I landed at San Francisco's international airport on a stormy afternoon. Home. But on approach, a bolt of lightning had struck the airplane. The plane quickly dropped hundreds of feet, all the cabin lights flashed, and some of the overhead baggage compartments flew open. The plane became unstable and rolled in both directions, while the nose dropped down. It was evident to all onboard we'd been hit.

Within seconds, we bounced along the runway, a hard landing, but on the ground nonetheless. All the passengers, including me—and no doubt the crew—were relieved to finally arrive at the terminal and get the heck out of that aircraft. It became apparent the storm had severely affected travel schedules; our plane was to be the last to land before the airport authority halted all incoming and outgoing flights.

After moving through international customs and picking up my two bags, I headed to the connecting flight to Sacramento I'd scheduled myself an hour between arrival and departure.

I checked in and sat down to relax, then noticed the monitors for incoming and outgoing flights were blinking; lots of action. The words DELAYED and CANCELLED popped up all over. The estimated time of departure for my Sacramento flight kept changing, later and later. Then the words 'FLIGHT CANCELLED' were posted. It was already too late into the night to call and bother family or friends to come and get me, so I decided to spend the night in the terminal. That decision was a lonely one, as I noticed how quickly everyone else left for hotels, or other transportation.

Well after midnight, I decided to sit it out on one of the hard, plastic chairs in the deserted terminal. They had metal handrails separating them so a person couldn't lie flat to sleep. I decided to use my time wisely and meditate. I sat upright and began doing my Kriya Yoga. No one was there to watch me, so I was not so self-conscious.

Within a few minutes, there was a presence. Someone was watching me. I opened my eyes and peered around. An old man stared at me from outside the window of the terminal building, through the rain-stained glass. I could see the runways and airport lights behind him. I looked directly at him, concerned. Perhaps, I was not supposed to be alone in the terminal. Then I closed my eyes and shut him out.

I meditated for about fifteen minutes. When I looked over at the large window, sure enough, the guy was still standing outside focusing all his attention on me sitting in the chair.

Then it occurred to me: Should I drift off into any kind of deep sleep? At some point, I could be in danger from a thief. But if this guy continued watching me through the window, it might deter anyone from lifting my passport and money; not that there was anyone around.

Another couple of hours went by. I opened my eyes from what was probably more sleep than meditation, and there he was, still watching from the same location. I returned to sleep. A few hours later, I was roused by sounds of people walking by. It was morning. I looked over at the windows. The man was gone.

I decided to walk over to the windows where I'd seen him and look outside at the runway. I was shocked to find where I saw the man standing was impossible. The terminal building was two stories tall. There were no railings or even ledges for anyone to stand on at any time, let alone all night long. There was no way anyone could have been out there looking in at me. I was baffled.

Not only had I seen someone there, but their image may have protected me from anyone who happened along. In any case, I'd been loved and protected as I left on my last leg of my flight home from India.

## Danica's Wedding

The moment I arrived home from India, I was packing again for San Diego, preparing to attend my good friend's daughter's wedding. I'd known Danica her whole life. Her mother, Mahalia, and I had dated as good friends back in high school. I was looking forward to seeing a few other classmates from high school there as well. In addition, there'd be a sprinkling of interesting television and movie personalities among the guests; Danica McKellar is perhaps best known for her roles on the TV shows, *The Wonder Years*, and *The West Wing*.

I planned to travel to the wedding with two old high school friends, Linda and Karen, and Mahalia's cousin, Carol. We organized a great road trip and decided we'd stay in the same hotel to keep it one long party. Problem was, it had been just a few days since I had been at the ashram in India, where I'd been meditating, praying, and surrounded with silence most of the time. Now I'd be in a highly energized social environment with lots of stimuli, which concerned me quite a bit.

When we arrived at the pre-wedding party at Danica's father's house, we walked in right as her grandmother collapsed. As she was laid out on a bed, my friend Karen, a nurse, took charge, while someone else called the Paramedics.

After several hours at the hospital, the grandmother was released without any further incident, but everyone remained alert.

One thing I noticed early on was I began picking up on people's random thoughts. I assure you there was nothing premeditated on my part. When we got back to the hotel I could hear all the people in the entire building, and I didn't know how to stop it. I was a psychic sponge, picking up thoughts, other energies, and information from everyone I came near.

The wedding was a real test. Carrying on a conversation was difficult. Being bombarded by the thoughts of others was exhausting. I attempted to explain it to Linda and Karen, who understand things 'happen' to me. I was working hard to shield myself, but failing miserably.

I finally returned home, only to be invited to Arizona to be a dinner guest, and to help on a short book tour with the Japanese water scientist Dr. Emoto. He is famous for his work with frozen water crystals, and how words, music, and even prayers can affect the very shape taken on by water molecules. After the dinner party, we went on the road to Flagstaff for a conference on water that the Hopi Indians had sponsored.

Again, I had the same issues with hearing people's thoughts. But by the time I returned home, one week later, I'd mastered how to prevent those intrusions.

## Radio Show Warning

After the wedding in San Diego, Linda, Karen, and Mahaila's cousin, Carol, and I headed north up Highway 5 for Karen's place in Gilroy. From there, we headed off in different directions. I hopped in my truck, parked at Karen's, and drove down the hill toward the main highway, very sleepy.

I tuned the radio dial into a strong radio station to help me stay awake. It was rebroadcasting a talk show about the dangers of driving while feeling sleepy—rather appropriate and timely—then the station identified itself as a Minneapolis, Minnesota AM station. *Odd, that's halfway across the country. I can't even get the signal from the Sacramento station eighty miles away.*

I found it both interesting and astounding that I was getting a radio show warning me of a current danger, but it did not deter me from continuing on without resting. I kept driving, despite the otherworldly message.

I'd been back on Highway 5 for a bit, heading toward Stockton, when I dozed off completely. I awoke to the sounds of vegetation—grass, weeds, shrubs—hitting the windshield. I opened my eyes and saw I was driving right down the median, between the north and southbound lanes. I raised my hands to grip the steering wheel, realizing I'd been asleep. As I did this, I noticed my truck was being steered without any help from me. It had maintained a straight path.

I then saw a cement barrier ahead, an upcoming overpass, and so I steered, under my own power, onto the paved highway. Fortunately, there was no traffic in any of the lanes I pulled into. I watched for the next exit and pulled off into a gas station, then got out and took a long, deep breath—long enough for the sleeping experience, inhale, and sigh to jolt me awake.

On a subsequent trip down that part of the highway, I noticed a trail about 200 yards long where my truck had plowed between the north and south lanes. It shocked me I'd traveled that far without steering.

The obvious question in all of this was: Why didn't I heed the warning? Once again, my guru was protecting me. One other small thing of interest that night was that the radio broadcast that night identified the date of the actual radio show as 6 months earlier that the year. So, it must have been a replay of an old show. Just good timing none the less.

## The Lady in Black

Around Christmas time, not long after I wrote my first book, *A Spiritual Warrior's Journey*, I received an odd phone call in the middle of the night from a publisher who owned a small book publishing company in Arkansas. He had identified with many parts of the book and had been emotionally moved by it. I waited patiently for him to say something like, "We want you to publish all forthcoming books with us," but that was not why he'd called.

After we'd discussed various stories from my book, perhaps for an hour, he got around to telling me about a woman I just had to meet. Coincidentally, she lived not too far from where I lived in the large central valley of California. He described her as one of those people who'd had an NDE (Near Death Experience) and who was lecturing around the country.

I didn't get around to contacting her until weeks later. Nadia McCaffrey, a naturalized American citizen who grew up in France, had married an American GI, and lived in Tracy, California. She was about my age and, at the time I contacted her, had recently lost her son who'd been killed in the war on terrorism.

We arranged to meet in Stockton, not too far from my home, as she was going to be there at a press conference with a small group of war protestors.

I wasn't keen about protesting any cause, let alone this war, but I did show up and found her facing several television cameras representing stations from across Northern California, including the San Francisco Bay Area.

Attired in all black, her blonde hair contrasted with the dark clothing. She spoke with a French accent, and appeared to be comfortable with the press. I stood off to the side, watching it all while trying not to get in the way.

Well…I had a very distinctive phone ring for when my ex-daughter-in-law, Syd, called. It was her actual voice 'shouting' for me to answer the phone. Suddenly, in the middle of an extremely serious live interview, my cell phone went off, Syd's voice shouting for me to pick up the phone. As I scrambled to find my cell, everyone stopped to glare at me.

That was our first meeting, but not the last. Our working relationship blossomed, leading us to co-work on her non-profit organization which helps PTSD veterans deal with returning home. I became the organization's chaplain and spiritual advisor, she became a good friend.

Her life story was truly inspirational. She'd had two near death experiences. The first was after a bite from a poisonous snake she'd received when she was a young girl living on a farm in France. She'd been in a coma for a long time and had one of those typical NDE events where one passes into the light. She said she'd been so overwhelmed with love, she did not wish to come back to her physical body.

Her next NDE was from her own hand, when she attempted to end her life. She had remembered how wonderful and loving it was on the other side. There are many details unaccounted for in this brief experience, but it became apparent to her she was here, in *this* life, for a greater purpose. She'd always had a mission, and now, at this stage of her life, after the death of her son, she knew what the mission was: she was determined to help other young veterans get their lives together upon returning 'home.'

She was truly a mother-like figure for these veterans. Her heart of gold held the worries and problems of many as she labored all over the country for the cause. She obtained old houses and farm properties to establish places where young men and women could come and get their feet back on the ground. Some of them might only need to stay a few weeks, while others may need six month or longer to readjust to life after surviving in a war zone. The places would be spiritual retreats without any formal religious overtone—spiritual-based, not religious-based living.

She had managed to find six houses in upstate New York, and a piece of property along the Russian River in Northern California. At the time of this writing, she was looking to raise enough money to buy an old abandoned college campus in Minnesota. It was a lot of hard work to raise awareness and funding. Therefore, her schedule involved cross-country speaking engagements to lobby for "her" troops.

One such speaking engagement took her to the far reaches of Northern California along the coast of Humboldt County. I volunteered to go with her for safety and to assist her. The drive north was over eight hours, allowing time for long conversations, where I learned all kinds of interesting things about her life and that of her son, Patrick.

She told me about how a big, white owl had shown up in her backyard in the daytime on the anniversary of the day her son was killed. It was as if he was communicating with her. She told me about all kinds of supernatural events surrounding his death, and how she found out he had passed away. I listened and could sense we were cut of the same kind of spiritual cloth. She was a mystic and had a powerful soul.

She understood my owl stories; how they always came to me as spiritual messengers. I've even had owls fly directly in front of my truck windshield to lead me down roads at night, and some have perched in my backyard in broad daylight. I also related the story of having seen two of them mating in a church bell tower at the memorial service of a good friend. (Several attendees and I decided this was to let us know she was fine.) Sometimes visions come when I am telling the story of one, like I did at the Hidden Valley Men's Ashram run by the Self-Realization Fellowship.

I had been walking with Lee, a fellow Vietnam veteran, in the back woods of the ashram, telling him how owls were my symbol. Whenever I needed encouragement or a spiritual boost in energy they would show up in my life. Lee interrupted my story by saying, "Do you mean owls like *that*?" There, just a few yards from us, sitting on a large rock in the bright afternoon sunshine, was just such an owl. The creature looked directly at Lee and me. Perfect timing. Lee was silent in respect of the situation. The owl's eyes lovingly watched us both until we walked away.

I finally ended my conversation with Nadia, saying something to the effect that most of those people I relate to best have had some kind of an owl experience with me, or on their own. I told her sometimes I go into people's homes and discover they have a large collection of owl statues, or pictures of owls, or artwork depicting them.

When we arrived at our destination, we discovered our host, a woman who owned the house where we would stay, had gone to work, leaving the keys for us. When we unlocked the door and went inside there were owl things all over her home. Even the kitchen towel had a series of owl images on it. We shook our heads and smiled. It was the right place to spend the weekend.

I found myself very ill when the time came for us to deliver a speech to a group raising money for a veteran project. I stayed on the sofa and, for the first time in my life, missed a speaking engagement. Normally, I would go come hell-or-high-water, but I was violently sick. I didn't move off the sofa until the next morning.

When I had gotten up, I found that Nadia and our host had been searching for the enlarged photos of her son that she takes to events. Nadia was frazzled that maybe she'd lost them, or they had been left behind at the event. She was beside herself with grief. Not only did the photos mean a lot to her, but it was her son's birthday.

After the two of them had gone through the house and car, they sat despondent. I strongly suggested they look again, which they did, making another sweep of the house. When Nadia went into the bedroom, where she had looked twice already, she saw them on the floor next to the bed. They had not been there earlier. She came out of the bedroom feeling divinely connected, somehow, with her son, since this was his birthday.

I proposed a little prayer ceremony for him, and suggested the backyard, a meditative area with a small water fountain and lots of open space.

We set up the photos next to the fountain and the three of us gathered to pray for her son Patrick. The moment we stopped praying, local church bells began to ring, overpowering the moment. When they stopped, I said a few words, then closed the short service. At that moment, the winds picked up. Patrick's photo fell over—face down onto the patio—and the wind chimes in the garden began to play delightful music. It was a powerful, spiritual moment. We listened and watched in awe at the magic unfolding around us.

When all the wind subsided, as suddenly as it had begun, it became totally silent; not even the chirping of birds.

We picked up the photo and went inside the house feeling Patrick had found a way to send his love to his mother from the other side. It had certainly made her feel wonderful.

## Visions of a Plane Crash

My son, Josh, had been flying airplanes since he was a teenager and even owned his own airplane when he was in the US Army stationed at Fort Hood, Texas. His enjoyment of flying extended to him becoming a certified flight instructor. A great pilot, safety was always foremost in his mind.

He'd flown into the Sacramento Executive Airport to pick up his son, Spencer, to fly him to the Truckee Airport. Spencer was about eight years old at the time, but had flown many times with his dad, so it was not a big deal to him.

I drove Spencer to the airport to meet his dad's flight and put him onboard. At first everything was okay, as we hung out waiting for Josh, but then I began to get a clear vision of a small plane crashing into the foothills above Sacramento. I could see the aircraft nosedive into some trees and catch on fire.

I wasn't sure what to do! Clearly, I saw a plane crash, but I didn't get any feeling of death or gloom for my son or grandson. Nevertheless, I did feel death for whoever was flying *that* plane, not necessarily my son's plane.

The vision and the images were so strong I began to second-guess my own sense of what was happening. If I was wrong, those I loved would be in harm's way. Normally, I'm good at sorting out the meaning of these things, but this time, as I watched Josh landing and rolling down the runway, I was concerned.

I looked at my watch. It was quarter-to-five; late afternoon. For some reason, I knew the crash I'd visualized had already happened. When I loaded Spencer onto the plane and waved goodbye, I perceived no danger.

Back in my pickup, I turned on the radio. A news story of a small plane crash above Sacramento broke into the programming.

Since I could still see Josh's plane gaining altitude, heading towards the foothills, I knew I'd been right. But I said a little prayer, not only for my son and grandson, but also for the unknown person or persons who had been killed in the crash minutes before Josh took off.

Later, the televised news showed a view of the downed aircraft as it had looked in my vision. Shortly after, the phone rang. It was Josh telling me they'd landed in Truckee and were on their way to Reno by car. It was such a relief to hear his voice again, so I told him I loved him. He must have wondered why I was so sentimental on the phone, but I didn't mind if he thought I was silly. Love is *never* silly.

## Book Award

In the summer of 2009, I was honored to accompany Gurunath to all his public appearances, except for one retreat in Oregon. I was asked to introduce him at events. What a great privilege!

In Los Angeles, at *The Skirball Center*, I was honored to present him with an award for his book: *The Founder's Award for 2008* from *The American Author's Association*, a prestigious award from one of the world's largest author associations. Previous winners had been authors who had sold millions of books and were world-famous writers, but this time the award was for a book that could possibly change the world. I really believed in the book and knew it was truly a spiritual classic.

The night began with me telling some stories of how Gurunath had helped heal me personally, and how he'd blessed my life. Next, a young actress, who was a yoga instructor, as well as a member of Hamsa Yoga Sangh (HYS), followed me. She told the personal story of how she had been dreaming about Gurunath teaching her to walk on water. She'd no clue as to the yogi's identity in her dreams, but six months later she'd attended an event and saw Gurunath in person. But before she could ask about her dream, he addressed her with some comments about what her dream of "walking on water" really meant. She was more than impressed. No one had ever heard it from her before.

The audience savored her story as Gurunath came into the auditorium. He sat on the stage and surveyed the sea of faces. It was as if he was greeting old friends from the past. Then the time came for me to present the award.

I gave a short presentation, moved forward to place the medal—on a red, white, and blue ribbon—around his neck. The award itself was rather large and looked like an Olympic Medal or a military award for valor.

I came so close our noses were almost touching. His huge eyes and mine were a couple of inches apart. For a moment, it felt like I'd done this before, déjà vu. The power of his eyes, so close, defies any existing descriptions of energy. I was slightly dizzy and disoriented from being so near.

As we stepped apart, both of us were caught by surprise when he received a prolonged, standing applause. The energy of the place was so powerful. I stole a glance at Gurunath's smile. It was a joy to be able to have had a small part in the proceedings.

*Photo David Schultz*

## Got Hope?

I was guest of honor of *The Military Writers Society of America* in Orlando, Florida in October of 2009. As the founder and first president of the society, I was rewarded with a free trip to their annual conference. The timing couldn't have been better. I could combine my work with HYS and meet the local team there.

While I was there, I participated in radio interviews for several stations and received some press, the stories of which appeared in many newspapers across the country that week, including Orlando, Chicago, and in the New England area.

The conference itself was interesting and featured the screening of a movie about the war on terrorism called *Trooper*. We were honored with the preview of the film made by Chris Martini, a young New York filmmaker, director, and actor.

The film depicted the plight of an army trooper returning home to New York from the war in Iraq; a fictional account of a PTSD veteran. The movie also dealt with the father of this soldier, himself a Vietnam veteran suffering from his own untreated case of PTSD from his long-ago war. The character of the father was portrayed as a heavy drinker in the throes of a terminal illness. The interplay between the father and son contained incredibly heavy, emotional acting. The storyline also contains the girlfriend who breaks up with the young veteran, leaving him emotionally isolated and physically alone. It reflected the aspects of PTSD accurately; its plot taking the viewer on a dark journey. The film's end had been edited in such a way it left a huge darkness on the heart.

When it was over, I sat there quietly while all the other authors praised the film.

After a time, Chris Martini stopped the feedback, pointed to me and said, "I want to know what Bill McDonald has to say about this movie."

I did not want to rain on his parade, yet there was something about the film that needed fixing. It left no hope or joy for viewers. A book or film, any story, needs to express at least a grain of optimism. So I carefully opened my mouth and expressed myself as gently and as kindly as possible.

"Where is the hope?" I asked.

Chris' face took on an unusual expression, possibly a questioning look, or a little shock. I wasn't sure if I'd offended him, but I had to tell him the film needed a more positive ending. He thanked me.

Afterwards, he joined me in the hotel lobby where we sat down and talked about what I had said. He told me, when he'd finished the film in New York and edited it, he'd been sure of its perfection. Then some of his production people and others in the film saw the original edit and asked him the same question, "Where is the hope?"

Then he went on to tell me about his trip to Florida and of his encounter with someone at the airport. A man came up to him, and was almost right in his face, wearing a T-shirt that read 'Got Hope?'

He then went on to tell me why he had a funny look on his face when I'd asked him "Where is the hope?" He figured the universe was telling him to change the film ending. So, he asked me how to go about doing that with next-to-no budget to work with. I suggested adding one brief scene where he could change the ending and emotional tone of the film and he promised me he'd do it.

He remained true to his word.

A couple of weeks later, I received a film clip of the new scene. He had improved upon my original suggestions with a dialogue that did exactly what was needed, and he'd shot the scene in a lush park. In the background was a pond with swans gliding gracefully about. I chuckled to myself. Of all things to see, those are Gurunath's logo and symbol.

He was very concerned about the music for the movie as his funding was limited. I later received a message that two music giants, Bruce Springsteen and Bob Dylan, who had watched the film with the new ending and allowed him to use some of their songs from their music catalog at no cost.

*Footnote: I received the following email message in December 2010 from Chris:*

*Bill, Sitting in the airport on my way to Frankfurt. On the TV, CNN story on LA. They had a shot of a road sign. In big letters it had one word: HOPE. I thought of you. Why does this always happen in airports??*

*A lot of positive movement on the film recently. I feel it's going to get out there very soon. This sign came on right after a PSA where Pat Sajak was talking about veterans and battle related illnesses.*

*Hope you are well, boss. Love always, Chris*

## Time Stands Still

I glanced at my clock—three-thirty in the morning—and noticed the second-hand was moving around the face, but the minute hand was not moving at all. I watched from my bed and wondered what was wrong. Perhaps fifteen minutes had passed by, with the second-hand ticking around, but the minute and the hour remained the same.

I sat up and wondered if the clock was broken, or if time could really be standing still. In either case, I set upon meditating and praying for my family and friends, but in particular for Daya. It was something I had to do right then and there. I offered deep prayers to Babaji himself; seeking his protection and intercession for my daughter and others.

I felt certain that I done this for over an hour, but when I opened my eyes, my clock was still showing the same time. I intensified my prayers to Babaji and continued. I checked again after about what felt like another lapsed hour of time. The clock remained fixed at three-thirty.

Then the clock slowly changed to six-thirty, just as I moved from the bed where I'd been praying and meditating. It felt like many hours had been spent engaged in my pleas to Babaji. All the other clocks in my house, *all* showed six-thirty. I had done all I could. The rest was up to Babaji. I remained uncertain as to what this was about.

Daya called me later that morning to tell me she had managed to miss being in a major freeway accident on her way to work, around *six-thirty*. The car in front of her had spun out of control and flown across all the other lanes, barely missing her. She commented on how lucky she had been; and that it was also rather odd no other cars were hit by the spinning car. In fact, even the spinning car ended up safely off to the side of the road.

Maybe the clock had become all-of-a-sudden broken and then worked again later on. It matters not whether time stood still. The real mission had been to send loving, protective prayers to my daughter. I answered that inner-call. No one can underestimate the power and impact of love and prayers. Who knows what might have happened if I hadn't prayed that morning to Babaji?

## Back to the Future

In the early hours of the morning I lay awake reflecting on the problems of Gurunath's organization, my family, my friends, and my neighbors. I foresaw all kinds of difficulties for a lot of these people. It was their karma, they had to work things out for themselves, but I still found myself feeling their pain in my heart. I was concerned they would be unable to handle things.

Sometimes I feel and sense too much about others for the good of my own physical health. My heart attacks and the chest pains I've suffered testify to this.

I was unsure how several situations would work out for certain souls in this lifetime. But in the higher sense, it all works out in the end.

As I remained in bed, I faded out of reality and went into a semi-dream state. I found myself back in Vietnam in 1967. I saw myself as a young man sitting on top of my old helicopter, repairing it.

In present time, I could recall this particular day.

I had been through some extra heavy combat encounters and our newest door-gunner was killed in a helicopter crash. He'd only had a couple of hours of flying experience. I had personally warned him not to get into that aircraft, as I'd had visions of it crashing and burning; everyone who flew on it the next time it went out would not come back alive. This door gunner was one of a few whom I tried to warn and protect in Vietnam, but all my efforts failed to keep them from their destiny.

As I reflected, I began watching my twenty-one-year-old self, sitting atop of my old Huey helicopter, in the darkness of the runway. My older-self of today was also sitting up there with the younger me. In a flash, I recognized this was what I had experienced that very night in Vietnam. Back then, I'd had an encounter with myself from the future; a more mature and older me imparting some wisdom.

The "younger me" sat and listened to the "older me" talk, who told me I would get out of there alive. Soon the war for me would be over, or so I thought. I re-minded my younger-self 'this, too, shall pass,' and so would these terrible times.

Then the "younger me" reminded the "older me" I could not save everyone; each had their own fates. In the same way, the "younger me" reminded this "older me" I could not save others from their karma now in the future. I could, at best, help and assist their learning process and be compassionate. In the end, I was told every person has their own karma to work through, no matter how painful it was for me to observe.

I totally remembered this encounter from both the past and the future. The "older me" then thanked my "younger-self," and vice versa. We had both helped each other to understand what we needed to focus on. It was an experience where I was both my future- and present-self, as well as the young warrior I had been. The conversation took place as if there were two of us.

I then faded out and returned to the darkness of my bedroom. I was all alone once again, but I understood I could not help change the karmic paths of all my friends and family. I was not responsible. Everything would work out for them as well. It always does, in the end.

## Shadows

It was early afternoon at my house. I was out in the backyard spending time with two of my youngest grandchildren, five-year-old Daylana and her brother Gianni, 18 months younger. They were playing on the swing set I'd built. Gianni was really enjoying himself, totally ignoring his sister's requests for her turn on the swing. As he went back and forth, he watched his shadow move across the ground under him. Finally, in frustration, Daylana told him if

*Gianni & his sister Daylana 2010*

he didn't let her take a turn she would steal his shadow. Of course, he laughed at her and stayed on the swing. She stood there with a determined look on her little face and crossed her arms across her chest with a very serious expression.

I'd been watching and listening to this when suddenly, the sky darkened a little. Gianni began to scream and cry, panicking greatly. His shadow had totally disappeared!

I looked at what he was yelling at. His shadow was really gone, but so were Daylana's and mine. I looked up in the sky and saw a small, dark cloud had moved directly into the path of the sun. The rest of the sky was clear and bright blue. The one little cloud now blocked the sunlight to our backyard and had stolen the shadows.

Gianni got off the swing, still crying. I comforted him by saying his shadow would be back. I pointed to the cloud overhead, but he was hysterical, saying his sister took his shadow. I had to hold back my laughter. The timing on her demand and threat was so perfect with the movement of that one tiny cloud above her head! Did she realize how close that cloud was? Soon the cloud moved out of the way and Gianni stopped crying and started chasing his reborn shadow around on the ground below him. Watching my granddaughter swinging away, I was a little wonderstruck by what had happened. Was this just a case of amazing timing and was all of this just some wonderous coincidence, or was it possible there something else going on?

## Cowboy Bob

I was stopped at a stoplight one afternoon in the fall of 2009 when I began to have this inner vision; a vivid and lucid daydream. I saw myself standing in front of a group of mourners at a church, giving a eulogy about my childhood best friend, Bob Amick. I saw a photo on the altar of Bob wearing his cowboy hat and sitting on a horse.

I heard the words coming from me in this dream-like vision telling those there about how we used to sing together in a folk singing trio called *The Midnight Three*. It was a joyful memory for me, as were many I recalled from our high school years together.

I also recounted our long conversations on the phone, regular check-ins, including one a couple of days before. In the last few conversations, we'd spoken about the possibility of him or me not being around much longer. Both of us had experienced the same kind of heart issues. He had chosen to have major surgery, while I had opted for the less invasive treatment of having five metal stents (at that time) put into my arteries to keep them open.

He told me, if he died the next day, or even within the hour, he was grateful and blessed for his life; how much he loved his wife and children and all his precious grandchildren. He was truly at peace with his life and all he'd achieved. Yet Bob was as healthy as he had ever been in years and hadn't complained about any health issues in a long time. He was busy planning to work his land and take care of his horse and other animals.

There was nothing out of the ordinary about these last conversations; we'd discussed these kinds of things before. We also had spoken of our spiritual involvements and our inner-most thoughts. In truth, things we never allowed others to experience. It was a sacred trust built on fifty years of friendship.

I sat in traffic reminiscing. We'd been there for each other through some of the darkest times of our lives. He was my supporter and best friend. I believed he felt the same way about me.

This vision of myself talking about him at a church continued, even when the light changed and I was driving once again. I shook myself back into reality and looked at the time; it was close to four-thirty.

Early the next morning, I answered the phone. Glenn, one of Bob's three brothers. I asked him what had happened to Bob. There was a long pause. He told me his brother had died the day before, between four-thirty and six in the evening.

My vision of his memorial service had taken place very close to the time of his death. I'd been given an early warning. Glenn and I spoke for a while, and I agreed to say a few words at the service.

Sutter Creek, California contains a small, old, wooden church. It was there I spoke about my friend, Bob. I looked around at the people sitting there, and saw the same faces from my vision. I even heard myself saying the same things I'd already spoken. Surreal. An all too familiar current of energy tingled in my spine. I hesitated, then decided to share the dream experience with those in attendance. Their faces were the very same ones I had envisioned. Such love radiated from the group as comprehension dawned upon their faces. Bob had found a way to show us all he would be okay.

It was a difficult memorial service for me. I'd truly miss having Bob to call up and talk 'life stuff' with. But he was honestly okay, and his family *would* carry on. True friendships this deep are extremely rare. It was a privilege to have shared those precious years with him.

My emotions deepened a few days later when I received an email from one of his children, who said her dad had sent her an email about eight years before; one she would never delete. She had printed it out and carried that copy with her in her purse. It was something I'd written to Bob and he'd forwarded to his children. She'd just noticed, after all this time, from looking at the name of the email sender, it was from me. She wanted to thank me. Little did she know how incredibly touched I was. It was amazing. Her father, my very best friend, would think so highly of my message that he'd sent it out to all those he loved so dearly. I was truly honored. When I finished reading her message, I let the tears roll down my cheeks—no shame, only love.

## Shouldering the Load

I was asked by Gurunath, in late fall of 2009, to help shoulder more of the operational load for his organization. I had been dealing with all the people issues and team building for Hamsa Yoga Sangh shortly after I'd returned from the ashram. Now I was asked to take a more direct hand in some of the operations of the organization. Of course, I would never refuse his request.

During a three-day spiritual retreat in the Los Angeles area, Gurunath initiated me and two others as Senior Kriyacharya. I believe this was more of a mantle of authority for the three of us to assist in leading his organization than as any sign of spiritual achievements. Regardless, in my opinion, those two other men could have been chosen absolutely for their spiritual attainments; certainly, they were people whom I admired.

Since I was so new to the organization—less than a year's involvement—the appointment was unprecedented. I was humbled by this honor, and most pleased to be of further service to him. Some of those present at this ceremony reportedly saw something unusual happen when Gurunath was blessing the three of us.

Apparently, when the three of us had our heads bowed, some people claimed to have seen me transform into some kind of Nath yogi, complete with some kind of a band across my forehead. I have no clue as to what they saw, for at that moment all I was feeling was the greatest of love emanating from Gurunath himself.

Soon after this, I plowed into the tasks; helping with organizational duties; diving in with all my heart and energy. Sometimes ten to twelve hours were spent on the phone or sending emails. There was little free time left for me, as issues related to the running of the organization rolled in.

I was beginning to feel the weight of the responsibilities. I visualized *all* of it on my shoulders and did not want to fail. I took on every organizational pain as my own and tried to give every ounce of me I could. It was then, in the middle of the night, in late October, I awoke in the greatest of pain. My shoulder was immobile. Cracked? Broken?

I rose, as I could not sleep, and found *any* movement in *any* direction caused sharp pain. There was no position where there wasn't any pain. Just sitting and not even moving was painful. I could not take off my shirt or hold a spoon or fork to eat. I went four days without sleep. I sat on my sofa trying not to move in any direction, but the pain never subsided.

I was invited to a dinner with Gurunath and a couple of other guests in the San Francisco Bay Area, and looked forward to spending this time with him before he left the United States. In too much pain to drive—impossible, in fact—a fellow devotee drove me from Sacramento. We arrived a little early, so we waited before connecting with Gurunath and his family. But the pain was too great for me to bear. I finally asked him to drive me the two hours back home; cancelling the farewell meal with Gurunath. I could not tell you what hurt more, the pain from the shoulder, or having missed spending special time with Gurunath.

Soon, I could no longer handle the intense pain level or the lack of sleep, so I went to Kaiser Hospital in South Sacramento and saw a doctor. He took X-rays and ran tests, then told Carol and me the shoulder was in rough shape and surgery was inevitable. The X-ray showed a possible fractured bone, along with a bad case of arthritis, affecting every movement within the shoulder. In addition, he told us there was serious tendonitis, bursitis, and shredded and torn tendons in the rotator cuff. He painted a rather negative outlook for the shoulder, saying he could not get much movement back with surgery, but could attempt to reduce, but not eliminate, the pain. He fully expected the shoulder to be in worse shape when he actually cut it open, and was determined to schedule the first date available for the operating room. This, he said, was of the highest priority.

I told him I was planning on leaving for India in December and would not be back until after the first week in April. He waved off my comments and went to his computer, scrolling through the surgery schedule—through the entire months of November, December, and then January—and found no openings. He kept scrolling until he finally found an open date on April 14, 2010—five months from the appointment; nine days after I'd return from India.

Rather strange. I had just been told I needed "immediate surgery," but then had to wait *five months* before I could get relief. I just sat and listened without objecting.

He set up a pre-surgery meeting the week before I left for India. He also had me undergo a series of new tests including an MRI with some colored dyes injected into the rotator cuff to assess the damage there.

In the meantime, the doctor prescribed a powerful pain-killer to be taken every six hours until the surgery. I honestly embraced the pills. The pain was so intense I could not sleep at all, nor move my right arm. I went home and took the pills as instructed. Two doses over twelve hours made me sick to my stomach and dizzy. Although, the pills did bring the pain level down to about half the intensity, enabling me to sleep a few hours, I wonder if I was simply so exhausted that I physically crashed.

The next morning, I made the command decision to stop taking the pills and live with the pain. I sat at my computer, unable to use the keyboard, and unable to remove my T-shirt. I sat there and silently cried out with a prayer for Gurunath to help me manage the pain, but not heal my shoulder. I figured, whatever the cause of the damaged shoulder, I was more than willing to work *that* karma out. All I asked for in my prayer was the ability to cope and manage the pain; not to relieve it or to even make it go away.

Within seconds of uttering this prayer, I went into a state of total pain-free-ness, a heavenly contentment. About ninety minutes later, when Carol called for me, I stirred from this restful, comfortable spiritual cocoon. The pain was totally gone.

The arm movement was still very limited, but I did manage to have enough to get fully dressed. I called Gurunath, who was in Los Angeles at the airport getting ready to depart for London, and told him what had happened. I got a huge laugh from him when I told him his love and blessings were much better than the drugs I had been given by the doctors. I told him "he was now my favorite drug of choice."

His laughter was the greatest medicine anyone could ever receive. It vibrated throughout my entire body; every single cell of my being trembled with his love and blessings. His healing hands were already at work on me as he said to listen to my doctor and do what I was asked to do.

The doctor I had decided to go see and listen to was Dr. Do Yoo in Sacramento. She used all the ancient healing arts from Korea including acupuncture and cupping. On my first visit to her, she advised me not to have surgery. She said if I listened to her and allowed her to treat me, I'd get some of my arm movement back and would not need any operation. After three weeks poking and sticking me with hundreds of needles, I recovered a lot of my movement and was mostly pain free.

Following this, I went through the new tests my surgeon had ordered, and I even kept the appointment with him. I went into his office wondering if my arm was better or if somehow, I was blocking out the pain, making my arm function by sheer will power. In reality, physically I was better, but wondered what the tests would reveal.

The surgeon had all the newest tests up on his computer's monitor screen when I walked in, but did not have the original X-rays. It had been several weeks and he did not remember who I was nor why I was in his office taking up his time. He studied the MRI images and looked at the results of the other tests, then asked me why I was there. I looked him directly in the eye and told him he had scheduled me to come for a pre-surgery consultation with him. He shook his head back and forth, very confused, saying he did not understand why I would be having surgery. There was not enough wrong with my shoulder—based on the MRI and other tests—to warrant my rushing into surgery. He could not see *any* bone fractures.

I briefly attempted to fill him in on what had happened, but he was not going to buy the help I got from an acupuncturist, and was certainly not going to accept that a guru somehow took away the pain and helped heal the bone. So, the conversation was very short. He told me maybe my neck or back had caused me all the pain. He never looked at the original tests and X-rays. At this point, there was no need for any continued conversation, as it would be a waste of both our times. He cancelled the planned surgery; said it could wait.

I left his office knowing my shoulder would be good enough and sufficiently pain free to return to India and spend several months at the ashram. Was it 100% healed? No way. But with it mostly pain free, I had just enough movement to function. My time with my guru would not be taken from me. I never did ask for a healing; all I asked for was to handle the pain and be able to function. I got what I asked for.

*Part Five*

# BACK HOME AT THE ASHRAM

### Return to the Ashram 2010
**The First Month**

I was looking forward to going back to the ashram. On this trip, I'd spend almost one hundred days with Gurunath. There was a distinct change in me from the previous winter there. It was with much anticipated joy I prepared to leave. My grandchildren would surely miss me, but I *had* to return to India.

Though I wasn't certain why I'd scheduled the trip as I had—December through April—there had been an intuitive feel to the itinerary.

I landed in Mumbai early in the morning, and joined with two others headed for the ashram. We drove all night and arrived before daybreak. There was a huge full moon, making the temple stand out in the darkness. Soon Gurunath joined us, leaving his personal residence to come out to give me a big hug. I was home again; back in heaven.

The first evening was New Year's Eve, and we joined a group of local Indian devotees around a campfire. All of us brought our blankets to lie down after we'd meditated. The fire pit was in the middle of the lawn, out in the open, allowing us to lie on our backs with a full view of the night sky, the perfect position to view the eclipse scheduled to take place around midnight.

As we lay looking at the moon, a huge owl flew over the campfire. Illuminated by the moon and the firelight, the owl's flight was perfectly timed to greet the New Year. It was a powerful moment for me, having just arrived, to see my spiritual symbol and messenger flying between the moon and the fire. We watched the night sky until around four in the morning. It was a perfect beginning to my second stay.

We later had visitors from Iran, who happened to accidentally find the jungle ashram. When they walked into the ashram they were fortunate to be able to chat with Gurunath. He surprised them all by knowing a great many details of their history, culture, and even religion.

When it came time for the guests to leave, they had to cross over the stream at the entrance of the ashram, in total darkness, and their car was on the other side of the water. There were no lights, and the path was down an inclined slope with lots of rocks. I decided to assist them and started off on the route they were to take.

Gurunath shouted to me, "Bill, let the younger men do that."

I took those words as a 'suggestion' only. Having a walking stick and a good flashlight, I was a bit over-confident.

Once again, he called out saying the younger guys should escort the visitors, but I ignored him, walking part-way down the slope toward the creek, stepping carefully over rocks.

The visitors were able to get across the water with the help of two of the younger guys. I assisted by holding my flashlight, affording them some light. Mission accomplished, I started back toward the ashram. Stepping on a rock, which moved under my weight, twisting my left foot, sharp pain thrust its way into my consciousness.

Now the words I'd taken only as a suggestion came back to me. I had failed to listen to and obey my guru's words. I humbly told him later of my error. But I also learned another lesson: gurus do not give suggestions.

Life continued at a pleasant pace at the ashram, with sacred moments and seemingly inexplicable happenings.

When a sweet, young woman from northern California was getting ready to return home, she could not find her passport. Her taxi awaited and she became panicked; time was ticking and she needed to get to the airport. When she insisted, she'd given it to Gurumata, Gurunath asked her to look in her copy of the book, *Wings to Freedom.*

She looked all around and through her bags, then she finally opened her book. Her passport was, as predicted, pressed between the pages. How it got there, neither she nor anyone else could say, but Gurunath was 100% certain it was there.

Wonders never ceased.

One night, when I opened the door to my darkened room, a large bat flew into my face. When I turned on the light, the bat continued to circle my room, inches above my head. I was rather amused this bat was not trying to fly out the open door. It simple kept coming right at me, just missing my head by inches. I stood off in one corner as it made dozens of trips around the room. I was not concerned about anything except the possibility this flying rodent might drop a load of bat crap on my bed, or on my head.

Finally, I tried shooing it away with a bamboo pole. Ten minutes later, it slipped out the door, unharmed, as I'd only used the pole to herd it in the direction of the door.

In short order, Gurunath came to pay me a visit. He sat down in a chair and I sat on my bed. We had a good one-on-one conversation. Nothing mystical nor spiritual, just some talk between a couple of men. It was good to have personal time with him. I asked him, only half-seriously, if having a bat in my room qualified as good luck. He smiled and held back silent laughter.

Gurunath was greatly concerned as he went next door to visit a devotee suffering from an illness. His fatherly instincts shown through as he gave advice to the young man. He left, then returned quickly with some medicine and instructions for the young man, giving them to Jay, who was in my room. Gurunath wanted all of us to make sure this devotee was taken care of as he was leaving the ashram that very night.

One day, I wandered onto the recently purchased piece of land adjoining the ashram where a group of young guys hacked away with machetes and axes, clearing the jungle. I went near an ugly, thorny tree with the longest spikes I have ever seen on any tree or bush; thorns like small weapons. The plant was more like a huge bush and almost totally black. It had an evil aura.

Nearby, I found two animal skulls: one was a monkey and the other could have been a small goat. I picked up the skulls and moved them away to the barbed wire fence separating the new property from the original ashram property. I placed them on two metal fence posts where an opening had been cut away for access to the new lands. I wanted the boys to see them when they returned to clear the land.

In late afternoon, I was with Jay when Gurunath joined us on a short walk around the ashram. I jokingly asked Gurunath if it was taboo to place the skulls on the fence, or if it was good luck. I went on and teased Jay by saying, if it was good luck, then I confess to having placed them there. But if that was a wrong action, then, of course, Jay must have done it.

The inside joke was good-natured. Jay would always get blamed for whatever happened at the ashram, even when he was a hundred miles away. Jay himself said he half-expected to have gotten blamed for the recent lunar and solar eclipses. Anyway, Jay laughed and Gurunath had a broad smile.

Gurunath said it wasn't necessarily a good thing to have them on the posts, so I removed them and sat them both back on the ground. Contemplating the matter, I could see there was more to these skulls, as well as the old, ugly tree where I had found them.

The next night we sat around the dining room listening to Gurunath expound on spiritual subjects. He then told us more about the black tree. A nature spirit had latched onto it and made it a home; apparently, an evil spirit. He went on about how these kinds of spirits can possess people. He'd already done some kind of ritual with his sacred sword to get rid of it.

He told us about the conversation he'd had with this spirit; totally strange and fascinating. In my head, I heard the old rock-and-roll song by Guns and Roses, "Welcome to the Jungle." Once again, I was reminded I honestly knew absolutely nothing about what reality was.

Gurunath told us many things the first month at the ashram. Due to the small group, we had lots of private time with him. Of course, we did a lot of physical work around the ashram as well, but there was no true way to pay back what Gurunath was giving to all of us. I was delighted to be back home.

## The Naadi Reading

Sitting around the ashram in early January, Gurunath told me I needed to get myself a Naadi Palm reading in Pune. I had no clue as to what he was talking about, other than it was a kind of "fortune telling" session with some Naadi guru/astrologer. I'd talked to a couple of people who had already had one done; their stories were too good to be true. I was not a real big believer in these things. I figured no one would be able to read me, and come up with all the information on my life, by just examining my right thumbprint. It wasn't something I would have done of my own volition, but obviously, I was fully aware Gurunath didn't make 'suggestions.' When I told him I did not believe in these things, he said what I heard that day would be true.

I was told, by using only my right thumbprint, readers could search through stacks of hundreds of thousands of old palm leaves and retrieve one that had all my basic life information written on it; information written before Jesus walked the earth. And, by answering some basic questions with either yes or no, a reader could discern *the* actual leaf for me. Of course, none of this made any sense to me.

Gurunath strongly insisted I do it and told me to make sure I had one of my past lives read for my most significant sins committed (karma), so I could remedy those now.

I could not see how there would be a palm leaf there with all my major life information on it, but I went along with three others to Pune—me, the doubting Thomas for sure.

The place was difficult to find, and one would *never* guess what was going on inside. It was fortunate one person in our group had been there before and was returning for additional information.

We sat and waited to be finger printed. When my time came to be interviewed, I wondered if they would look for clues and read me like some good mentalist act in Las Vegas. So, I was going to stick to yes and no and provide zero clues. I was told to put the first initial of my name next to the thumbprint. I put down "W" for William, my legal name, but a name I've never used except for my passport and legal documents. My friends all referred to me as Bill, so I was wondering how this might trip them up.

After about an hour, I was called into a small, dimly-lit room for the reading that looked and felt like a tiny temple, and was filled with religious and sacred items. Smoke was billowing up and filling the room from candles and incense sticks. I sat down in front of a large altar-like table. The reader then pulled out a small bundle of about twenty leaves. Each was attached by a heavy string through a hole drilled through them. It kind of resembled Venetian blinds, all stacked with a cord running through.

There was extremely old writing inscribed on the body of each palm leaf. The entire edges were trimmed back to create a solid piece of palm wood on which to write.

I answered each of their questions with either a yes or a no. The questions dealt with my name, parents' names, wife and child information, and career stuff. Six leaves were rejected before the man discovered mine.

And then the conversation went like this:

"Is your name a four-letter word beginning with B?"

"Yes." (I was already wondering how they ignored the 'W' I'd provided.)

"Your name is Bill."

"Yes." (They hit this correctly and did not go with William. So far, they were correct, but I remained unimpressed. Maybe they'd heard me called that by one of the people I'd come in with.)

"Your father had the same exact name as you."

"Yes." (Okay, this peaked my interest. I *am* named after my father. We have the same full name, except I am a junior. I shifted a little in my seat.)

"Your Mother's name was Marcella."

"Yes." (Not only was that her name, but it also finally dawned on me he had used terms for my parents indicating they were no longer alive—'was' instead of 'is'.)

"Your parents have been dead for several decades."

"Yes." (He confirmed what I had been hearing from him; they are no longer here in the physical world. Maybe this was a good guess because of my age, but they both had died young and could have been alive without being too awful old. For the record, my father died in 1973 and mother in 1990. I did not learn my father was dead until the year before this reading.)

"You are married and your wife's name is Carol."

"Yes." (I was now blown away. Not even those people whom I'd traveled with had this information. Oh, they knew I had a wife, but I did not throw around her name to the group. I became more focused on the possibility this palm leaf contained some real information, but I could not understand where that information came from. I sat there waiting for the next facts he would throw at me. I also looked at the leaf itself and saw her name written there in English, as well as my mother's and father's names.)

"Your wife is a university graduate and very intelligent."

"Yes." (She graduated from The University of California – Berkeley)

"You have two children and both are married."

"Yes." (I have two grown children and both are married. So, what was going on here?)

"You have a good relationship with them both."

"Yes." (This was correct, but certainly not impressive. This could have been a good guess.)

"Your children are a boy and then a girl."

"Yes." (That was the correct birth order. My son, Josh, was born first, followed a year and half later by his sister, Daya. Again, I was not overly impressed. He had a 50/50 chance on that one.)

"You are a foster child." (This question confused me, so I hesitated and asked for a clarification. I was told they did not have a closer word to use, but what he meant was that my father had left me. I had a stepfather, or perhaps had some other circumstance in my life where I was separated from my parents for a long period of time. Then this would qualify for a "yes" response. I did have a stepfather. I had also taken ill and spent almost a full year in the county hospital with very little contact with my family. That happened when I was around eight years of age. So, I answered 'yes' to this question of fact. But it was an odd question.)

"You are a writer."

"Yes." (I had written several books and, even though my income is very limited by this late-life career choice, I had to reply yes.)

"You are *right now* working on a spiritual book about your guru."

"Yes." (This statement amazed me as I was working on this very book.)

Then he asked me a question that would show this was indeed the right time and place for me to get my life reading. This question also threw me for a loop. These leaves were written over two thousand years ago. The statement was: "You have recently worked on a movie, but not as an actor." (He went on to add this choice of words, "movie" instead of "play", was an intuitive one on the reader's part. Since there were no movies when this was written, "movies" was the correct question to ask.)

"Yes." (I had to reply "yes," as I had helped write a new ending for a movie called *Trooper* just weeks before coming to India. But I wondered how in the heck all this could have been predicted some two thousand years before the invention of movies. I was now sitting there in a daze. I was still trying to figure out where this was all coming from.)

Then the reader stated, "Your birthday is March 16, 1946."

I was temporarily speechless and then quietly uttered, "Yes." (I could not figure out how my fingerprint could have given them all that information, *and then* to have it all recorded on some palm leaf. I looked at the writing on the palm leaf and saw numbers that looked like my birth date. I also saw the names Carol and Marcella written on the leaf before he shifted it out of my view. It confirmed to me they were in fact reading from the palm leaf itself. This was spooky stuff.)

"You were born between 1:10 and 1:15 in the morning. I am unable to tell the exact time for some reason."

"Yes." (This was the oddest piece of information he gave me. There was in fact, confusion at the hospital about the precise time I was born. I was born while waiting for the doctor to come. The time of birth was just a close guess for the birth certificate. How could this problem be known about over several thousand years before?)

I was then told Shiva was my guru. But a few moments, later before I could reply, he said my guru's name was Gurunath. I cocked my head, slightly confused as he stated I had two gurus…or were they truly one and the same? Also, no one can be a direct disciple of Shiva.

Another great mystery.

There were about thirty more pieces of personal information given, all matching perfectly with my life facts. I was now totally bewildered by how someone could write about me from so long ago and predict I would come in to seek this information at this time and location, *and* these palm leaves are scattered over various locations in India.

Assuming this was my basic reading, I'd reached for my money to pay the reader…but he stopped me, saying that was just my "index". From this information, they would then do a complete reading of my current life and touch on past lives. I left the little room and came out into the lobby shaking my head. I sat in the lobby with the guys, all of whom had experienced similar results pertaining to their lives.

We sat for many more hours waiting for them to do our Naadi charts. I was quiet. The others left to get some food from the German Bakery down the street. I chose to sit, with much to ponder, in the lobby of the building where the readings were given.

In the meantime, I began doing some basic math and determined I did not have enough money for the full reading and all the remedies. When my fellow devotees returned, I told them of my dilemma. One of them kindly volunteered to advance me a sum of money I could repay at the ashram.

When my time came, I was called into an upstairs room, where I was joined by a translator. The reader pulled out my chart and began the reading of my present life. There are some things better left unsaid about the reading due to its personal nature, but I chose the following to share publicly:

The reader began with the recent past, this lifetime, and moved forward. He told me my real spiritual life and work did not fully begin until my 62nd year, the year I first meet Gurunath. In this current life, I was told I have already been visited by Shiva many times in various disguises and forms, but have not fully recognized Him. From this point on, and up until my death, I would continue to be blessed with visits from Shiva, and would begin to see and recognize Him in all his different forms and disguises.

Shiva, at some future festival in or near a Shiva temple, will inhabit my body and dance or sing, while most people will just assume I am some old fool, or I'm crazy. My love for Shiva will continue to grow and I will feel more and more of His harmony. I will become a "fool" for Lord Shiva.

My mission in this lifetime is to write books and help lead people to Gurunath, thus to Lord Shiva. Although my books would also bring attention and fame to me as well, I was advised this cannot be avoided nor should I be concerned. The pure intentions of my heart and writings would always be on my guru and Shiva.

At some future time, a couple will come to me for advice. I will recognize them as Lord Shiva and his wife. Latter on water and oil will fall on my head as a blessing from Shiva.

I would experience major health issues with my skin.

I would spend more time in India working for Gurunath and writing more books. "The key focus in your life will be to inspire others to seek God through your guru."

I am supposed to tour Shiva Temples and write a book about the experience.

My hair, beard style, and over-all appearance will change.

Within the next four years, whenever motivated by LOVE, I am to go to a specified Shiva Temple in Southern India and walk uphill for four hours. There, waiting for me, will be all the rishis. They will impart knowledge to me so, after this time, I will no longer have questions as to why we are here or what life is about. I will understand.

I am to help pay for, or help to rebuild and repair, or build a new Shiva Temple.

My life will end with an appearance of Shiva in a blaze of light, as I consciously leave my body and enter into Shiva as rainbow light. I was told this is apparently how I have ended my previous lives.

There were many more personal and spiritual predictions and facts about this current life I am reluctant to share; some about my family. The basic reason I am unwilling is my ego; one already much too big. Besides, who really knows how much of this is really going to happen, or has happened? God only knows. Nevertheless, after getting the basic index information on my life, I am inclined to accept the possibilities.

The following was said about a past life of mine that impacts me today:

In a previous lifetime, I was the senior and most trusted priest at an ashram. I had an impure thought about a married woman and fell emotionally in love with her. Although nothing had happened, or was planned to happen, the guru read my mind and put a curse on me, making me wander around like a fool in a daze for an unknown period of time.

While I was bathing in the Ganges River, I emerged from underwater to see Lord Shiva, who forgave and spiritually healed me. I left my body consciously in a ribbon of rainbow light with Lord Shiva; the end of *that* lifetime.

That guru at the ashram was none other than Gurunath in a previous lifetime.

So, my worst and most significant sin of my past lifetime was an impure thought! Back then, Gurunath had zapped my mind and sent me away to wander the fool's life.

Musings on the past life reading:

When I returned from Pune to the ashram, I was met by Gurunath, who wanted me to tell him all the details of my reading. I said I was a little reluctant to believe it all. He looked me directly in the eyes and stated, "For you that was a true and accurate reading."

I spoke to Gurunath about being cursed by one's own guru. He said it was all a part of the Divine play and even he'd had been also cursed at least four times. Being "cursed" sets up a connection to this lifetime and is a part of the overall spiritual mission. It has nothing to do with the guru being angry with the disciple.

Apparently, I have consciously left in a 'rainbow body' in many previous lifetimes. This is nothing new to me. My Vedic charts give the same message about leaving each lifetime in a 'rainbow body.'

There was much more to the reading, but these were the basic facts I want to address publicly. At some point in time, I will write a more detailed accounting of what was predicted, and how those predictions turned out after a period of time. When I wrote this chapter, only some of the predictions had occurred. Now, as I am editing this for publication, I am realizing almost 95% of what was told me has already happened as foretold. There are also predictions I will never tell anyone, like when and how I am going to die.

Author's Note: Here is a very brief explanation of Naadi/Nadi Palm Readings from my unenlightened western point of view. I was totally ignorant of what a Naadi was, let alone the history. I went into this process without any knowledge about it at all. I certainly was not a believer and expected it to be a huge waste of my time and money. I had not wanted to get it done. I am simply sharing some of what I have discovered, been told, or learned.

Naadi astrology is a form of Hindu astrology practiced in Tami Nadu, Kerala in India. The belief is that Hindus could see the past, present, and even future lives of every human being and the universe. These predictions were made between 2,500 years ago to more than 5,000 years ago by great rishis. They would channel information about people, have scribes write them on palm leaves, and then put a kind of clear material over the leaf to preserve it. The texts are written in Vatteluttu, an ancient Tamil script. That is why, when one gets a reading, it takes two people to read and translate.

Originally, these were stored in one location in the Saraswati Mahal library. The British took some of them, and there was also a fire which destroyed others. Subsequently, they were moved to various locations around India. And so, if you have a reading, it can mean searching across the country to find the right location containing 'your' palm leaf.

There are many false and fraudulent online readings claiming to be correct, as well as some readers in India who are suspected of being dishonest. Getting this done in person is best, almost essential, to get valid information. Never give any information beyond yes and no answers to the questions. The only way to truly know for sure about your own reading is if your guru orders you to get it done. Unless you are personally ordered to have a reading, do not subscribe to one, but keep an open mind and never count on it being 100% correct. Do not ask your guru if he or she wants you to participate in a reading; he or she will tell you.

## I Touch My Guru's Feet

When we returned from getting our Naadi readings done, Gurunath asked the three of us to share our results with a small circle of devotees gathered around him. I was asked to speak first. It was apparently important to Gurunath, so I did. He listened attentively to my story and then asked the other two to give an account of their readings.

Many *pujas* (acts of worship) the Naadi reading called for me to do, began immediately. The first was at the location where I'd received the Naadi reading. It consisted of purchasing some fruits and a coconut, along with a flower garland, and then performing a ceremony in their small altar room, comprised of some chanting and burning of incense.

One of those *pujas* needed to take place for 244 days inside a Shiva temple, reciting a special chant and mantra daily. I was allowed to hire a priest to do that for me. At the end of the allotted time, I would be sent an engraved metal tag indicating it was complete. Since I would be leaving India many months before this could be fully done, this was the only course of action to take.

There were another three *pujas*. One was for the rest of my life and consisted of waking at four each morning and giving my love completely to Lord Shiva. Another involved performing a ceremony involving Gurunath. It was to take place on a guru's day; in India this is each Thursday. Since my "significant sin" was directly involved with Gurunath himself, in a previous lifetime, I needed to come to him personally for my *puja*. In my case, I needed to ask for Gurunath's forgiveness and give him my loving service.

Each week I went to him and told him I needed to do one of my remedies for my Naadi with him that Thursday…and each week he would say to remind him later. Weeks passed with the same "remind me" routine. It was like he was toying with me, yet I kept preparing myself emotionally.

On one Thursday night, after failing to do the *puja* with him, I had a deep dream/vision. In this dream state, I was stretched out on the ground before Gurunath with my hands wrapped around his bare feet. I had placed a flower garland around his neck and then pledged my service and loyalty to him as my Satguru for as long as time and space existed. Although very real, a part of me knew I had already completed the *puja* at some other level of reality. So, waiting for "the" *puja* was simply a formality since I'd already performed it with him in the dream state. To me, there was no difference.

When the day finally came for me officially to do my *puja*, he kept me waiting all day, then at the last moment said, "Let's do it."

I had lovingly made a flower garland from all the different flowers growing around the ashram grounds and placed it in the refrigerator in the dining room so it would be fresh for the *puja*. He had told me that morning to sit and meditate for about ten minutes, but those ten minutes were more like four hours. I was being taught some much needed humility, as well as patience. The "ceremony" was originally going to be private, but as it turned out he invited many other devotees to observe.

I placed the garland around his neck and then grabbed his feet much like I had already done in my dream. Naturally, in my dream state, my body was much more limber and my back did not hurt to get down on the ground. He did not wish to endure lots of fuss with a very formal ritual, so we kept it rather simple. It occurred to me I had just pledged myself in service to him and his mission until the end of time and space, a vow I took seriously. The weight of the world lifted from my shoulders. My spirit was free.

Reflecting on my Naadi reading's message, with the most significant karmic issue still causing me concerns in this lifetime having been my guru's curse, it made a lot of sense for me to be having such great difficulty with my brain this lifetime.

It is most interesting, within ninety minutes of meeting Gurunath (and without telling him about my brain seizures or health issues) he gave a very public prayer for the healing of the brain, while he looked in my direction with those powerful eyes of his.

His first gift to me was to heal me of my brain seizures; one that made great sense to me now. I believed it was all true; all a part of some divine plan. It also told me I was long-ago forgiven; that asking for forgiveness was just a formal recognition of my error.

## Who's in Charge?

At the end of the first month, Gurunath and his wife, along with everyone else at the ashram, joined a large international group for a tour of Southern India. I stayed behind to be "in charge" of the ashram. For some reason, Gurumata was unusually concerned about me falling or getting injured. She and Gurunath strongly suggested Jay stay behind and work on re-editing Gurunath's autobiography, *Wings to Freedom*. I think we both knew *he* was there to babysit me, and *I* was to make sure he stayed out of trouble. In other words, we were meant to look after each other.

After everyone left, I was technically in charge of half-a-dozen or more servants and several construction crews working on projects around the ashram. My task was to make sure things did not get too out of hand. None of them spoke English, and neither Jay nor I could speak whatever Indian languages the others spoke.

It is interesting to note: the mood of the place changed. The workers took on a bit of a holiday spirit. Jay and I worked on our separate book projects almost full time, with Jay beginning late in the day. He'd sleep late, do his meditations, and then work until four or five in the morning. We noticed he was most creative after ten in the evening.

I, on the other hand, got up as early as possible. I would meditate on the rooftop of the temple for a couple of hours before sunrise, work by myself in the ashram office on my computer until about one, and then finally take my first meal break.

Jay and I became like two ships passing in the night. We spent a few hours, in the middle of the day, together. Jay could write up a storm while listening to rock and roll; a practice that would reduce *my* productivity to zero. So, by midday I'd finished most of my writing and was editing.

We handled all kinds of visitors to the ashram and answered the phones. The only issue we had was with some loud arguments going on between a couple of the servants, a husband and wife, who lived on the ashram property. They yelled and screamed into the early hours of the morning, causing their children to cry. I could hear it all. Very unnerving. I lay on my bed and fought back dark memories of my own step-father and mother fighting while I was growing up—terrible times as a child; always in fear of their bickering inevitably exploding into violence.

Overhearing the couple on the ashram property opened old wounds. I spent the next several nights making peace with my past. When I was ready to emotionally move on, to truly bury these past issues from my childhood, the fighting at the ashram ceased and it was quiet again. The husband had left his nagging wife to spend three days with his mother in the village. Everyone got some much-needed rest!

An interesting thing happened: I kept hitting my head on a low tree branch hanging near the dining area. It became such an event; all the women servants would sit and wait for me to walk by. I swear they must have had a betting pool on when and how many times, I would bang my head on the same branch. Each time I'd hear their laughter as they enjoyed my daily show.

One day, as I sat in the hanging bamboo swing, my feet propped up on the wall of the porch, the weakest link on the old, rusted chain decided to break. The seat was about three feet from the ground, and came down, with me in it, onto the hard concrete. The impact caused a huge jolt to my tailbone, and my neck snapped. The sound of the crash alerted everyone in the entire ashram. Soon, about a dozen people stood over my crumpled body, stuck in the chair now lying on the porch.

Everyone was happy to see me move, including me. I was lifted out of the chair by several sets of hands. Although nothing in my body appeared broken, I felt like I'd fallen off a cliff, having experienced that before. Once everyone was sure I was okay, the servants all smiled and started talking to each other about what I'd done. Again, I'd fulfilled their daily dose of comedy. And in this case, I truly was the butt of the joke!

Jay took off for a few days before everyone returned to the ashram; wanting to journey to a temple he'd heard about. Alone, in some ways, it was wonderful. It was also easier on the staff. I did not demand any attention, tea, breakfast, or dinner. All I needed was a light meal at lunchtime. I was able to get back to writing this book and also got better rest.

The previous year at the ashram, I'd not had much sleep *or* rest. I'd operated on as little as four or five hours of sleep a night. The work on Gurunath's organizational issues took a lot of time, and I had spent hours speaking with visitors or on the phone. Now, on this trip, I was getting a chance to catch up on much needed sleep without any guilt attached.

One night, I heard the dogs barking. Lots of animal sounds came from the ashram's newly acquired property. The next morning, one of the servants informed us a large panther had carried away the big, black dog hanging around the ashram; had dragged the poor dog into the jungle and eaten him. The dog was a good-sized animal weighing as much as my youngest grandson. Two nights later, one of the guys reported seeing the panther's shining eyes when he'd turned his flashlight on him on his way to the bathroom.

One aspect of Indian culture still eludes me: I seem to be stuck in this Western way of thinking that says, "One doesn't walk on or through cow poop, especially barefooted." But at the ashram, they take perfectly good, clean concrete areas and mop over it with a mix of cow manure, mud, and water. It is said to be 'healthy.' The claim is it keeps away flies and other insects. Over time, I observed its truth. I never saw any bugs on it or even near it.

The justifications for this practice go even further, but I am stuck in a world where we don't walk on poop of *any* animal. When I moved across the ashram into the newly constructed rooms, I discovered there were no walkways to them, just dirt. I could handle dirt; that was a nonissue.

When I was resting in my new clean room, I heard the women working outside, talking and splashing liquid onto the dirt. I got out of bed to look. There was instant mud all around! I could not understand why they'd want to add water to the dirt and make mud...then I saw the cow-poop-soup. My world was surrounded by cow dung; very *wet* poop. I was told it would eventually dry, but first they needed to do this for many days, over and over, to build up a good thick layer of cow mud.

The women all laughed at my concerns, and merrily continued their daily task while I gingerly walked through the cow poop coming and going from my room. I have to admit, in a week, when it had dried, it did keep the dirt from blowing around. And unbelievably, it did not smell.

I needed *no* reminders to remove my shoes when I went into my room. I still did not relish walking barefoot on those covered surfaces. Every night I thoroughly washed my feet before jumping into bed. Maybe it is just an American thing. I truly love the people, customs, culture, and great spiritual wisdom of India, but this is not something I will ever incorporate on my patio at home; at least not in this lifetime.

A couple of days after my fall from the porch swing, Gurumata sent someone to check on me. The first question she was instructed to ask was, "How is your back?" I was a little surprised at the question. *No one* had told Gurunath or Gurumata about my accident nor about the injury to my back. My back and neck *were* hurting still, and would make my meditations very difficult for my remaining time at the ashram, but my reply was I was just fine. I didn't wish to worry Gurumata any more than she might have been already.

## You Only Need A Little Duct Tape

We received a phone call one night from an enthusiastic devotee in Los Angeles, who said she and her committee were sending a young filmmaker from New York City to make a couple of short films for the organization. Recently returned from making a documentary in Africa, the filmmaker's efforts would be funded by the devotee's all-women committee.

When the filmmaker arrived, she experienced a cultural surprise. Yet, I did my best to accommodate her needs, even gave up my room. I did everything I could to ensure she had all the assistance she needed, including assigning several young men to carry her equipment.

There were some contractual issues on the use of the film, but in the end, through some tears and laughter, we all established a good working relationship.

We ended up shooting at other locations, one of which was an orphanage outside Pune. While walking around, the filmmaker cut her big toe. It bled profusely in her sandal and on the ground. When I put a disinfectant on it, she freaked out a bit—not the best patient—then I pulled out a roll of duct tape and some gauze. I had been waiting for such an opportunity. I'd dreamt of duct-taping a bleeding wound several nights prior to this event. In the dream, I'd taken the tape and wrapped the foot to keep the wound clean. Well, I took her foot and did exactly that. I wrapped the toe so thoroughly it was protected from the dirt and further injury as well. I kidded her and others that a guy only needs two things in life: a roll of duct tape and a can of WD-40!

It was late when we arrived back at the ashram. Gurunath had just been speaking about the uses of duct tape; had even given an example of how it could be used in such a way. It was a well-timed appearance as the filmmaker hobbled in with her wrapped toe. No doubt, Gurunath and I had been on the same "duct tape" page that day.

The next afternoon, I used another roll of duct tape to wrap up some of the guys' hands who had blisters from hacking back growth with machetes. I also patched up some thorn wounds on the bottoms of their feet. My duct tape was the perfect product for our medical triage.

Before she left, the filmmaker, a wonderful young woman, stood talking with me as Gurunath came by. He later told me he felt a 'father-daughter' vibration between us. I really had been as concerned for her as I would have been for my own daughter.

## Happy Birthday

In India, there is a special holiday known as Maha Shivaratri; a celebration for Lord Shiva. The ashram holds a big, all-night party celebrated by those staying at the ashram, as well as the local villagers. The event includes a spectacular fireworks display over the temple, and a laser light show on the temple itself.

Gurunath gathered most of us in the dining room to spend the night together singing, talking, and sharing fellowship. His power was fully charged. I could feel energy ripping through my body. Everyone present could feel this vitality. At one point Gurunath waved his hand and a group of about 12 people sitting next to each other with their eyes shut meditating, all fell backwards as I watched. I was immediately stuck to the back of my chair by the same the power being transmitted to me. Later, he simply waved his hand, a gentle wave in front of himself, to make a point, and an energy softly entered my body and those around me. I could see people physically being affected by his burst of loving energies. It was truly an amazing night.

Around four in the morning, Gurunath began to request songs. He asked a very wonderful Indian woman to sing. For some silly reason, I started laughing at her singing. I tried to suppress it, but I couldn't. Contagious, it made about a dozen others join in. Soon, the room was filled with laughter. When I *could* get control, I was ashamed of my rudeness, so I stopped. But everyone else continued to laugh. Then I acted all innocent.

One surprise of the evening was the opera singing of Dr. Dan Kogan, a long-time, young, American devotee who'd attended medical school in India. He sang an Italian opera to perfection. An outstanding performance! Then Gurunath went around the room asking individuals to sing.

Suddenly, I jumped up and stood in full view of the whole group, stating I wanted to sing "Happy Birthday" to myself. I wanted everyone to join in with me seeing as they would all be gone when my birthday came the following month. I had all of them sing to me while I danced around like some kind of old fool directing them. It was all grand fun and everyone lightened up and laughed. I finally sat down and wondered to myself why I had gotten so inspired to get up and make a public spectacle of myself and sing the birthday song. It made no sense.

After the sun was up, the group was gathered outside around Gurunath. Unlike all these young guys, I had chosen to sleep for a couple of hours, and so was a bit tardy. Gurunath said something about me having sung the birthday song hours before. I took that as an opportunity for an encore presentation.

I seriously addressed the group, telling them I was going to do something I'd never been done publicly, on TV, or even live on stage before: I was going to sing the entire "Happy Birthday" song backwards. I paused for effect... Then just before I started to sing, I turned around backwards so my rear end was facing them while I belted out "Happy Birthday." It got a *huge* laugh. Once again, I sat down and wondered what I had done and why.

Sometime thereafter, Gurunath told me in private that both times when I sang "Happy Birthday" it mentally loosened the whole group so he could really blast them with his energy transmissions; making them all receptive.

And much later, Jay told me, before I had joined the group in the early morning and sung my "Birthday" song, Gurunath had just finished telling the group this celebration was like a "Happy Birthday Party for Lord Shiva." Then, guess what? I came into the group and sang the song to myself. Jay tapped me on the shoulder and 'reminded' me of my Naadi prediction, of Lord Shiva himself inhabiting my body, dancing and singing, on some holiday for Shiva, and everyone would just think I was an old fool, or crazy.

Wow.

Getting up in front of everyone and being silly is not totally out of the norm for me, but choosing to sing *that* particular song was *so* impulsive. Who knows what really happened. Maybe I was just an old fool.

## The Bombing in Pune

For several nights at the ashram, I had a recurring dream in which I saw a group of terrorists sneaking up on the ashram. I suspected they were going to try to kill the Westerners at the ashram. Of course, being my dream, I was the ultimate hero. I not only stopped the impending attack, but single-handily took them all out. I was like an old, short, fat Rambo. I didn't see it as a visionary message, yet when I awoke, I was always a little uneasy; something I could not quite put my finger on. In my heart, I knew the ashram was the safest place to be in India, but I continued to have concerns about terrorist bombings in the area. My senses heightened after having a similar dream for several nights in a row.

It was late at night when we received news of terrorists bombing our favorite place to eat in Pune, *The German Bakery*, a wonderful place well-known to western travelers in this part of India. In fact, Westerners were the main customers. We went to the bakery often. It was just down the street from where we'd had our Naadis done.

Tragically, the place had been leveled. Over a dozen people were killed and several dozen more were wounded. The entire block, where it once stood, was a big pile of rubble. The news hit the ashram emotionally hard, as if we'd received a direct attack ourselves.

Gurumata called the local police right after we heard the news. Within thirty minutes, four well-armed policemen were stationed on the road to the ashram. Over the next couple of nights, we had a low-key and out-of-sight presence outside of the ashram. We were safe and sound.

Within a few days, I drove by the site. There were military men surrounding it as others sifted through the debris looking for evidence. It was painful to see. We were reminded of one inescapable fact: the war against non-Muslims existed; a radical few wishing to make it a living hell for those who did not believe as they did. It's heartbreaking to see such hatred and violence in this world, all in the name of God and religion.

## Old Message from The Past

A dear friend, and excellent Vedic astrologer, had been reading star charts for many people in my circle. So, he did mine, sharing it with me on the phone. He confirmed most everything my Naadi Palm reader in India had said.

He also told me about my "life mission" according to the charts, but sharing it here would not serve any great purpose. I only mention it because I was using this as another tool to help me move forward in my own spiritual journey. It provided insights as to why certain things were happening in my life.

One thing to keep in mind with readers of charts, Tarot cards, or other methods: *no one* is one-hundred percent correct. *No one.*

The information provided is always filtered through the reader's own life experiences and personal belief systems, and is limited by their spiritual level of understanding. In other words, they are human beings, not gods. It's best to use these findings or readings as aids to discover your shortcomings and strengths. Using this information, one can improve and evolve along a spiritual path.

Knowing who you were in some past life may give a false sense of identity and, in my opinion, serves little purpose other than to inflate the ego. The only thing you really can count on is who you are right now. Because of this certainty, it's best to deal with those facts in "the now."

This astrologer and my daughter Daya had ongoing conversations—via email and phone—for several months while I was at the ashram in India. When Daya expressed concerns about some things on my chart, the astrologer went into its deeper meanings. He sent her an email, using a word she did not fully understand: "covenant." He used it in relating to my life mission.

Normally, she would have gone online for the definition, but for some reason, she pulled out her twenty-five-year-old dictionary; the one she'd used throughout her high school and college days. When she turned to the page where the word was listed, there was a message written from "me" to "her;" a note I'd written more than twenty years before. The message was extremely personal, sharing how much I loved her. I'd even added a smiley face at the end.

It touched her heart. She felt close and connected to me. It had been waiting for her inside the dictionary all those years, yet she'd been directed to look for it exactly when in need of my personal encouragement. When she told me about it, even I was amazed. I'd had no recollection of having written the note with any predestined purpose. However, it did what it was supposed to do: show her how much I loved her.

## Speaking in Mumbai

One afternoon, I received a phone call asking me to speak and introduce Gurunath to an audience in Mumbai at the *Hall of Culture, Nehru Centre,* and at *The Gyan Sagar Amphitheatre.* This was a huge honor, totally unexpected.

I was humbled by the invitation, yet a little confused as to why. It had been planned on a *"Pride of India Night"* and I am *not* Indian. At first I was reluctant to accept, but Gurunath himself asked me to do it. Once he did, I pushed all my concerns aside.

As plans were made to attend, and the event neared, I stayed with a wonderful young Indian couple, Swanand and Aassavari Thatte. Super nice people. They even bought me new Indian clothing so I would look my best when I was on stage, and fed me as if I was a king.

An interesting thing happened as we were getting the paperwork done for the event. Swanand was on his way to the police station for a permit when he discovered he'd lost the original paperwork, but he called someone and they redid the necessary papers. We then made another trip to pick it up. I told him this would change the timing of his being at the police station. This could make something special happen that would not have taken place had he not lost the paperwork.

When we got there, it looked like it was going to be a long ordeal. But as he walked up the stairs of the station house, he ran into an old high school friend from almost twenty years before. The man was now a police officer. After exchanging news and updating each other on their lives, he took us to the right office to see the man who could help us with the permit.

Walking back to our parked car several blocks away, we crossed to the middle of a busy street, where an older man joined us from the other side. The traffic was moving briskly in the two lanes on either side of us. As we stood there, the man took out a large conch shell from a cloth bag and blew it loudly, right next to me. He did this repeatedly. We looked at him, wondering what was going on, then crossed the street to the other side. He kept blowing it, facing in our direction. I turned and glanced at him, but walked on. He did not stop until we were out of sight.

I was still thinking about the man and the conch shell as we entered Swanand's home. His daughter was watching cartoons on an Indian cable station. The show just coming on was about a spiritual character who finds a magic conch shell. The episode title was "*The Conch Shell.*" I looked at the TV screen and pointed this out to Swanand and his family. We all nodded in knowing a stranger had just blown one in my ear.

Swanand retrieved a conch shell from his own collection of things and gently placed it in my hands. I put it to my lips and tried blowing to get a sound. The first few times were not very magical or tuneful. But after several attempts, I managed a powerful, energetic blast. I then blew several longer blasts. How wonderful to once again blow a conch shell! The last time was when I lived in Hawaii as an eighteen-year-old.

Swanand had to meet the Vice Mayor of Mumbai to finalize the permits for Gurunath's events, so I tagged along. When we entered his office, we placed one of the event posters on the table featuring a wonderful photo of Gurunath with his white beard and long hair; a classic photo for sure.

The Vice Mayor picked it up and studied it closely, glancing at me several times, sitting across from him. We chatted a little, then he said to me, "You know, Gurunath, you are going to have to learn to speak much better English if you want to successfully talk to all these people in Mumbai."

My friend could not help but giggle. I humbly told him I was *not* Gurunath; that I was an American. He looked at the poster again and then at me, totally ignoring what I had said. Swanand and I looked at each other and smiled. Gurunath was taking care of everything.

The permit was issued in quick fashion and all the paperwork completed for our events that week.

At the first satsang, where I introduced Gurunath, someone asked him why there weren't any more miracles like those in Yogananda's autobiography. Gurunath told the man he had not listened well enough to "Bill" in his introduction, when he mentioned many such miracles. The audience smiled and nodded in affirmation.

At the second event, in a large Amphitheatre, I mentioned to the audience that some of them were there because of friends or relatives, or perhaps they had read or learned about the presentation, but some might have accidently come upon the event and joined the group. I told them there were no accidents; everyone was supposed to be there that night.

Then Gurunath took questions.

One of the very first people to ask him a question mentioned he was brought there by "Bill." He'd heard me talking as he was walking through the park. Gurunath was pleased with the remark. I'd earned my money and done my job of introducing him to Mumbai.

*Author's Note: In November 2014, on the big island of Hawaii, I was with my buddy Dave Nye. We found a large conch shell at an open-air market in Hilo. I walked over to the table and picked up the shell, then proceeded to blow a long and loud musical sound from it, pitch perfect. The air had actually vibrated when I blew it. I was told it could probably be heard at least a mile in each direction of downtown Hilo. The man wanted $125 for it, saying no one else had ever gotten any sounds from it. As I stood there, several others came and tried. All failed. I decided I did not need to buy it, but I had felt the need to blow it—good enough for me.*

## Being Careful with Mantras

One morning at the ashram, while talking to a group of Indians, Gurunath mentioned he normally avoided giving Americans and western people mantras because of their difficulty in pronouncing the words. He went on in some detail about how each word creates certain sounds and vibrations, and how variations of those sounds may cause problems.

According to Gurunath, there are dangers with repeating words one doesn't know or understand. I wondered why he would speak of this subject to a group of Indian devotees who *did*.

An hour later, I was in the ashram office working on this book when I answered a phone call from a devotee in California. There was stress in his voice as he requested to speak to Gurunath as soon as possible. I told him Gurunath was currently speaking to a group of sixty, but if he would tell me the problem, I would get the information to Gurunath.

He insisted it was *very* important, and *only* Gurunath could help. It was about a mantra sent, in a box, to the caller's mother. After she'd read it, all kinds of supernatural things started happening; not good things, either.

He and others were frightened, worried, and unsure how to undo what was happening. It was like they had opened a Pandora's Box. Terrible things were happening around them even as he spoke to me on the phone.

I took the phone to Gurunath as fast as I could. This was the very issue Gurunath had warned everyone about that morning. I interrupted his talk to request he take the call.

Gurunath took the phone and listened to what had happened. He asked several questions, including ones about the container in which the mantra had been delivered.

Gurunath then told him to put the written mantra back into the original container, go to the Golden Gate Bridge, and toss it out into the water. If they were not close, they should locate a bridge nearest them. He said not to throw it away; rather they should release it.

Listening to how he handled the phone call, it clicked why I had been given *that* information *that* very morning. The timing made perfect sense. I certainly understood the full importance of doing mantras correctly.

## Guru Causes A Storm

In the late afternoon of the first day of the Indian spiritual retreat, Gurunath had been playing around with a small battery-operated, personal-sized, cooling fan. He held it up to various devotees and let the fan's blades cool them down. Gurunath teased us, saying he was creating a windstorm. He was also showing us how he was serving humanity. It was all fun and games.

Then we went outside to walk on the new ashram land with several of those he had been fanning. Within minutes, the wind outside picked up speed and strength, and we found ourselves being blown around with the leaves and various debris. Lightning flashed across the sky and loud claps of thunder followed. Heavy rain began to fall. Within five minutes of rushing to the safety of the office, a torrential rain soaked the entire ashram. It lasted for a couple of hours; mud and water everywhere.

I looked at Gurunath and wondered if his little playful attempt at cooling us with his fan may have kicked off this storm; one that came out of nowhere. We jokingly blamed him and told him to be careful about how he used his fan in the future. He humbly smiled, a twinkle in his eyes. *Was it his fault?*

Ironically, up to that point in time at the ashram—I'd been there six months over the last two years—I'd never experienced a rainy day. After the storm, the weather returned to hot and dry, at least for the three weeks I remained there.

## Sacred Sword

I'd heard stories from Gurunath for two years about his sacred sword called the *Chandra Has*. It was said to have supernatural and mystical powers, much like King Arthur's sword, *Excalibur,* he had pulled from a stone. But apparently, the *Chandra Has* was not straight. It was curved like a crescent moon.

We'd been told of how Gurunath charged it up with chants, prayers, and special mantras. The energy in the sword was used to fight off negativity. On one occasion, we heard about some spirits he had chased away or sliced up with this spiritual sword. He would take it into his hands and whirl it around while in his underground meditation cavern directly under his small temple at the ashram. No one had seen him do this ritual, so it was all just an image in our collective imagination.

One night, after the end of the spiritual retreat for Mumbai devotees, when almost everyone had left the ashram, I found Gurunath's grandson's plastic toy sword lying on the ground. Looking directly at Gurunath, I held the sword upright with one hand while making a fist salute across my heart and chest, much like the Roman gladiators used to do. It was an odd gesture from an old and mature devotee to his master and Satguru. I questioned myself why I'd done such a foolish thing. I was slightly embarrassed, but Gurunath gave me a far-away look, with a slight smile.

About twenty minutes later, he called all of us who had remained to gather outside his small temple at the entrance to the ashram. As we settled on the stone-paved patio, he informed us he was going to bring out his sacred sword. To my knowledge, few had ever seen it, perhaps no one outside his family; even though, over the years, many devotees had asked to repeatedly.

He asked us to remain quiet while he retreated to the temple. Watching him descend the stairs, we heard him chanting a mantra as he slipped below the temple floor. He emerged with the *Chandra Has*, resting on a wooden display platform. It was as he'd described: about three feet long and curved like a crescent moon, with a double-edged blade containing sacred writing. Apparently, the message was about protecting the righteous and destroying negativity. The sword was designed for a king's use.

He invited each of us to enter the temple and personally view it, to bow down to it if we wished, but forbade us to touch it; only to kneel and observe. I went first. Gurunath lifted the sword and showed me the writing on the blade. I stood there transfixed for about a minute before returning to the group, allowing another the privilege.

When we had all viewed it, we regrouped, and Gurunath brought it out and began to swing figure eights above his head. As the blade swiftly moved through the air, I saw the sword itself become flexible. It transformed into a cobra! Gurunath was no longer swinging a sword through the air but a dark snake! Although the image of the snake was intermittent, when his sword was rotating in a certain way, it was clearly a snake. I was not the only one who saw it.

*I cannot help but be reminded now, as I write what happened, of the story of Moses turning his staff into a snake.*

Some saw blue flames coming from the blade; others witnessed some of the seven colors leading to violet. Though I did not see the energy in a lighted-color, it pulsated through me. Gurunath later said we would have seen the colors we were attuned to.

One man from the Mumbai group, who had stayed on for an extra night, suffered from Parkinson's disease. His body—hands in particular—had been shaking violently up to the time of the sword swinging. But some of us noticed whenever Gurunath swirled and moved the sword through the air, this man's body became steady, not shaking at all. Whenever the sword stopped, the tremors began again. (I also observed the next morning, when this same man sat near Gurunath and focused on listening to him, he was in complete control.)

Gurunath then grabbed a piece of citrus fruit, cut it, took it out from the temple, and tossed it beyond the ashram. As he cleaned the blade, he recited another mantra and put the sword down. What joy for all who sat on the temple steps and listened to him speak about the sword's history, what it represented, and how it was going to be used in the future.

My western mind, along with my total lack of any knowledge or understanding of these things, hampers any ability to fully report the full significance of what really took place. I'd spent my entire lifetime knowing the myth of King Arthur, and now I was told *he and his sword* were real. Gurunath enlightened us by saying King Arthur was one of Swami Sri Yukteswar's previous lifetimes. Although his words did not all register with my physical mind, I embraced them with my heart. I understood everything, even though I could not put any of it into words.

There was absolute silence as Gurunath spoke of the sword of King Arthur and the importance of "The Four Horsemen." When Gurunath finished speaking, we slowly rose and left in silence. In awe, I was still wondering what we had all witnessed. This was a sacred moment and a major blessing for all of us; a moment in time and space which had altered a part of who I am.

## Who Is A Disciple Of -Babaji?

Gurunath was working on his book, *Babaji: The Lightning Standing Still,* and was attempting to write about who a true disciple of Babaji might be. He came out of his office to meet some new arrivals; people attending a week-long ashram experience. One of those was a fifty-year-old Indian woman named Savreet Brar.

She and I had met the month before when she'd traveled to the ashram to meet Gurunath. Unfortunately, he had been away from the ashram and she missed him by a day. She'd brought her daughter and son-in-law, and was disappointed her family could not meet Gurunath.

Elated, she and Gurunath were now engaged in a short conversation. She told him it had been predicted she'd meet her guru after she turned fifty. She'd had a Naadi reading in Pune about seven years previous, and asked for her tenth chapter to be read; a chapter dealing with one's spiritual life and guru.

The reading had noted her age and stated her guru was Gurunath Siddanath, a disciple of Goraksha-Babaji, and she would meet him in the same town the Naadi reading was done (Pune).

A couple of years later, she met a doctor who was talking about spiritual matters. Curious about why he was interested in such things, she asked him if he had a guru. He said he was a member of Hamsa Yoga and he did, indeed, have a guru. She asked if his name was Gurunath Siddanath, and he replied with a yes. Then she asked if he was associated with or was a disciple of Goraksha-Babaji. The doctor confirmed this. She finished her questioning by asking if this guru was in Pune, which again prompted an affirmative reply.

The doctor had, in fact, been using her intuition; connecting the dots with the information she'd been given: a name, location, and a way to find her guru.

A few years later, she attended a banquet in Delhi and discovered Gurunath was nearby giving yoga classes. But by the time she'd received this information, he'd left. She finally made a trip in January 2010 to his ashram outside Pune, where she met me and missed Gurunath by a day. The day she spoke with me she did not mention any of this story. I'd simply suggested she sign up for the Indian five-day retreat taking place the next month.

An interesting fact emerged: she had turned fifty on February 23rd, just three weeks before the five-day retreat. Thus, the prediction of her meeting her guru after she was fifty came to pass.

The other predictions were also true; the mailing address for the ashram is in Pune, where Gurunath also has his personal home.

The conversation might have also put some focus on the very question Gurunath had been asking himself. He was being told he was and is a disciple of Shiva-Goraksha-Babaji. Although he has been reluctant to openly claim or acknowledge this as a fact, all of us who had heard this story understood this was a revelation for Gurunath, as well as ourselves.

## The Forest Fire

Gurunath had left the ashram and would be away for a full week in the Himalayan Mountains to negotiate a land purchase for an ashram. During his absence, there were about a dozen people staying at the ashram.

One afternoon, we saw a fire crawling along the hills on the south side of the ashram above the temple. As it neared the property, we sent several of the men staying at the ashram to stop it from burning the grass area close by. They all returned tired and smelling like smoke, but feeling good about what they had done. They'd stopped the fire's path to the ashram.

On my way back from the village, I saw the entire hillside above the temple engulfed in flames. The grass and trees where ablaze, shooting up into the night sky. The smaller afternoon fire had morphed into a raging forest fire several miles across, from the top of the hills to a few hundred yards from the temple itself. Its path was on a collision course with the temple and the ashram!

I returned to the ashram to find a small team of firefighters having tea. They were watching the progression of the fire as it neared the ashram. A red line of fire moved down the face of the hillside for as far as I could see; we'd be up all night monitoring it or fighting it.

Several people and I climbed onto the roof of the temple to get a better view. From my vantage point, it looked even closer to the ashram than from ground level, and much more out of control. The grass was a couple of feet high and there were dry branches, sticks, and leaves on the ground, perfect kindling for a huge blaze. Enough fuel for it to burn for several days!

I phoned Gurunath and advised him of the situation. Not seem too concerned, he said, in the worst-case scenario, we would have to dig trenches and fill them with water in the morning—or even do nothing—but we should not worry about the fire. Gurunath said it would be okay; gave the impression he was going to make it stop. At least that was the feeling we were left with.

Most everyone went back down to the center of the ashram to relax and have some tea, but a young man from San Diego and I decided to stand fire-watch on the roof of the temple to make sure we did not have any problems.

The night sky was smoky and glowing red; the smell of burning grass and trees thick in the air, uncomfortable for our eyes and lungs. We kept watching the huge flames leap skyward each time they consumed another tree. It looked like a war zone, and brought back not-so-fond memories of Vietnam jungle fires in which we had to land our helicopter.

A few minutes after our watch started, we noticed the fire had stopped advancing. No movement down the mountain. The long line of flames began to break; a solid red line reduced to several separate ones. The flames turned to embers. The fire was going out...on its own.

Next, we heard the sounds of the forest department's firefighters with some of the ashram's servants, walking up the hillside, south of the chapel. They'd decided to fight the fire...now that it was going out on its own. I had to smile, certain they'd get full credit for extinguishing the entire forest fire. But by the time they reached the ridge, just yards from where the fire had been aggressively eating up the trees and grass, it had already faded. There were hardly any signs of embers. It was amazing to watch as the entire red line of fire went totally dark within less than an hour.

We climbed down from the roof, figuring our services as firewatchers were no longer needed. On the way down the steep hillside behind the temple, I became concerned about the young man following me. He did not have a flashlight and was also walking barefoot on the rocky ground—this guy never wore any shoes, even when working or hiking in the thick forests around the ashram. I cautioned him, saying he could easily fall and slide down the hill and get hurt.

I turned around and aimed the beam of my flashlight on the ground in front of him so he could see, but was also looking behind me as I walked down the hill. That was when both of my feet flew up. I landed hard on my neck and back, then slid on my backside all the way down the hill until I hit the base of a tree with my feet.

I lay there trying to look as dignified as possible, but in of a lot pain as I looked up at his concerned face. He helped me up and I brushed off the dirt and rocks. I said I was okay, but I wasn't.

When we joined the rest of the group near the dining hall, there was only one small red spot on the entire mountain, and *that* receded in a short time. The fire had gone from a several-mile-long raging battlefront to a campfire. I'd been a witness to many California fires in my lifetime, even fought a small fire when I was twenty-three. Fires don't just go out on their own like this one had. I'd never seen anything like it.

Two days later, my young friend and I went for an early morning hike up the hillside to assess the fire damage. We hiked about four miles across the hills, following the path of the fire. Of course, he was walking barefoot through the burnt forest. We did not reach either end of the fire line, but we did find something interesting at the line where the fire had stopped. What we saw were half-burned tree branches and leaves. Some were totally consumed by the fire, but inches away, the other half remained untouched. There was tall grass where the fire blaze had stopped; fuel for continued burning was in great supply along the entire path of moving fire. We were baffled by this barrier and wondered about what forces could have caused the abrupt halt.

Maybe scientists could give a logical reason for what happened, but I *know* what I saw. Someone or something sucked the very energy out of that fire, saving the temple and the ashram.

Gurunath was right in telling us not to worry. I believe he did something to stop the encroaching inferno. And of course, being the very essence of humility, he would never make a big deal out of it, let alone admit it.

## Door Latches and Visualizations

There weren't many of us left during my last few remaining few days at the ashram. So, I helped prepare for a large group coming from Germany for a retreat; about two dozen arrived extremely early in the morning. I quickly made friends with two men, David and Lars; old souls, old friends. I spoke to the two of them about the power of visualization, giving examples on how they could manifest events, changes, and outcomes using the power of the mind; by visualizing what they wanted. This approach would help them in the near future; developing these skills could help shape and change their lives. At some level, they each needed to hear this message, to learn whatever lesson was coming through for them.

Shortly after, late in the evening, Lars and David went to their bungalow—right next to mine—to retire for the night. When I arrived at my bungalow, I heard all kinds of banging. David came to me complaining. Somehow the inside door latch had closed shut and locked the steel door from the inside.

I later learned there was never any history of this having happened with any door at the ashram—not ever.

There was no way the door could be locked from the inside without someone on the inside sliding the bolt, but there was nobody inside, and all windows were grilled. If the door latch had been partially open, it would have hit on the metal door jam and the door would not have been able to be closed. It was a huge mystery on how it could just lock as it did. We all looked at the locked door. They demonstrated to me it was locked by shaking the door and banging on it. I told them not to worry about it, assured them I'd handle it in the morning, and, while I slept, I'd be visualizing the door unlocked. I received a quizzical look from both men before I sent them to another room to sleep. And clueless as to how to physically open the door, I went to sleep by just affirming it would open for me in the morning.

On waking, I returned to their bungalow and found the door remained locked. I stood in front of it and visualized the door opening. I gently touched the surface of the door with the fingertips of my left hand. Then, in my mind, I saw the door open. Seconds later, I simply pushed the tips of my fingers on the door itself. As I did, the inside bolt rolled back and the door opened wide.

I stood there, a little amazed myself, thinking it unfortunate no one had been present to witness it. The event had totally proved my point about the power of seeing what you wanted done by using your mind first.

Then I went to the Earth Peace Temple to meet David and tell him about the opened door. The very moment I reached the top of the stairs, David walked out from behind the temple. He'd just finished his meditation on the roof and was not surprised at all when I told him I'd just opened the door. Through visualization, he had seen it all. I asked if he saw me opening it, and he replied, "Only the outcome; the opened door."

When Lars came down, we told him what happened. He was quite puzzled.

Though I'd made my point, perhaps there was a silent disbelief within them.

Later, I pulled out a plastic chair and sat on my porch waiting for them to return from their afternoon mediation. I mentally sent David a message to come and see me, then I sat for about five minutes. Next thing I saw was David's face sheepishly looking at me. I asked him why he was five minutes late. In reply, he asked if I'd been sending him a message to come see me. When I confirmed I had, he said he'd heard it, but wanted to put it off for several minutes and finish his meditation.

We both smiled and started to talk about our families. A few minutes later, an Indian devotee, Rajesh, joined us. As we continued to enjoy our conversation, David asked Rajesh and me if we'd like to see some pictures of his wife and children. When we said we would, he went over to his bungalow to retrieve them. Shortly, I heard banging and pounding again; on the very door I'd previously opened.

David returned and announced the door was once again bolted shut from the inside. Unbelievable!

I asked him to sit down and spend time visualizing it opening for him. After he'd done this for at least ten minutes, we all walked to the door. He tried doing what I'd done, but nothing worked. Then he pounded the door with both hands, then his feet. He grabbed the outside door latch and shook it, trying to loosen the bolt. I then asked Rajesh to try to open the door. After hesitating—the situation puzzled and scared him a little bit—he attempted to open it by shaking it.

I asked them all to step aside and showed them the door was still in fact, bolted, there was no movement at all. Then I stepped forward and told them to watch what was going to happen. First, I stated the door would open, then I gently held my hand about an inch away from the door and touched only my fingertips to the surface. I could sense and feel the latched bolt moving. The door flew open like when police kick in a door; flying back on its hinges, making a loud sound.

I was as surprised as the rest, but I had my back to them so they could not see my face. I wanted to say, "WOW! That was something!" But it would be more dramatic to turn slowly, without any surprised look, and walk off, as if this kind of thing happened every day. In truth, it would have been very exciting to be a bystander and have watched someone do what I'd done.

As I left, no one said a word.

I smiled inside, gave thanks, and prepared to leave the ashram.

Interestingly enough, my energy had been building the entire stay. It certainly made for a very dramatic exit; just as much of a gift to me as it was for them. I was left wondering how the experience might affect them.

### Abbreviated/edited email from Lars in Germany – May 12, 2010

*Dear Bill,*

*David told me you are thinking about publishing the story of our ashram house door locking on its own in your new book.*

*Last night I had an interesting dream about the ashram story when David's and my little house in the ashram was locked from the inside. I wanted to share with you.*

*It was like getting a kind of an explanation for this happening. The house was symbolizing the inner-self, being locked from inside for some unknown reason.*

*After you had opened the door, something in me still wasn't able to believe it was safe to take rest in my inner/higher-self, symbolically, so the door closed again and you had to open it a second time.*

*Nothing "just" happens in the world without a deeper sense, so I start thinking about all that now. Somehow meeting with you (holding the key, the ability to open the door) seems to facilitate an important change in me.*

*To say it short. The key to me seems to be to have faith in God. Therefore, I had to read your book* A Spiritual Warrior's Journey.

*I can't give it a name, but it's happening. Though I didn't change much in my Yoga classes, the students are glowing, having out-of-body experiences, and lot more things since I came back from the ashram.*

*Somehow it feels like being the man delivering the divine mail from God, and in India I received a big bundle of letters for me to read and for my Yoga students to deliver. And somehow just being with them in the Yoga classes, I'm delivering the mail, without even being aware of it and they are receiving their messages.*

*You see it still needs to come to some order. The basic trust in me is growing though sometimes there is a voice inside telling me "Lars, you might be getting crazy now."*

*It's not that this man writing is of any importance, but still he's very grateful to have God's mail delivering job.*

*But what so ever I'll let go and let God.*
*All the best*
*Lars*

## Mumbai Airport Encounter

I left the ashram and headed off to the Mumbai Airport to catch my early morning flight, arriving about six hours too early. A crowd pushed up against the doors, as police and military men turned people back. I heard them say no one could enter the building until two hours before their scheduled flight time. People had to stand outside the doors and wait.

I wanted to get inside way ahead of schedule, so I could check my bags as early as possible, and sit and relax. I had been having slight chest pains and wanted to rest. I watched a uniformed man with an automatic weapon turn away a large family of Indians who were three hours early. Still, I handed my tickets to him. He examined them and directed me inside, stating I'd not be allowed to come back out. It was so smooth, without a hitch. Interestingly enough, it was just what I had been visualizing to have happen. Though I was not surprised, it made me smile.

I went inside and made my way into a huge waiting room near my assigned gate. Though I had an excellent seat, I experienced an urge to move across the room to another row of seats. Once settled, I fooled around with my laptop, played some Indian chants, and viewed some photos of Gurunath.

Shortly thereafter, an Indian woman in an airport wheelchair —her name was Regina and she was forty years old—rolled into the seating section across from me. She looked frail and weak. There were bruises and small cuts on her hands and face; absolutely beaten by life.

Her eyes searched my soul as she got out of her wheelchair and shuffled over. Standing over me, she said, "I believe you can help me with my spiritual problem." Looking at my computer screen, at a photo of Gurunath, not knowing who he was or anything else about him, she blurted out, "All I see are sunrays surrounding him."

Now, she had my attention.

I studied her. It was obvious she needed spiritual help. She then blinked her eyes a few times quickly and told me, "This might sound strange, but I see you as one of The Knights of The Round Table."

I was stunned. I'd been thinking about all the references Gurunath had made about King Arthur and his Knights of the Round Table; that it was not merely some myth but a fact-based period in our human history. Even though lots of the stories have been fictionalized and distorted, there really were such great souls. He had flatly stated Sri Yukteswar had been King Arthur, Merlin had been Lahiri Mahasaya, and many who follow him are those same Knights.

In particular, Gurunath and I had been talking about one of those famous Knights, Sir Lancelot, and how he'd done a terrible thing by having an affair with King Arthur's wife. He'd looked me in the eye and uttered something to the effect of, "*For you*, that was not such a terrible thing to do." What a strange way to reply! I was left wondering if he really meant "me."

So, there I was at the airport thinking, no, wondering what Gurunath had been trying to tell me, when this woman rolls in and tells me I'm a Knight of the Round Table. She'd done so totally out of the blue, with no prompting or clues. I was speechless. She'd just answered a question I'd been asking.

She went on to say she saw me in the dark robes of a monk in another time period. She would get these intuitive flashes and could see who people were in their past lives.

Finally, she revealed she was being attacked by people using tantric magic and other forms of curses on her and she'd been suffering for years. She took out some photos, explaining the attacks came when she was sleeping; that she was physically assaulted in her dreams. When she woke, there would be cuts and scratches and bruises all over her.

I did not have much time to help her before our plane was to board for Frankfurt, so I did what I could and gave her my walking stick to use as a cane. She abandoned the wheel chair and found the energy to walk to another gate when our gate number changed.

We got on the plane together, though our seats were many rows apart.

At the Frankfurt Airport, we had to go through security to get to our connecting flights. I helped her with her baggage, then stopped at the baggage X-Ray machine and handed her bags back to her. In my mind, I saw the security guys opening her bag, thinking it was my clothing, and I didn't want them to think that those were mine.

When her bag went through the machine, the security personnel *did* open it up in front of me. Right away I said it was her bag. They took out a few handfuls of her undergarments, but since it was not mine, I was spared any public humiliation.

At this point we were to part, as we had different planes to board. She asked me to bless her and pray for her, which I did. I sent her off with whatever energies I could spare, and we exchanged phone numbers so she could contact me later. I was concerned about her spiritual and mental health.

## Thoughts on Leaving India 2010

I found myself, once again, heading back to the USA, reflecting on the extended stay with Gurunath at his ashram. So much had happened! What did it all mean?

On Good Friday, two days before I was to leave on Easter Sunday, one of the German visitors walked from the temple crying, claiming she'd just seen Jesus and He'd spoken to her. She was not the first to tell me such things; I'd heard it before on my previous two stays at the ashram. Remember, I, too, saw Jesus; not as a vision, but very much alive inside the giant Mercury Shivalinga resting in the center of the temple. Those images played with my mind as I sat in my cramped airline seat.

This visit had been different—in many ways—than my first time at the ashram. Even though I rested more, my energy was not always there. I found myself winded from walking up the steps to the temple. A few times I experienced sharp chest pains. Gurunath never pushed me physically and had made sure I rested; suggesting a few times I should take a nap.

This trip I'd spent more personal time with Gurunath and now had a better understanding of what he expected from me within his organization. More importantly, our personal relationship had grown in profound ways. I did not feel any need to ask him any questions or to engage him in conversations. Tranquility was found in his complete silence. I found the quiet time spent with him to be more powerful than when he was talking. It really made little difference to me if I was physically there with him at the ashram or in California, there was a total connection. On a personal and human level, I would miss his physical and emotional presence. He had become so much more than my Satguru; I was his friend.

Some of the things Gurunath talked about during my first visit to his ashram—things I did not understand—now resonated within me with some degree of comprehension. Though I might never fully understand all he'd given me, I'd gained new insights. The thing was, he had continued to reveal so much new material it was impossible to grasp and remember everything. I had long ago given up on using my mind to intellectually decipher all these things. I just let my heart listen.

Working alongside Gurunath, while he dictated his book on Babaji, was beyond any known experience I'd ever had. One night, I was sitting right next to him for a period of four hours; our heads inches apart. I had to lay down on the sofa, my head was so dizzy with bliss. I'd 'overcharged' all my energy levels. It was so powerful! What memories! I just knew when I read his finished book all these same feelings would return.

As I headed back home to my wife and family, I reflected on things discovered, things about myself; some of which surprised me; some of which humbled me. My Naadi reading was still an issue burning within me. Knowing the future is not always such a great thing. But for me, it was good to see my mission and life purpose were reconfirmed on so many levels.

I looked forward to being home, my other home. I'd missed my family so much I'd been counting the days. Not that I'd wanted to leave India, but I wanted to be with my wife. If I could have found a way to be in both places at once I would have. (Note to higher self: I need two bodies.)

Then there was the phone conversation I'd had with Daya. She'd called me at the ashram from California and confidently stated Gurunath was Sri Yukteswar. She had reached this conclusion without me having told her, but was looking for my confirmation to support what she knew in her heart to be true. Her only question was how he could be in two places at once. According to Yogananda, his guru was in a higher world helping souls evolve. (She was referring to the subtler astral heaven of Hiranyaloka mentioned in *Autobiography of a Yogi*.)

This was all still true, and yet Gurunath was also the soul and very spirit of Sri Yukteswar working through an earthly body to help Babaji with his evolutionary mission for this earth cycle. She totally got it and understood. I wondered if others would, and pondered on how many others had reached this same inner knowing about Gurunath's identity.

*In this book, I have officially let the cat-out-of-the-bag, but I only exposed a not-so-well-hidden secret among Gurunath's closest disciples. Not inclined, but overcome with such a strong inner urging, I knew it was the right time, and this book was the proper vehicle. He would never reveal this on his own. So, if it was ever to be, it was going to have to come by others who have accepted the Master's identity for themselves.*

*Part Six*

# LIFE OR DEATH - DECISIONS OF THE HEART

### Heart Journey Begins – Warning Signs

While at the ashram, I had been having sharp chest pains. Knowing something was not right with my health, I'd put off all thoughts about what it might be and fully embraced all the organizational work I could do for Hamsa Yoga Sangh (HYS).

Gurunath had tasked me with helping to coordinate events for HYS in the USA. I saw my over-all task as mainly getting everyone to work together harmoniously. There were many good people around who knew what had to be done. To that end, I found myself working twelve to fifteen hours a day on emails, and with phone calls, smoothing over people's issues, and helping others set up a USA summer tour for Gurunath. The main part of my mission was to get people to communicate and to work together without friction. I flew to Florida and spent some time there with those running the Florida HYS organization.

On the flight to Florida I had terrible chest pains. I began to think I was dying, the pain was *so bad*. I managed to get there, but did not say much about it. I spent my four days there presenting an informal workshop on non-violent and compassionate communication skills. It was the same kind of training I had participated in at the Self-Realization Fellowship years back. I remember how it gave our SRF Sacramento group some excellent tools to help build more compassionate interpersonal skills. I wished to do the same with HYS.

On my first full day in Florida, we drove north of Orlando to do a small workshop at the home of one of the young men in the group. In attendance was Regina, the Indian woman I had met at the Mumbai Airport when I was flying home. She'd been invited to come to Florida so she might learn something to help her with her spiritual and emotional issues. Physically, looking much better, she was being helped by one of the young yoga teachers in Florida. More relaxed than the last time I saw her, she sat there with all of us, fully engrossed in what we were doing.

Peering about the room, I envisioned a scene from a past life. I saw these very same people sitting around a campfire on rocks and on the ground listening to me talking. I was about to go on and describe what the place looked like when Regina interrupted me and filled in all the missing details.

I sat there totally amazed and dumbfounded. She was seeing the exact same things I was—the rocks and trees, what each of us was wearing, and even what the surrounding area looked like. I'd never had others see or share such things with me before, except at the ashram when I saw those ancient beings from Easter Island, so this was a most interesting confirmation of my vision.

The next couple of nights the group spent in Orlando at the team coordinator's home. This way we could maximize our time together. We were all sleeping in various locations around her home. Fortunately, I was sleeping in the family meditation room, seeing as I was getting up at two each morning and would meditate until about four or five. To my delight, others joined me. It turned out to be a real bonding experience for all of us. I called that time of day 'my magic hours with Lord Shiva.' The stillness and quiet made for some great, sacred, uninterrupted meditation time.

There was a group of young men sleeping in the front room on the floor in sleeping bags. For reasons known only to them, they decided to go out for a walk sometime after midnight, without telling anyone. They proceeded to get lost while wandering around this typical Orlando neighborhood, which looked the same on every block. They had been gone a long time and weren't too successful in finding the house again. It took a while, but they made it back. They told me what had happened in the morning when I got up and we all had breakfast together.

They said, after realizing how lost they were, they decided to stop aimlessly walking around. None of them had a cell phone. In a strange but imaginative act, with closed eyes, each spun around, the idea being that when they stopped, maybe they would all face in the same direction. They reasoned, if they were lucky, they might be able to divine the right way to walk back to the house.

As luck would have it, they ended up facing different directions. But when they saw a small armadillo scooting down the sidewalk, they decided to follow it, hoping it would lead them to a familiar street. So *that* is just what they did. For whatever reasons, they actually ended up finding the right house. They came back inside just before two in the morning. When I got up to meditate, they joined me.

As I listened to their story, I smiled. I'd had a very realistic vision/dream while they were gone, where I was outside the house in the same neighborhood. I had seen them wandering aimlessly and went to meet with them. I walked up to them, chiding them for not having a phone. I was not sure they could see or hear me, like I was having an out-of-body experience and was not fully able to communicate with them.

They were spinning around with eyes shut trying to find out which way to walk. All I could recall from the dream was a small animal wandering into view as I became conscious. Perhaps, for a moment, I somehow had become the animal, but I was unable to recall nor confirm this.

I found it rather interesting and a little amusing. *I* was dreaming of *their* night excursion, and was not sure what *any* of it meant. A part of me felt I'd really been with them, but all I had was a vision/dream experience and no hard evidence. Whatever the reason, I was not seeking to impress them with any possibilities. I was just happy they had made it back safely.

I was exhausted when I got back home from Florida. I experienced chest pains on the return flight as well. The very next weekend, I drove 450 miles to Los Angeles and facilitated another workshop for nineteen people. I gave them all the physical and emotional energy and love I could. Some wonderful personal and group things happened there; some dramatic, soul-awakening experiences. I was told many of these things happened afterwards, but a number occurred right then.

I was sitting there with the group, simply listening, when I got an abstract image in my mind's eye. I saw myself like a huge vacuum cleaner sucking up everyone's hurts and pains directly into my heart; an odd visualization for sure.

All this time, I continued to experience extreme chest pains. I did not complain, but some in the group noticed I was grabbing my heart area with my hand and squeezing and massaging it. Allie, one of the women there, a psychic card reader, went over to me on one of the breaks. She placed her hand directly on my chest while her other hand was on my back. She told me she'd had an inner message from Gurunath to do this; to channel his loving energy and light to my heart. She did so for several minutes, then stopped. My heart stabilized enough to finish up the workshop. Everyone was in such great spirits! True fellowship flowed through all the hearts there.

I left the next morning and drove all the way home. My only hope and prayer was for this fellowship and positive experience to last a while longer. I had given them everything I could. I was drained physically and emotionally.

## My Heart Attacks

I was to give five public talks on military and veteran issues; scheduled every other day for the entire Memorial Day week. I started off on Sunday spending almost the entire day in Sacramento, giving an early morning talk, following up five hours later with another talk. I was exhausted and having chest pains the entire day. When I returned home, I almost collapsed.

A couple of days later, in the Sierra Nevada foothills, during a keynote address in front of several hundred people, I felt as if my chest was going to explode, like someone was stabbing and twisting a rusty knife blade between my rib cage and my heart. I continued speaking, finishing up about fifteen minutes later to a standing ovation. No one there was aware I was in extreme pain. I left right away and drove fifty miles home in extreme agony.

Major chest pains continued for several days, and resulted with me collapsing on my sofa several times. Friday morning, while my wife and grandchildren were at the Sacramento Zoo, I could not take the pain any more, and dragged myself to the next-door neighbor's home, who kindly called an ambulance. I was transported to Sacramento Mercy General Hospital where I was greeted by about ten medical personnel.

Once stabilized, I was taken upstairs into the operating room. The procedures took about two hours. Before the doctors finished, I had another heart attack right there on the operating table. The next hour was spent with me lying there with several specialists watching over me.

It was as if I had left my body several times—in and out.

The medical staff told me bluntly, of the five stents I already had in me, two of them were totally blocked by blood clots, and an additional artery (without a stent) was completely blocked, so they added an additional stent, for a total of six. They could not unclog one artery and would have to leave the clot there; hopefully to be dissolved. I was given blood thinners to work on that particular clot, and kept under close watch.

My family and many friends came by while I was in the hospital. One loving friend, Bill Gunther, drove up from Hollywood just to say hello and then drove back home; a twenty-minute visit. I was honored by such friendship. I received dozens of phone calls, cards, balloons, flowers, and even fruit. Ironically, I spent all my time cheering up those visiting or calling me. I was truly loved and blessed by all the love and prayers I was getting.

At no time did I ever think I was going to die. Even with the doctors telling me any of the five major heart attacks I had over the previous six days could have and should have killed a normal person, I knew Gurunath was watching over me. He called me from Europe, where he was on tour giving lectures, and told me not to worry; everything would be okay. I heard his words of encouragement while I was lying in my hospital bed with IVs in my arms and an oxygen tube in my nose. IT WAS THE TRUTH. I thanked him for calling me and for taking care of me. It was wonderful to get his phone call, even if I already knew he was there with me in the spiritual sense.

It was not my time to go. According to my Naadi Palm Reader, I still had many missions yet to accomplish, of which writing this book is only one part; inspiring readers to pursue their own spiritual journey is another. Emotionally and spiritually, I was alive and full of joy, even if the body was totally exhausted. Gurunath was there for me, regardless of my physical situation. I fully trusted in the Divine and rested in the fact I was loved.

## Losing Face

I spent as much personal time with Gurunath as I could the summer of 2010, introducing him at events in Los Angeles and such, but I could not be at all of them due to medical appointments. This time they were not related to my heart, but to the cancer I had on my nose and other parts of my face and head.

Normally this should not have been a big deal as I had fought skin cancers for over thirty years—most of them removed without resorting to surgery—but had a few cancers over the last couple of decades *requiring* surgery. In 1998, I was off work for five months for cancer treatments on my face.

So, in 2010, when the doctors cut a good-sized tissue sample from the area next to my right tear duct, I was not overly concerned about it. *Two months later*, I was informed it was a bad cancer and would need surgery to get it all.

One day, in the mail, I received several notices from doctors informing me of several medical appointments that were scheduled, including two for surgery. I had no clue as to what it all was going to entail and how invasive it might be. So, when I went to see an eye surgeon, who was also a plastic surgeon, I was wondering why.

The doctor, the area's best at what he does, lacked any bedside manners. As I entered the room, he did not ask any questions about me personally, just went right to the area around the eye. Examining it, he told me it was much worse than he had been expecting; that it might even involve the removal of the right eye, parts of my lips and my ears and it would involve several follow-up surgeries.

His words came at me from out of the blue. I had no idea it was *that bad*. I had reported these cancer issues, *to my doctors*, about *two years* before, and they had treated it for a year with medication. Now I was being told this was a 'grave situation' and they would be performing several surgeries *on my face*.

It took my breath away to hear the doctor go on about how they would have to rip up my face to fix it; how they'd cut my forehead and parts of my ears to rebuild the area around the right eye, eyelid, and the nose. He casually reminded me he might have to remove my right eye, then went on with more, but I'd stopped listening; numb from the hard-hitting news. I went in thinking this would be a little cut and some sewing up, but discovered my face would be almost removed and rebuilt with some of my own body parts.

While I was sitting there, he took out a couple of very long needles and poked them into the area next to my right tear duct. I wasn't mentally ready for *that* either. He went on to say the cancer could have grown and rooted out into my cheeks and eyelid, and even the tear duct and behind the right eyeball.

I staggered out of his office.

Downstairs, I found myself sitting all alone in my pick-up truck in the hospital parking lot. I was stunned to say the least. I had to catch my breath and examine what had happened. I got on my cell phone and called Karen. I told her what was said and she filled in some of the missing information on the procedures I might be getting. I thanked her for her help.

I then called Gurunath and left him a message on his cell phone, telling him I would do whatever I had to do, even embrace this karma and make the best of it.

I admit to feeling a little down and bummed-out for about an hour. Then I took a deep breath decided this was something I needed to do with courage and great trust. If I could go through all of this, no matter the results, it might inspire others facing difficult life situations. I was determined to just do it and not worry or complain about it. I was *not* going to be a victim. I had the opportunity to be a positive example on how to face and handle these kinds of issues. I had successfully talked myself into seeing all the good that could come from it.

My family took it rather hard when I told them, even though I made sure I was fully positive. I refused to have a "Why me?" pity party.

My heart doctor was concerned about me being able to handle two back-to-back surgeries less than 24-hours apart. So, the day before the first operation, I was sent to get a physical exam. They wanted to make sure my blood pressure would not be too high. The nurse called me to come forward and sit down. She took my blood pressure—105/59—and was surprised at how calm I was the day before my surgeries.

She took my wrist, looking for my pulse. By now, I was even more relaxed, like I was in a different state of mind and body. She kept moving her fingers around on my wrist and arm seeking to find my pulse. She could not find any, so she rolled over a machine that measures heartbeat and pulse. She hooked me up and turned it on. It was working, but showed nothing for the pulse; no numbers posted on the digital screen. She fooled around with the machine for five minutes and couldn't get any pulse reading. She said the machine was working, but for whatever reason it was not registering my pulse. She theorized it was just too low, and went back to trying to find it manually…unsuccessfully. I smiled to prove I was not dead. She was speechless.

When I left there, I continued to experience a Divine sense of calm; ready for whatever was waiting for me.

## Face Off

My first surgery involved the removal of the cancerous tumors from my face. I went in early in the morning to see the surgeon. He took one look at my nose and around my eye and made the same kind of comments the eye surgeon had, that it was worse than he had previously diagnosed and could take several surgeries to repair. I sat listening to him drone on about the long process…He was going to cut a few layers of tissue at a time, while going only so deep with each cut. Then he would send it to the lab to look at each tissue slice. There they would chart out where the cancer was growing and thus follow it along my face. Meaning, he would only cut as deep and as far as needed. He'd inject me with painkillers all around my eye socket, nose, and face before cutting, then burn my skin to keep it from bleeding, throw a bandage over it, and send me out to the waiting room for an hour or longer to await the results. When he got them and determined what else had to be done, the doctor would cut another layer; a process that would continue for as many hours and times as needed.

With each trip back into the surgery room I would get all those shots again in and around the face and eye. Several of the needles went deep into my nasal cavity and eye socket areas. I could taste blood or chemicals trickling down my throat from the injections.

On one of my trips back to the waiting room, there was a young woman, perhaps in her early thirties, who was being brought in by a couple of her friends. They held her steady by each arm and helped her sit in a chair, but she was not emotionally ready for this process. She was visibly frightened, so I offered up some encouraging words about how it was not much worse than a dentist visit.

She looked at me from her seat and then proceeded to verbally abuse me for thinking she was just some poor female who could not handle this surgery. She went on about how she'd done this process before and could handle it without any of my macho crap. She sat there holding onto her friends and gave me one of those hard looks like I was a chauvinist male pig. Wow. I thought I had read her situation correctly, but, oh, how wrong I was.

When the nurse came and told the young woman the surgeon was ready for her, she almost collapsed onto the floor of the waiting room. Her friends and the nurse all took her limp body into the room for surgery. They all stayed inside with her. In short order, there were bloody screams and yelling vibrating the walls of the waiting room. It was a very brief surgical procedure. She came out with a very tiny Band-Aid on the side of her left cheek, which looked to be a cut maybe the size of a small pimple. She was still limp. She then curled up into her seat with her friends talking to her like she was a baby.

I watched all of this without any expression. Although I must admit, an evil smile emerged from within me. Inside, I was saying something like, *"Okay lady, now who's the big baby!"* I was relishing her pain and had to stop myself from laughing at her or saying anything. I almost felt guilty, but I decided I would live with that small piece of evil karma and enjoy it. This certainly proves I am not a fully enlightened being by any measure.

She never went back in again. Her total medical process was just one very small cut on the cheek. When I went back for more cutting on my face and eyelid, the doctor, nurse, and I all laughed about it as the doctor poked more needles though the area around the tear duct. It was odd to be laughing while getting poked with a needle near the eyeball.

The surgery was not comfortable at all. I could hear the sounds of the doctor cutting the nose. I could feel the cuts in my eyelid and all around the tear duct. Every time he finished up, he would burn it all so it would stop bleeding. I could see the smoke rising from the flesh being burned and could smell it while blood was pouring down my face.

Finally, it was done. Just before I was bandaged up for the last time, the nurse pulled out a piece of gauze stuffed into the hole between my nose and eyeball. I watched as she pulled out over 3 ½ feet of bloody material from the hole in my face. It made me ill to see it. I had to refocus my mind and take a deep breath. I asked to see what I looked like. The doctor did not want me to look into a mirror, but he did take a photo and showed me. They had to send the photo to a plastic surgeon for review. He had to be made aware of what he would be dealing with in the morning when I returned for surgery.

I gasped. They had cut off a large part of my nose around my right eye. Several holes were visible in the top of my right eyelid and there was a *very* large hole in the center of my face! My mind flashed, *how in the world would they ever be able to close that up and make it look like a human face again?*

## Pain, Blood, and a Visitor

When I left the surgeon's office, he instructed me to pick up two bottles of heavy-duty pain medicines; that when the shots wore off, my whole face would feel like it was on fire; that without any doubt I'd need the pain pills every day for several weeks. We parted with his warnings about the intense pain to follow.

When I arrived home, Carol asked if I was planning to take the medication, knowing I usually would not take any pain medication, not even for dentist visits. I looked her in the eye and said, "Real men do not need pain medicines." I was determined to handle this without the aid of drugs.

My face was totally wrapped in bandages, covering my right eye completely, most of my nose, some of the cheek, and a small part of my forehead. I looked like I had been wounded on some battlefield.

As I stood in the kitchen, I noticed the effects of the shots were wearing off. My face began to feel warm, then hot, and next like someone was holding it down on a hot barbecue grill. My face was ablaze and my right eyeball felt like it was skewered onto a metal rod and placed on a spit rotating over a white-hot fire.

I pounded the top of the kitchen counter for about ten minutes, thinking maybe a 'real man' could take a small amount of drugs for pain. After all, this was serious pain; the kind when, if asked to rate it from one to ten, I would have answered, "More than twenty-five!"

I grabbed the bottle of pills and took a half-dose, just wanting to stop the extreme pain, then said a quick prayer to Babaji to give me courage to handle it all and to bless the pill, which I popped into my mouth followed by a swig of water. But before I could swallow both—but not stop the swallowing action—the agony stopped. All pain completely subsided. Gone! The pill was still in my throat on its way to wherever it was chemically intended to go, but the pain was already gone. Not only had the intense burning stopped, but I was overcome with the power of PEACE. I stood there, in the kitchen, amazed by what had happened. Carol saw it all.

Fully exhausted, I told Carol, since there wasn't any more pain, I'd take a short nap. I needed rest before the plastic surgery scheduled the next morning, and so went upstairs straight to bed. I woke up about three hours later with all the bed sheets and pillows soaked. I could feel the wetness, but *could not see* hardly *anything* with one eye patched and my face so swollen. Warm liquid rolled down my cheeks as I headed downstairs to tell Carol her wimpy husband must have been crying like a baby; that the sheets and pillows were soaking wet from his tears.

She shot me a curious look (I must have been a Halloween horror) and went upstairs. Minutes later, she came down with her arms filled with bedding. I had not been crying, but had bled all over the sheets and pillows.

I was so pleased, I smiled, with blood running down my face, and said, "Thank God it is only blood and not tears!"

Carol was blown away by my remark, but I was serious. I was happier to have the bloody sheets than to think I'd been crying that much. But what a mess!

I went back to bed as soon as my patient and loving wife had it remade. We had to leave early in the morning for the hospital, thirty-five miles away in Folsom.

I'd slept soundly until around four in the morning, when I was awakened by a sudden burst of light. I rolled over, opened my left eye, and saw something like a blazing sun next to my bed. The light should have been physically blinding, brighter than any person could look at, but I was focused on it.

I saw an arm reaching out from the center of the LIGHT. The fingers on a hand spread out and covered my face and all my wounds. A solid hand, not some dream vision of a hand! It was physical, having discernable weight. It touched me; caressed my face and embraced my entire soul. My whole body remained in bed, absorbing the LIGHT and the LOVE.

I never questioned why It was there or who IT was, just accepted IT as reality. Yet, a part of me knew who IT was; even expected it to happen. I remained in total peace, filled with infinite love and compassion. A complete state of total contentment.

Speaking was unnecessary. I understood what was happening. I was greatly loved. Everything happening to me was ordained, a part of my destiny. I gently closed my eye. I was being healed beyond physically. I was being restored at levels I could never fully realize, express, or describe. There was more to this visitor's touch…much more.

I had been renewed, altered, changed, and born-again in the truest sense of the expression.

A while later, Carol came to wake me up. I told her what happened as we drove to the hospital for the plastic surgery.

At the hospital, when I was taken in for prep, the surgeon spoke to Carol and me before I was rolled away on the gurney. He said he would have to cut parts from my ears to help rebuild the holes in my face and nose. He also said he would graft skin from my forehead, seven inches wide at the top, then overlap and fold onto my face and nose. Once in place, he'd sew it all down. Later, he'd operate again to reduce the bump on my forehead and make repairs to areas where the grafts had been harvested.

He continued talking to me as I was given a shot to knock me out, but I remember asking him how it all looked.

With his not-so-wonderful bedside manner, he said it was much worse, a deeper hole than he'd expected. He said it would take a lot of work on his part. He continued speaking, but I drifted off under the influence of whatever drugs he'd given me.

When I came to, I was in the recovery room and Carol was talking to me, wanting to know what happened to my face. They'd not cut my ears or forehead, but there did seem to be a stitched wound on my left shoulder. She asked to speak to the doctor and, when he was located, she wanted an explanation.

This is what he said. Once he got into the operating room "it all changed"—"it" being somewhat a loose term. Somehow, he'd been inspired, at the last moment, to use flesh from my shoulder for all the open holes and wounds on my face; opted to completely forego the procedure he'd planned.

I was grateful for his skill; to perform the operation without using tissue he'd usually have used for my situation. It also meant less or perhaps even no plastic surgery later on.

The surgeon prescribed painkillers and said to use them daily. He warned me about what was coming. I had dozens of stitches in and around my nose, eyelids, and shoulder.

When we arrived home, I put the bottle of pills in the cupboard with the other two unused bottles. I trusted I would not need them. After all, I had my favorite drug, Gurunath!

As the drugs used in surgery wore off, I remained pain free. I was even amazed myself. I went to bed and slept soundly until around four in the morning. Again, I was awakened by the presence of a bright sun-like sphere. Its LIGHT graced my room. The same arm and hand reached out from the white, glowing, radiant mist. It was totally Biblical! There isn't anything else to call it. A loving hand held my face and fed my soul with LIGHT and LOVE. I was infused with the energy of that LIGHT, and I knew who IT was. No need for any conversations or questions, I was at peace.

Whatever had happened twenty-four hours before was happening again to me. More of the old me died and the new me grew stronger. I was not "me" any longer. I did not know *who* I was, or *what* I was going to become, only that things would never be the same again. Truly, I was not me anymore, and it was inexplicably and amazingly good.

## I Learn the Identity of the Visitor

Ten days after the plastic surgery, the surgeon prepared to take out the stitches. He was his usual self with his terse bedside manner, but even he was surprised at what he discovered. He took off all the face bandages, looked at the stitches on my face and shoulder, and said he'd never seen anything like it.

When I asked him what he meant, he told me all the areas he had stitched had skin growing over them; a phenomenon unheard of in ten days.

I asked him how long he'd been a plastic surgeon. He replied his career had spanned over thirty years.

To remove some of the stiches, he had to cut through new skin, and to take out the others, he pulled hard.

When I came out of the doctor's office, Carol had a hard time looking at my face. I resembled a monster who'd come apart and been sewn back together. All I needed was a metal bolt for my neck and I could've given Frankenstein a run for his money.

White puss oozed out of the tear duct area, an infection. Each cut looked huge and flaming-red. I looked into the mirror and tried to picture it healed, or at least not oozing and bleeding. I was determined not to concern myself with the details of my healing process. I figured, no matter how it came out, it would be okay. If it ended up "ugly," then I might look macho. If it healed well, then that was fine, too. I had no expectations. I embraced the situation with total acceptance for whatever would be.

My face may have looked terrible to others, but inside there was nothing but joyfulness and thankfulness, owing to the two middle-of-the-night visits. I was not the same guy any more. I had a different view of life. Nothing was so important as to make me angry or become depressed over. Everything was "small stuff."

And something else happened to me, something much harder to explain. I could sense new things about people I'd not been able to before; as if I was a spiritual doctor. I could distinguish where spiritual illness or pain came from.

Yet, I couldn't go around telling everything to everyone, so I set about finding a way to use the knowledge without interfering with others' free will and karma. Some people cannot handle the truth and would not listen even if they said they wanted to know.

There was a joyful buzz within me. I could not help but smile for all the wonder I could see and feel around me. Although, on the exterior, I looked like damaged goods, within dwelt a wondrous depth of astonishing proportions.

One morning, I looked in the mirror and saw the exterior ugliness. I'd not be going out in public for a while. Then I received a phone call from Gurunath, who said he was in the San Francisco Bay Area with his wife, and they wondered if they could come and visit me. A three-hour drive. I was amused he had humbly 'asked' to come over. Heck, I was thrilled! I replied with a resounding "yes," and offered to take everyone out for dinner.

I examined my face in the mirror just before Gurunath and his wife arrived. I was concerned his wife might be upset about how I looked. But when I saw my reflection, I was surprised by how much I'd improved from earlier in the day. In fact, I estimated my looks had improved about fifty percent in a matter of a *few hours*.

When they arrived, I apologized for looking so good. I told Gurunath I was losing the compassionate vote from others, as I was healing so fast. It was a most amazing experience to have improved so much in such a short time.

I decided my face looked good enough to accept a wedding invitation from a good friend. She was getting married in Napa Valley and had wanted me to be there. So, all of three weeks into the healing, I would be going out in public, sporting an eye patch and showing off a little discolored skin; all passable in the outdoor light.

People said they were amazed I could attend, and I was thrilled to be a guest. At the wedding dinner, Gurunath talked about my morning visitor in the light. He told all of those sitting at our table what happened to me was not a series of dreams, or visions, but a real visitation. He told us it was 'The Big Boss.'

I was blown away when he confirmed what I intuitively knew. He said it was true, and that it really happened as I had said it did—twice. For those close to him, Gurunath refers to Babaji as 'The Big Boss.'

Though I wasn't sure how to fully respond, I chose to sit quietly and savor the information. There was such peace in the validation the visitor was real and not my imagination.

## Burning Man to Rainbow Man

My face looked better each day. Due to my surgeries, I'd missed all but one of the retreats that summer. It was important I be there, in Los Angeles, to help support the group. For me, that meant basically holding hands and talking to people. It was imperative I show people how well Gurunath had been taking care of me; my healing was certainly a testimony to his love.

Just before the retreat, Gurunath had posted a video on You-Tube with a provocative title, "From Burning Man to Rainbow Man." It was an inspiring talk referring to the annual "Burning Man Celebration" in the state of Nevada. Gurunath took it to much greater spiritual heights, relating it to the burning of our karma through Kriya meditation, which ultimately leads to one becoming a "Rainbow Man."

About the same time, I'd sent out a link to a video about an Indian man called "The Fire Guru." This video shows a fully-clothed guru lying on top of a large pile of wood totally consumed in fire. The guru has fire all around him, yet neither he nor his clothing burns. He claims he becomes one with the fire. Therefore, he does not get burned. It was some of the most amazing video footage I have seen. I copied the email to several of the young men in the organization who might enjoy viewing this mysterious occurrence. Though I was unaware at the time, this set the tone for my spiritual retreat.

On the first morning of the retreat, I had the opportunity and privilege to speak to the entire group. I wanted to relate the experiences of my recent operations on my face; an indisputable testimony of major healing.

Though I was unsure exactly what to say, the words just flowed, unaided by any notes. I spoke totally from my heart. Those present embraced it as much as I did.

After my talk, I found several people wanted to speak to me about their own lives. I'd opened a door of trust. I was honored.

When one woman, from Arizona, approached me to address a personal issue, I gently stopped her before she began. I had a story she needed to hear. I told her about my experiences with kidney disease, and related to her how I'd embraced it, surrendering it all to Divine will. My story ended with me expressing how my willingness to embrace the pain, the disease, and the results had led to my learning a huge spiritual lesson.

She stared at me in loving acceptance, as my personal story related to the subject she wished to discuss. Her own kidney issues caused great pain and concern. She thanked me for giving her the answer before she'd had to ask.

Many others approached with different questions, but one man came to me to express he was upset with how he was received by Gurunath. He went on about how he'd found his guru; how when he'd finally walked from the cabins to the hall with Gurunath, he'd not been recognized nor welcomed formally as a devotee. He'd wanted confirmation of the relationship, and was visibly bummed-out by being ignored.

He was 'expecting' and 'demanding' a specific kind of welcome from the guru. These expectations and demands were his ego. He had not opened himself to whatever the universe might wish to give him. Sadly, my answer did not make any points with him. We parted ways in the dining hall.

On the last day of the retreat, the organization held a drawing, a kind of "select-a-name-from-a-hat" type of door prize. Two names would be randomly selected, and each would receive a personally signed book, handed over and blessed by Gurunath in front of all the attendees at the retreat.

It was with great pleasure I heard the complainant's name called out as the winner of the final book. It was moving to see the look on his face as he walked past me and made his way to Gurunath. I watched as Gurunath looked directly into his eyes and held the book out for him. There was a moment of obvious recognition, by both. This was a destined connection. He staggered, vibrating with joy, back to his seat.

Shortly after, I approached him and placed my hand gently on his shoulder. He turned and looked at me, his face illuminated with peace. His tears were those of joy.

I looked into his eyes and asked him if he now understood. His look, followed by his humble words, demonstrated he not only got it, but he was experiencing transformation before me. His manner and voice were so gentle and loving. I smiled. Something special had taken place. The universe had delivered more than he could have asked for. He'd received his reception.

Gurunath called me and several others to come and sit on the stage with him on the last day. I sat directly next to his feet with my back up against a tall candleholder, one I had not noticed or paid any attention to.

But while I was sitting there, a great heat surged through me, like my head and back were on fire. This went on for almost an hour with me squirming around feeling great discomfort from the hot sensations down my neck and back.

Eventually, we were released and asked to return to our seats in the audience. I rose slowly and walked away with a feeling I'd been on fire the entire time. As I left the stage, several people called my attention to the back of my sweater. It was coated with wax, some of it still warm and moving down my spine. I removed the sweater and looked in amazement at the thick layer of wax coating my back, then I saw the candle and stand I'd been leaning against.

The candle had been nested right at the nape of my neck, its flame directly under my skull and hair. It was obvious, I should have been burned or set on fire, but neither had happened. All I'd experienced was the dripping wax as evidence of what had transpired. Several of the people there kidded me saying I *was* "The Burning Man."

As the retreat ended, I went about my plans to drive home—about 450 miles—but Gurunath was concerned and asked me not to drive home that night. He invited me to spend the night where he was staying; the home of a devotee. I accepted, and we gathered there, had dinner, and talked until two in the morning. I slept until just before four, and then got up to begin my long drive home. I wanted to get out of Los Angeles and avoid the morning commuters.

I got into my pick-up, zipped out of the city, heading north on Highway 5. But I kept hearing Gurunath's voice telling me I needed to sleep to be safe. As soon as I came down from the mountains into the big valley, I pulled into the first rest stop, parked, and tilted my seat back. It wasn't difficult to fall asleep. I was truly tired and needed rest.

I awoke to the sunrise. And with that sunrise, I returned to the highway, deciding to pull over at the next rest stop and take another long nap, which I did. I also stopped for gas and food, taking my time going home, making sure I was alert and awake.

When I pulled into my driveway, I checked the clock. Somehow, I'd managed to use the same amount of time I usually needed to drive back from Los Angeles, and those trips did not include rest stops. I was amazed I could stop and sleep and still make the same time as I normally would have. But then, these kinds of things happen often around Gurunath. I smiled and walked into my house knowing, once again, my guru continued to look after me.

## Self-Realization Fellowship Meeting at Mother Center

I'd only been home a day-and-a-half, and had more surgery booked a few days later, when Gurunath called me around ten in the evening. He wanted me to return to Los Angeles so I could go with him to the headquarters of The Self-Realization Fellowship at Mount Washington. He was an invited guest and was to be given a tour of the grounds and meet with several of the monks there. I told him I would leave early in the morning and meet him at the Mother Center (the name SRF calls their headquarters).

Gurunath asked if someone could come with me. He did not want me to drive alone. I answered saying, "I never drive alone, 'God is my co-pilot.'"

He laughed and said he'd see me tomorrow.

I rose early and drove to Los Angeles, then up the mountain to the Mother Center. So much peace and love pulsates there! The grounds still have that wonderful energy and sacredness Yogananda established. One can feel his presence everywhere.

The grounds were decorated for Halloween. It looked like a fantasy world for small children. Each year, thousands arrive from all over Los Angeles to enjoy the festive celebration organized by the nuns and monks. But I was not there for fun and games, I was there to enjoy seeing Gurunath and the monks.

I arrived early, so I sat in the lobby of the main building and meditated next to two paintings: one of Yogananda, and the other, Yogananda's guru, Sri Yukteswar. When I opened my eyes, after my long meditation, I saw one of the monks standing near me, smiling. He looked at me then declared, "Aren't you the guy on the You-Tube video doing a testimony about Gurunath?"

He said he'd just watched it before coming out to greet me and had been impressed by what I'd said. We went on to talk about some of what was on the video so he might have a better understanding of Gurunath.

When Gurunath arrived, with a group of several young devotees, we were taken into the library. The organization had sent four monks to greet Gurunath. We all sat and listened to Gurunath enlighten us on the great spiritual mission Yogananda had carried out and SRF continues to honor. Because of Yogananda, others, such as himself, could come to the west and carry out the mission of Babaji by teaching Kriya Yoga.

Gurunath continued to talk about how SRF needed to expand its worldwide reach; that all organizations teaching true Kriya, as taught by Shiva Goraksha Babaji, should embrace each other as spiritual brothers and sisters. Gurunath spoke of his love for Yogananda, then took a flower and placed it near the painting of Yogananda. There was a long moment of silence, then the monks gave us a tour of the upstairs bedroom of Yogananda; pristine, left exactly as it was when he left his body in March 1952.

I was honored to accompany Gurunath into the bedroom. It was rather an odd and wonderful moment knowing Gurunath was a reincarnation of Sri Yukteswar. What a sacred time, following Gurunath around the bedroom of his own devotee.

Gurunath almost floated through the bedroom; steps so gentle so as not to mar a sacred surface. It was touching for all of us to be a witness, even if the monks had no clue as to the depth and significance of the event. Afterwards, we all meditated downstairs, then the monks presented gifts of books, fruits, and flowers to Gurunath.

When it was time to leave, we said our goodbyes outside. And, for the first time ever in our relationship, I approached Gurunath and asked him for a blessing to help me with the surgery I had to undergo the next morning in Sacramento. I was facing surgery on my skull, ears, legs, and arms. I was told they'd be cutting away more cancerous areas, and to expect lots of stitches. My ears were my biggest concern, as they would lose lots of tissue.

Gurunath looked me over, then placed his hands on the top of my head to bless me, then he slid them down over my ears. Like always, he told me not to worry, it would be okay.

We all drove off our separate ways.

As I headed down the Grapevine on Highway 5, it began to get dark. Suddenly, a huge owl swept into the path of my truck; side-to-side, across the front of the truck as I drove downhill. It was a magnificent sight. I reflected how owls have always been my personal spiritual messengers and bearers of great blessings. This was truly a good omen of things to come.

The next morning, I went to the hospital for my surgery. The doctor, a beautiful Indian woman, examined me, then pronounced it wasn't as bad as it had previously looked. In fact, one ear had no cancer at all, and on the other ear she could remove it with liquid nitrogen, stating, "I will just burn this cancer off."

She began to spray. It hurt, but I was smiling. I was being "burned" once again. Then she looked at the top of my head and said she could do the same thing there as well. She proceeded to cauterize the top of my head. It burned maddeningly, but I had no complaints. It beat being cut up and stitched.

She proceeded to burn all the cancers on the rest of my body. The good news: there was no cutting, no surgery, and no stitches! I was truly a 'burning man' once again!

## Big Basin Redwood State Park

There are times when being with Gurunath is such an unexpected delight. Toward the end of his stay in the US, I was able to join him for some driving excursions around Northern California, including the Monterey Bay area, and around the Santa Cruz Mountains. One such adventure was to *Big Basin Redwood State Park* with a married couple and their young daughter. They were long-time devotees of Gurunath who always made it a point to ensure he enjoyed some recreation time.

Although Gurunath enjoys the outdoors and being close to nature, he was exhausted from many months of speaking engagements and teaching tours around the world. I'd never seen him so tired. He needed to recharge his body, and the redwood forest was to provide energy and inspiration to him.

We stopped at the park's headquarters where he got a cup of hot coffee. I watched him with it outdoors, at the picnic table, and witnessed the cup jump up about three inches in the air, turn upside down, and spill the beverage onto his clothing. We were both startled at what happened; perplexed at what could have caused it. Gurunath stated it was an attack by a mischievous nature spirit. With his energy low, the spirits could attack him.

I was shocked, but Gurunath was undeterred and wanted to take a walk through the redwood groves to recharge.

We ended up, a short time later, sitting at the foot of a massive redwood tree fifteen-hundred years old. The center of the tree was hollowed from previous forest fires; a cave, the size of a small room, inside the enormous trunk. Gurunath went inside the tree-cave and peeked out at us. It was certainly a magical moment; all of us engrossed in the beauty of the place, as if the tree was loving us and delivering a spiritual hug. Totally embraced by the Divine.

It was obvious, we all sensed something. The very air we were breathing was so thick and rich one could caress it as it flowed past and around us. I could touch it as I might a river of love. We breathed it into our lungs and agreed it was a phenomenal experience. In all my life, I have never breathed in any richer or more satisfying oxygen. It was an energy drink for the soul. We bathed in it, luxuriated in it. The trees were recharging Gurunath with loving energy, and we were benefiting from it by being near him. What a blessing!

When we'd filled our bodies and enriched our spirits, we walked out of the redwoods and returned to the van. I noticed there was more zip to Gurunath's steps.

We drove up to the top of the mountain road and stopped to watch the sunset. Outside the van, each one of us faced the sun and did our surya. It slipped away just as Gurunath finished.

When we climbed into the van, Gurunath took out his harmonica and began to play Christmas songs. We all sang along as he played his music, making the trip back a truly delightful experience. Gurunath's personality was alive and revitalized by the journey to the redwoods. Nature had been there to humbly serve him. He was ready for his remaining weeks in the US.

## Fire Ceremony and Film Premiere

It was completely appropriate for Gurunath's last official events in America in 2010 to be highly charged and life-changing. He'd been interviewed and filmed for the documentary *Tapping the Source*. It was given an official red carpet, Hollywood premiere style, and Gurunath as one of the guests of honor.

It was wonderful watching him walk down the red carpet to be interviewed by several people with television cameras, equipment, and personnel with them. He was the center of attention and focus, his energy brighter than the spotlights. I was proud to be a witness to this triumphant finish to his USA tour.

Everyone who was someone in the "New Age" world of writing, acting, or motivational speaking was in attendance. Actresses Mariel Hemingway, Cathy Lee Crosby, and others were present, as were many bestselling authors of inspirational and New Age books. It was packed with celebrities, but Gurunath stole the show and the imagination of the audience.

After the film was shown, Gurunath sat near the middle of the panel assembled for a discussion, trying not to be noticed. He spoke briefly, and when he did, he knocked everyone out with the sheer volume and power of his personal energy.

The highlight of the night was near the end of the program. He took the microphone and told people he was going to have them personally experience "the source." He then proceeded to impart his no-mind state.

Those sitting in the audience experienced an incredible phenomenon when Gurunath clapped his hands and the whole place fell totally silent. People stopped moving and thinking. The place was electrically charged, and yet it was filled with loving silence. He then brought everyone back.

When he asked, who had experienced a "no mind state," about ninety percent of the audience raised their hands, including every member of the celebrity panel. The demonstration had stunned; a performance no one could surpass.

That weekend there was a special fire ceremony for an invited group, including many in the film. The setting was sacred and inspiring. The fire pit was at the head of a long swimming pool illuminated by underwater lighting and dozens of candles floating on the surface.

Gurunath beckoned people to come forward, two at a time, to participate in the ceremony. Afterwards, he had people sit inside the lovely home where the celebration took place. He mesmerized them for six hours while they sat patiently, absorbing everything he gave them. It was a night of reformation. People left there in a different state than when they'd arrived.

Gurunath had finally been discovered by the west! I left there knowing the world was about to be changed forever! Shooting stars filled the skies over Los Angeles that evening as we drove north. A deep gratitude filled my soul, so much appreciation for the past two years. I was a new man. Nothing was ever going to be the same for any of us.

*Part Seven*

# DON'T GIVE UP HEART

## Germany and India Journey 2011
### Germany – January

Before I was to leave on my winter journey to Germany and India I had this overwhelming feeling of dread; some physical issue within me. I scheduled a complete physical at my HMO, asking my doctor if I was in good enough shape to travel for four months overseas. I was given the all's-okay/bon voyage, but something wasn't quite right within my physical self.

As Carol and Daya dropped me off at the airport, I announced they should not be surprised if I returned sooner than scheduled. They said their goodbyes with puzzled looks. I continued to feel apprehensive on the flight to Frankfurt.

When I landed in Germany, David, one of the meditation teachers of the German Hamsa group, greeted me; the same man for whom I'd "unlocked" the door to his bungalow at the ashram the previous year. We took the train to the small city where he lived with his wife and young family. I also stayed at the home of Lars, the other German who'd experienced the "door opening." I was energetically welcomed.

We went to the yoga studio Lars owned and operated, situated on the top floor of a building in the downtown area, whose access required climbing several flights of stairs. Ascending the staircase, I registered a tightness in my chest.

The studio was quiet and emitted a sacred energy. I was informed there would be a gathering of over two-dozen people, and a workshop, from noon to eight. This sounded quite special and, despite the nagging pain in my chest, it felt good to be in the fellowship of so many loving people. I failed to realize I was "the workshop," and had zero time to plan anything. My only actual concern was to get someone to translate what I said into German.

About five minutes after informing me it was *my* workshop, I was introduced. I stood in front of a wonderful group of young German yogis. I was given eight hours of freedom to say whatever came to my mind. Even if I had known before about doing this workshop, I would not have planned anything more than I normally do, which is nothing. Everything I do comes directly and spontaneously from my heart. My attitude is simply to flow with the energy to see where it takes the group. I always follow the same process when speaking publicly. I just relax, open my mouth, and allow whatever is ready to materialize to happen. I never honestly consider where any of my talks are heading or even the subject matter. My style is just to trust the universe to provide the words. It is always as much of a surprise for me as it is the audience. My presentation style can only be described as walking a tightrope without a net. It takes solid faith and trust in the Universe. It never fails me.

I began by finding someone to translate my English into German. I would speak in slow, short bursts, and then wait for the translator to inform the group of my message. About seventy percent of the participants understood English, so I could see how my words were comprehended. I had no problem filling the entire time, and I was able to get short breaks to rest while the words were being translated.

Near the end of the workshop, I decided to ask the group to individually tell me something about themselves. I asked them to speak in German, and requested their words not be translated; to tell me anything they wanted about themselves. For instance, like how they'd met Gurunath, something about their own spiritual path, or an interesting aspect of their lives.

And it began. One at a time. As each person spoke, I focused my fullest attention on his or her body—on the face, especially the eyes—trying to pick up the sense and feeling of his or her message. Although I am only familiar with about a dozen German words, each person's statement entered my heart. I did not listen to the words. No. I simply opened myself to what each individual "told me."

From all the messages, I asked for only two questions to be clarified. One was to a young woman I sensed was dying of cancer. I wanted to verify my feelings. She was, and I did.

Afterwards, I revealed what I had heard with just a couple of the Hamsas; a personal focus and observation on those who had spoken. I had connected with the essence of what had been said, even if I hadn't understood everything.

The wonder of it all—about the messages and the personal declarations, or even private thoughts—amazed even me.

Through this involvement, I directed some of my attention to the woman dying of cancer. She was looking for a miracle to cure her, but I saw no future in this lifetime. She would be gone before the summer arrived, and she passed away just a few months later.

Doing this workshop, I could feel Gurunath's presence beside me as I spoke to his devotees. It was as if he was physically present in the room. The group of souls glowed, literally, as I saw huge auras of white light around them. They radiated and resonated with what I was telling them, but also with each other. The funny part is I really have no clue as to what I told them. I just opened my mouth and let the words flow from my heart.

## India

Traveling from Germany to India was completely exhausting. I arrived at the ashram in rough shape—physically shattered—not the best way to begin a long stay. There were only five others at the ashram in January, but Westerners would arrive mid-February to fill the place. It was kind of nice to be able to spend some quiet time there to work on this book and meditate.

One of my first nights at the ashram, we spent more than four hours listening to Gurunath deliver an insightful and inspirational discourse on a variety of spiritual subjects. It is hard for others to fully understand or even imagine how much he gives of himself to his devotees. His words and his silences transform those present to the degree of each person's sensitivity and openness allows. Every moment spent with him is savored; a personal treasure.

**Notes from my personal diary:**
**My first week in India.**
*I'm working on this book while sitting in Gurunath's ashram in India. It's a cold January morning as I write these words; still dark outside. I've been reflecting on all that has happened in the last several years, and how truly blessed it has all been. Everything has drawn me to the feet of my master, even the so-called bad things. I feel rather inadequate to describe my time with Gurunath. There is no way I will ever be able to fully capture who he really is, at least not from any description in a book. I do not believe any author will or could. His energy and power do not translate to mere words on paper, nor does his love. His abundant presence can only be truly known by sitting with him in deep meditation.*

*My body is exhausted from the past year of health issues, but I trust Gurunath is looking after me, enabling my body to somehow finish my mission. I have been told my time is limited, so I need to focus on doing what I am fated to do. This is no different for anyone else in terms of birth, life, and death; something we all must experience. The difference is, I* know *my mission* and *how long I have.*

### January 20, 2011

*Last night, Gurunath called me at the ashram from Pune, where he has spent most of the week with his family, saying he was scheduled to speak to an important women's organization at a large hotel there the next week. He told the organizers that he wanted me to introduce him at the event. When he told me this, I was, once again, truly humbled by the honor.*

*While I was on the phone with Gurunath, he pointedly asked me how I was feeling. I told him I was not physically well. I'd been blowing my nose and coughing around the clock. It had exhausted me. He said "not to worry," he'd send healing energy my way. After I hung up the phone, I was empowered. I was able to finally sleep, the cough no longer an issue. This morning I feel fully rested. It was amazing, once again, how receptive my body and mind are to his words. A suggestion from him sends healing energy to my body and soul.*

### January 24, 2011

*I introduced Gurunath today, in Pune, at a function attended by more than three-hundred business leaders; a phenomenal representation of the most influential women in this part of India.*

*The leaders of this group told me, in clear terms, not to exceed a two-minute introduction. Gurunath told me not to cut my introduction short, but to say all I normally would say; not to worry about their rule. He then went on about what stories to talk about in the introduction. What he wanted was about a twenty to thirty-minute presentation; impossible to cover in two minutes unless Gurunath could stretch time itself.*

*I silently said a prayer to him as I approached the podium. Then I opened my mouth, with no idea of what I was going to say, and proceeded to talk for what could have been half an hour. I covered everything I'd wanted to convey, including what he'd advised me.*

*Afterwards, in the hotel room the organizers had given to us to use as a Green Room, the leaders came in to speak with us. Well, in truth, they wanted to be with Gurunath. He asked them how my introduction went and the woman in charge said it was truly amazing. She mentioned it was wonderful; that I'd stayed within my time limit for the program "precisely," she'd said, "right to the second, just two minutes."*

*She then thanked me. I smiled and replied with something like "it was my pleasure"—it truly had been, and always is—but I was amazed, cognizant I'd taken much longer. Gurunath had pulled one of his time-warping tricks.*

### February 8, 2011
*And again, Gurunath honored me, asking me to introduce him to Indian audiences in Mumbai. Each event was comprised of huge, enthusiastic crowds.*

*At the last event, an early Sunday morning, I was watching him teach a large group his techniques for charging and healing the body through sunshine. This lesson was carried out at sunrise. During his lecture, I began to experience sharp pains in my chest. I became dizzy and weak, the same kind of symptoms I'd experienced before my last major series of heart attacks. I grabbed at my chest and massaged it, attempting to survive a serious medical situation. I pulled out my bottle of nitro pills and took several to ease the pain.*

*But I fell, and ended slumped over on the cement step in front of me. I remained there, lightheaded and disorientated; the nitro pills had had no effect. The pain had overpowered me, and I ended up laying on the cement step in front of the bench where I'd previously been standing.*

*Meanwhile, Gurunath had everyone standing for the healing exercise. He couldn't see me from where he demonstrated. I heard him change the direction of his teaching, telling the group to visualize the healing power of the sun in their heart lotus. He went on and on, talking about the healing energy flowing through the hearts of everyone there, but he was totally focused on working me over—twenty minutes of heart healing visualization, during which I found myself becoming fully stabilized and out of pain. The dizziness was gone. He had come to my aid.*

*At the end of the event, he called for me to come on stage to be thanked and blessed for my service to him and his organization. When I arrived on stage, I thanked him profusely for showering his healing love and energy on me. He looked at me knowingly, with the greatest of love. He'd saved me, again.*

*Regardless, his wife, Gurumata, insisted I be seen at the hospital. She made her feelings known this was much more serious than others were treating it. I did go to the local medical clinic, but by this time my heart showed no sign of trouble. She still had doubts about my situation, and shared her worries with Gurunath.*

*Returning to the ashram that afternoon was like attending a cosmic circus. First, a man riding a white horse greeted our vehicle and traveled beside it; a nice touch based on my past experiences with Gurunath.*

*Next, the sound of an emergency vehicle came up behind us, then overtook us. The printing on the back of the ambulance stated: "Emergency Cardiac Care." How appropriate it was to see the flashing lights on our way back to the ashram.*

*I was traveling with others—Gurunath and his wife were several miles behind us—and our driver kept telling me Gurunath would take care of me, and I should not go home as his wife suggested. He went on and on about how I should ignore her warnings and concerns. Then his cellphone rang. He put the speaker on so we could all hear the phone call. Gurumata seriously ripped into the driver, stating she hoped he was not trying to talk me out of going home and telling me NOT to listen to her. It was like she'd listened in on his previous conversation. He went silent. We'd all heard her. Her timing was amazing, and what she'd said was accurate.*

*When we arrived at the ashram I was exhausted, again. My heart reminded me of its needed attention as soon as I returned to the USA.*

*Gurumata had called my family deeply concerned; insisted I change my flight home. She said it was time to go home! Her feelings were so strong I had no choice.*

*That evening, when four of us westerners were having dinner in the ashram dining hall, something wonderful and sacred happened to give me closure; to confirm I was doing the right thing by leaving.*

*I was sitting in a chair with my back to the kitchen door when I felt eyes boring through my back, watching me from the doorway. I turned around. Someone was standing there. I rose and walked toward where I saw him. Gone. No one was physically there.*

*I asked the others if they'd seen someone standing there. To my surprise one of the young men, Brian Yosowitz, a young lawyer from California, admitted he had. He described to me exactly in detail what I had seen. Another stated he was touched by a presence, an energy coming from there, but could not see anyone. One young woman said she'd experienced nothing.*

*The man Brian saw looked exactly like Sri Yukteswar and stood as Gurunath does, with his hands behind his back. We had both seen the same image. This was precisely what I'd seen. Of the four people there, only the two of us saw him. It was time for me to go home.*

*When my flight was changed, I packed my bags. I was going back home, nearly two months early, as was predicted before I'd left the United States.*

*I spent my last few days at Gurunath's home in Pune. I could not have asked for a better way to leave India. Gurumata told me I was not to return to India until I was healthier. She knew more serious things were coming at me.*

## Returning to the USA

I tried to get some assistance with boarding at the Mumbai Airport, showing my medical files from the hospital in Pune to the ticket agents. I told them I was not physically well; that I was experiencing weakness. I showed them my swollen hands and feet and my records from the emergency room of the hospital in Mumbai where I'd gone after my heart attack. What I needed was someone to get me across the terminal via a wheelchair, but my pleas fell upon deaf ears. The agent said there were still several hours before my flight was to leave and I could walk slowly to the gate.

I left the ticket counter, dragging my bag behind me, more drained than when I had arrived. When I looked back, I noticed two wealthy-looking, Indian women in their fifties receiving wheelchair assistance from the same agent who'd told me I could walk slowly. I had to laugh. They'd appeared in good health when they'd followed me into the airport.

My feet and ankles continued to swell on the flight to Germany and my lungs filled up with fluids. There was no comfort to be found in the middle seat sandwiched between two extremely overweight travelers; a prisoner for the duration of the long flight.

When we landed at Frankfurt to transfer planes, I could hardly move. I faced the daunting task of getting my bag and myself across to the other side of the airport where I had to go through another security checkpoint. I asked the flight attendants if I could get some wheelchair assistance, but was told because I had more than six hours until my connecting flight, I'd have plenty of time to arrive at the departure gate. It was a Mumbai rerun.

At the security area, where I complained about having major physical troubles, I breathed a sigh of relief as they pulled me aside. Finally, I'd have some assistance. But no, they directed me to another line where I stood for twenty minutes. Staff took my laptop computer, demanded my passwords, and then proceeded to check my files, photos, and emails. There was no place for me to sit down, and when I asked about getting a chair I was told to be patient. The experience was sheer agony.

Hours later, I collapsed into my seat on the flight to Denver, coughing and wheezing all the way from Germany to Colorado.

When we landed in Denver, I stumbled with every step. A US customs agent sent for the paramedics when I almost fell in the customs line. As I was rolled away, the medics ran an EKG as well as several other diagnostics. When I told them I was going through to Sacramento to see my heart doctor, they were reluctant to release me.

I was asked to wait in the quiet VIP room, where they had a sofa, television, and some food. I waited there for six hours before they came to determine if I was okay for the flight home.

I was informed I'd be allowed to board the flight, but I must seek immediate medical help when I arrived in Sacramento. With the flight attendants fully informed, I boarded. I probably should not have flown again, but I wanted to be home and not in some 'far away' hospital away from my loved ones.

Several hours after landing, I was on a surgical table undergoing angioplasty.

Based on the dye patterns providing a picture of the blockages in the arteries around the heart, the news was stents would not be an option. We were talking by-pass surgery. Gurumata had been correct, my illness was much worse. I was thankful she'd insisted on my return.

## Heart Surgeries

You know you're in trouble when your doctor takes one look at you, orders you into a wheelchair, and rolls you directly to the Emergency Room.

After I'd been diagnosed with major heart blockages, much like the previous one where I'd received stents, he insisted I be kept in the Intensive Care Unit for at least four days to stabilize me before surgery. It was a good call on his part; my body was beyond exhaustion. And it was advice I followed. My mind floated in and out of focus as I adjusted to the sterile surroundings of ICU, and became reacquainted with a concept called bed rest.

From there I was sent to a hospital specialized in heart operations. I arrived at eight o'clock at night by ambulance and was scheduled for open-heart surgery at six the next morning. Even with the stabilization days in ICU, I was still totally spent.

Carol and her sister came to see me before dawn; both observably worried. Doctors and nurses poked me with needles and attached tubes. Carol hovered, and at one point asked whether I was going to make it.

"It's not my time to go," I assured her. But the truth was, if it was my time, I was ready. I could surrender.

Soon, I was rolled away, and lay in a cold operating room, surrounded by machines and tables covered with strange-looking instruments. As the surgical team prepared, I asked the doctor whether I would be totally unconscious.

His answer, "In some cases, around five percent, patients had reported they were semi-awake; at most sensing something going on around them."

He also warned me that when I was put on the heart-lung machine I would be receiving less anesthesia, and, for some people, it was an issue, but just a small issue.

The operation would be brutal. Surgeons slice the chest down the middle with a tool resembling something designed for shearing large tree branches. Next, the ribs are spread open with a device created for that specific purpose. The heart is then attached to a heart-lung machine, so oxygen and blood continue to circulate through the body. Essentially, the organ we call a heart has then been bypassed by a machine, and made available to be worked on in the same way as a non-working limb. The machine enables the body to work while the heart comes to a dead stop.

The key is the heart must be still so it can be worked on. Surgeons harvest arteries from other parts of the body—arms and legs—and spend a great deal of time reattaching them as bypasses around the blockages. When the procedure is finished, the transfer from the machine to the original heart, with its brand-new routes, takes place. For this to happen, the heart must be jump-started.

No matter how many of these surgeries are successful worldwide, it is extremely serious surgery. And it isn't painless or comfortable. When it is happening to you, all the statistics about safe bypass outcomes are meaningless. They're just numbers.

I drifted off into darkness aware I was under anesthetic in the hospital, but I was in Southern India, too. It was a beautiful day, and I was walking uphill away from a temple. And not just any temple! No! This was *the* temple mentioned in the prediction at my Naadi Palm Reading. I was to walk for several hours until I met a group of rishis.

The rishis, about two dozen men sitting cross-legged on the ground, were waiting for me on a hilltop. I knew all of them. They invited me to join them. As I sat and listened, they told me things, things embedded in my soul. They were just 'reawakening' my access to it. I said little. At the same time, I could feel pushing, pulling, poking going on inside my chest, even though I was also detached from my body, seemingly in some altered state.

I continued in conversation with these holy men for what seemed like weeks. My guru, Gurunath, joined us. He was serious when he told me he was there to make sure I did not give up. He kept telling me, "Do not give up heart!"

There was an extremely powerful female energy present. She was so beautiful, although I could not really see her face. Awash in bright light, her voice was seductive and loving. She kept telling me all I needed to do was to let go; give up fighting and enjoy the bliss. She promised great peace and love awaited me. All I had to do was stop breathing. She promised me NO MORE PAIN. Said I'd done enough and owed no one anything more. Others could carry on. I had completed my duty, and now it was time to give up my heart.

Then I heard my guru's voice repeating over and over, "*Do not give up heart!*" He insisted I stay and fight so THEY could assign me *more pain*; that in the past I had always been rescued from my deepest suffering by Divine Grace and my guru's love, but now I was being asked to experience it as normal humans do so I could inspire others with real physical and emotional afflictions. It was my duty to take on more pain. It was my destiny. I had volunteered for it.

A sea of faces—men, women, and children of all ages—surrounded me. Some familiar, but many were strangers. I had to help them with their spiritual journeys, *and I knew why*. My spiritual heart hurt for all of them.

I looked into the eyes of my guru. "I am offered peace and love and no pain and all you have to counter with is a promise of more and greater pain?"

My guru folded his arms and nodded. "Yes. It is your dharma!"

I would have this same vision, or delusional dream, about my spiritual battle repeatedly over the next twelve days and nights in the hospital.

Now, as I looked around the group of men sitting there, the light around us grew more brilliant. We all faded peacefully into the light.

At that moment, something powerful pulled me back into my physical body on the operating table. My body jerked upwards. My heart began to pump, and my blood began flowing through it. But as I regained consciousness, I could not move or talk. My eyes felt glued shut. I wanted to cough. I wanted to drink some ice-water, but there was a long tube down my throat. I could feel more tubes in my stomach and arms. I remained there, listening to the medical staff talk about me. Machines pumped fluids, beeped, and made metallic noises like those in the lobby of a Las Vegas casino.

I wanted to cry out for help, but I could not. I was totally separated from everyone. Then abruptly, I was pulled back to the hilltop where the rishis were waiting patiently for me.

This back-and-forth process went on and on; part of me struggling to wake up and fight, another part wanting to give up.

When I was finally able to open my eyes, I was no longer in the operating room, and the breathing tube had been removed from my throat. I gasped for water and was given a few pieces of ice. What luxury!

I could barely talk, so I whispered, "I love you" to Carol. I'm not sure whether she heard me, or if I'd even made any real sounds. I cycled between my hospital room and my holy friends on the hilltop. I could not distinguish between dream and reality; both existed in the same space and time.

My wife looked worried, so I tried to smile. It didn't work. I touched her hand and gazed into her eyes to reassure her. My problem was I wasn't sure I wanted to be in the hospital room. I missed my hilltop. I missed my Divine friends. I wanted to return. It saddened me to be lying there in my damaged body. I fought the desire to leave it all. Back and forth. I was willing to give up the heart and go back. Then I'd see all those faces and feel the connection to duty.

## My Hospital Stay and Recovery

Several fitful days and nights in the ICU and I was still being sucked back into my delusional world on the hilltop with my divine friends and my guru. The scene and conversation were always the same. Two offers: escape to paradise and peace, or Gurunath's call to duty complete with more pain.

As I fought the battle over my destiny, my body grew weaker. I had difficulty breathing and less desire to live. The pain was great and I was weak.

When I slept, I'd see events happen in the hospital. When I awoke, all I'd witnessed would occur. It was as if I was about five minutes ahead of everyone else. Talk about a delusional state of being!

I'd lost a lot of blood and was told I'd had to have five blood transfusions. Even though there was a constant delivery of blood dripping into my veins, I continued to grow weaker.

One night, around ten-thirty, fluids were filling my heart cavity and/or lungs. The doctors ordered an emergency MRI. But just as the attendants were about to transfer me to a gurney, the phone rang.

"Hello," I said weakly.

The familiar, strong, loud, and energy-filled voice of Gurunath announced, "This is Gurunath from India. DO NOT GIVE UP HEART! You can skip a few beats now and then, but do not give up heart!"

I was speechless. I had been hearing him say these same words on the hilltop every day and night, over and over. Now he was on the phone, in the physical world, saying them again.

Gurunath told me he had instructed everyone at the ashram—well over one-hundred people—to meditate and pray for me. He reminded me he would continue to send healing energy. He added, "I love you."

"I love you, too," I said.

The attendants transferred me to the gurney and rolled me downstairs for the MRI, and for some other tests.

When I returned to my room, Carol was waiting. I told her I could not bear the thought of disgracing my guru, tarnishing his word, by dying in the hospital. He had assured so many people he was sending me healing energy. "I'll be home in thirty-six hours," I said.

She looked at me as if I was crazy. I'd been fighting for my life for almost two weeks.

The next morning, I asked my attending physician what I had to do for him to feel confident enough to release me from the hospital. He was surprised I asked, but gave me a list. Fairly easy, except it was going to be painful. I planned my actions, but refused to show any pain. Certain vital signs were required to be discharged; a daunting task.

About mid-morning, I asked a nurse to watch me do all the physical things: walk, sit, stand, eat, and use the toilet. Other nurses took my blood pressure, body temperature, blood counts, and heartbeat. I was still ill, exhausted, and in the greatest of pain, but I was not going to let Gurunath down. I was not going to "give up heart" and die.

Less than thirty-six hours later, I packed for home.

## Water and Oil

Just before I was discharged from the hospital, I had perhaps another delusional event, but thankfully a pleasant one. As I was sitting up on my hospital bed, a sphere of protective light surrounded me, then I saw the figure of the ever-youthful Babaji with his long, dark, flowing hair and shiny skin. He had taken off his shirt and was standing in front of my bed pouring oil and water onto my head. He touched my forehead at the spiritual eye location. I was unaware of anyone else around me. This was my own private experience. I was so happy I did not care whether it was real or a dream. There was simply so much love! Truly it was a gift, no matter the source.

Once home, Daya visited me and asked whether I knew our neighbor, David, had gone to the hospital to see me.

"No," I said, puzzled.

She related David's story: He had gone into my room, but stayed only a few moments because a young, long-haired, shirtless Indian man had been pouring water and oil onto the top of my head, while chanting in a strange language, as I simply sat on the edge of my bed. Quite strange, but he'd left out of respect for the private ceremony.

Describing my vision to her, I began to wonder what other parts of my delusional dreams had been real. I couldn't explain how David had witnessed what I'd considered to be some kind of dream state. In the end, all that mattered was I had felt, and still feel, sublime love and joy.

## Another Heart Procedure

A couple of weeks after I came home from the hospital, I began to complain. I wasn't any better. I didn't feel right. Nothing had changed much since the surgery. There was still shortness of breath and chest pains. It was disappointing and a bit scary.

My doctors were reluctant to be too aggressive in investigating the complaint, preferring to wait for me to get better. But when I didn't improve, they decided to do an exploratory angioplasty—perhaps pacifying my complaints—hoping they would find no issues.

I registered at the Cardiac Catheterization Laboratory at six in the morning. At the time, my back and hip were bothering me, so I had pain just walking into the lab. I had additional concerns about having to be flat on a steel table for a couple of hours.

The staff did the best they could do to make me as comfortable as they could, then drugged me, shot some black dye to contrast the arteries, and then cut a hole in my groin so they could place the catheter, with camera, inside me.

They soon discovered one artery graft was not visible. None of the dye had gone into that artery; totally blocked. There were also some early stages of blocking in other areas. Disheartening.

The best thing they could do was to leave all catheters in place—in the open cut—so this opening could be used later. An ambulance was scheduled to take me to a hospital specializing in heart procedures. I was instructed to stay still, not go to the bathroom, nor eat or drink anything until the operation had been performed.

The ambulance arrived in late afternoon. I'd been lying uncomfortably with tubes and equipment hanging out of my groin all day long. I was thirsty. I had back and hip pain.

Twelve hours after the groin incision had been made I was taken into surgery. An Indian doctor greeted me. He impressed me as being a little overweight, with good bedside manners. I began complaining about why I couldn't go longer than two months between heart procedures, and went on about my great vegetarian diet and my healthy lifestyle; no booze, no drugs, no meat, no candy, no…

He stopped me and said something about how Krishna and Arjuna had their famous talk about having to fight a battle against family and friends. The bottom line was, when he got through telling that long story, I understood we must all embrace our karma and perform our duty. Just do it. It was my dharma; what I was supposed to go through and do.

I looked at him and smiled as the nurse asked me if the doctor had answered my question. I told her "absolutely yes." I did understand.

By now, my hip and back were in terrible pain. I was laid out naked on a cold, metal table. Finally, someone thoughtfully tossed a sheet over me, providing a little relief from the cold.

And then it happened. Right smack in the middle of surgery. Suddenly I was looking down from the operating room ceiling. Looking down at my own body below. My physical eyes were open wide. I was not unconscious. At various times, I could watch from the table looking upward, or watch myself from the ceiling, looking down at the table. I did not fully understand how I could leave my still-very-much-awake body, which was certainly not dead.

When the operation ended, the surgeon pulled down his mask and looked at me. I told him what had happened with me looking down from the ceiling.

He wasn't the least surprised or even skeptical; only smiled.

I mentioned he must have Krishna and Shiva with him.

He replied. "Oh yes! All the time!"

It wasn't until almost three in the morning when they finally finished closing my wound. Then to stop the bleeding, they set a twenty-five-pound bag of sand weight on top of the opening at the groin. A metal clamp followed, tightened to the bed frame. The pressure was created by physically tightening a screw. It remained in place for one hour. I was so happy when it was removed, I could go to the bathroom, and have some water to drink.

The next afternoon, I went home in great pain. I could not walk upright. My hip and lower back were at the highest levels of pain I have ever experienced. I could hardly get into the car to be transported home. At home, just climbing my stairs to go to the bedroom was almost impossible; five minutes to cover twelve stairs, in tears.

I remembered the visions and dreams I'd had during my earlier open-heart surgery. I'd been promised much greater and more powerful pain, and I had not been undersold on that promise!

I could not sleep, sit, stand, walk, or get into any bodily position without physical distress. It never let up, even when I was still. I called a couple of my friends and did something I had never done before—complain!

After three full weeks of hell, I finally took a couple of pain pills so I could take the edge off. I'd let the pain grow to a level where I could not use my mind to control it. The whole experience was something new to me, but it gave me greater insight into how others suffer. My empathy grew, as did my love for others.

Pain can and will drive people insane, if they do not have the skills to handle it. The option of drugs, for some, I now understood. For myself, I wanted to avoid the drugs; making them the last resort. But I allowed myself that option, if all else failed.

The doctors had told me I would need a left hip replacement and surgery for my lower back and neck. I chose not to. Once I had made up my mind to deal with it, I was able to focus my attention away from the pain. Though it never completely left, it has become more like soft elevator music in the background of my life; no longer front and center.

## Gurunath and Gianni Save a Bird

In the summer of 2011, I went with my youngest grandson Gianni, to spend an afternoon visiting Gurunath at a devotee's home in the San Francisco Bay Area. When we arrived, Gianni, without delay, engaged in a long conversation with "his friend" Gurunath. He had brought along his own digital camera and began doing a photo-shoot of Gurunath posing and smiling.

After a while, I asked Gianni to share with Gurunath the "bird story," which might be amusing, and possibly inspirational. It turned out to be both.

Gianni began by telling Gurunath about a small bird flying directly into the closed glass patio door at their house, hitting his head hard, and falling to the ground. The little bird lay with his feet up in the air and his head limp to one side. It was a sad sight for him to witness, so he'd asked his family to see about the bird.

As they stood looking at what appeared to be a dead bird, Daya suggested they pray to Gurunath to either help heal the bird or take the bird to heaven.

Then Gianni asked his dad to get a glass of water, and he did. With the glass of water in his hand, Gianni told everyone what was to be done. Then he poured the water on the bird. Within seconds, the result surprised everyone. The bird hopped up and flapped its wings, then took flight as if nothing had happened.

Gianni concluded his storytelling by declaring it was he, Gianni, who'd healed the bird.

Gurunath looked at little Gianni and said, "No, it was I who healed the bird."

Without any doubt in his voice, Gianni replied, "No, it was I who healed the bird!"

The exchange went on for a couple of rounds before Gurunath looked directly at Gianni and said, "Okay, it was *both* of us who healed the bird."

Satisfied with the compromise, Gianni smiled, and the two of them hugged.

## Blood Clots

I continued to have concerns about the latest procedure—two months and I was still out of breath all the time. Walking across a room was a physical burden. Even when I attempted to sleep, I had chest pain and shortness of breath. I went back to see the heart doctor, and he decided to take another look at the arteries and heart.

I was scheduled for the following Monday. Same venue: the cardiac catheterization unit. Same show: angioplasty. Same scene: naked body on cold, metal table. Act one: cut groin, inject dye, and insert tubes and camera. We had all been there, done that before. Not our first rodeo.

I lay there, my back and hip in pain, and endured the examination.

The surgeon performing the procedure said the health issues might be related to blood clots. When the procedure was finished, I was told someone would get back to me.

So, they scheduled me for a chest X-Ray, an MRI, and a CT scan.

A whole week went by and no one had reported any findings. I figured since they had not gotten back to me, I was not in any danger, even though I continued to suffer from all the symptoms.

It was Friday night, almost eleven, when I heard the phone. I'd been sleeping and did not want to get up to answer the call. But when the answering machine came on, I heard the concerned voice of my cardiologist leaving me what he termed a "very important message." I raced to grab the phone before he hung up.

The specialist disclosed the test results, stating he'd found some evidence pointing to blood clots in my lungs. Left untreated, the clots could become lethal, under certain conditions.

Instructing me to head to the hospital's emergency pharmacy, he called in a package for me, including a large case of syringes filled with Lovenox for pickup. I'd need to inject myself in the stomach every twelve hours. Along with this, I'd require Warfarin, aka Coumadin, a strong blood thinner.

I put my jacket over my pajamas, got in my truck and drove six miles to the hospital; not the brightest thing I could have done. I walked into the ER and was sent to the pharmacy to pick up all the drugs and equipment my heart doctor had ordered for me.

When I arrived home with the drugs and filled syringes, I found no instructions on how to inject the product. The pharmacist had said to follow my doctor's orders. Well, there were none, other than inject myself every twelve hours.

I had no *idea* how to give myself a shot.

Once again, I called Karen, in the San Francisco Bay Area. By this time, it was very late; she was either working a nightshift, had one in the morning, or both. She said she would be there as soon as she could. She drove 100 miles in the early hours of the morning to show me how to do this. At about two in the morning, Angel Karen knocked on my door. I was ever so grateful.

She instructed me on the fine art of stabbing oneself in the belly with a needle. With some hesitation, and a little blood, I managed to do this for myself. She then said good-bye and drove off into the dark, misty fog hanging around through the early morning hours. Overwhelmed by her love and our bond of friendship, I wiped a teary eye.

The injections became part of a routine, along with the new blood thinner and two others I'd been taking for my heart. In total, I was taking four blood-thinning medicines. I went to the lab several times each week to monitor blood levels—thick or thin. They didn't want it to coagulate too quickly. A too high reading would indicate danger of bleeding in terms of not being able to stop the flow; too low indicated there was danger of clotting. It was a balancing act. Several times a week the doses were adjusted. The kinds of food I ate affected these levels, too, so I attempted to maintain the same diet to assist in keeping my system even.

The second week on the drugs, I bit the inside of my cheek—normally not a big deal, just a little nick inside my mouth. It started to bleed in the early morning hours, before I was even out of bed. Blood flowed all over the place. I was spitting blood all morning and afternoon. Nothing would stop the hemorrhaging. After twelve hours, I was directed to Emergency to have the bite treated.

While I lay on the gurney in the ER with gauze stuffed inside my mouth, Rudra, Gurunath's youngest son, called me on my cellphone. I mumbled I could not talk because I was in the ER being treated. Moments after the call, I was miraculously better.

Seven days later, I ended up in the ER again. This time, I could not breathe. I wasn't getting enough oxygen. Supposedly, blood clots were moving or blocking something in my lungs. After six hours of being given oxygen, I was much better.

The following week, a spiritual retreat took place with Gurunath in Joshua Tree, California. I had been looking forward to being with him and was determined to go, despite my medical issues. I'd talked to Chris and Dan Murphy, two brothers from Florida who were planning to attend. I asked if they could fly to Sacramento instead of Southern California, so they could drive me to the retreat. It was out of there way by over eight hours, but they were glad to help me get there. I did not trust myself to go so far alone as messed up as I was.

The retreat property was in a magnificent desert location, just a short drive from Joshua Tree National Park. It was also in close proximity to The Self-Realization Fellowship's Ox Bow Retreat Center in 29 Palms.

Checking in, we were delighted to be given a bungalow sharing a wall with Gurunath and his wife. We were as close to the energy source as it gets!

The next night, Gurunath and his wife invited me to their room for dinner. He was curious how I could be there just days after being in the ER. While I was talking and eating my food, my nose began to bleed profusely. I grabbed about a dozen dinner napkins and held them on my nose. The blood soaked right through and continued to pour out of me. Once again, I envisioned a trip to the local ER. I'd been having major issues with bleeding for two weeks already, with blood coming from various places in my body, but this was the worst I'd had so far.

I was embarrassed about how I'd ruined their meal. The blood continued to pour. But in a matter of seconds, Gurunath shoved his pointed finger directly at my nose, just a couple of inches from touching it, and shouted, "STOP!"

Everyone in the kitchen heard him…and felt the energy. But for me, only love and energy vibrated from him. I put the bloody napkins down on my plate, knowing it would stop. It had no other choice.

I think all of us agreed, consciously and subconsciously, there was no way another drop of blood was going to defy the order. And not another droplet dared to show.

Gurunath made no big deal out of it. He never spoke another word—took no credit—just went back to eating his food. I could not help but smile at the hemorrhage following his order, and be awestruck by his humility and love.

Near the end of the retreat, we had the opportunity to go swimming with Gurunath in the large pool. I then discovered Gurunath transmits energy while in the water. It's like swimming with electrical eels. One can detect a slight electrical current emanating from him. This man was so much more than he, himself, presented.

Before I left, I decided to call a friend in the Bay Area whose sister had been diagnosed with blood clots in her lungs the same week as me. Seeing as I was managing the same issues and believed they would be resolved, I was not overly concerned.

When my friend answered, she proceeded to inform me she'd just arrived home from her sister's funeral. I was speechless. A young woman, diagnosed with blood clots in her lungs, buried ten days later. She'd bled to death internally due to all the blood thinners she'd been taking. I was in emotional shock; perhaps taking my blood clot issue far too casually. I thanked God (and my Guru) for taking such good care of me.

On the way home, escorted by Chris and Dan Murphy (twin brothers) who'd come to my aid and become my chauffeurs, several entertaining, interesting things happened unexpectedly.

At one point, we drove past fields of cotton with white balls hanging on the branches. A song about cotton that was a big hit in the early 1970s, by Credence Clearwater Revival "Cotton Fields," came to mind. I sang a few bars.

They laughed at me, and teased, thinking I had made up the entire song; thought I was spinning them a tall tale. Then I reached over and turned on the radio. And lo and behold, the song was playing. The music and words came rolling out. When I joined in with the radio, we all burst out laughing. The timing could not have been better. What were the odds?

When we arrived back at my house, the guys told me they needed to leave the following morning for their flight. I drove them to the airport, but about four hours after I dropped them off, I received a phone call from them. They were on their way to Mount Shasta. A computer error had caused a glitch; their flight was not for two more days. They had decided this was a gift; a way to take advantage of the situation and see Mount Shasta. They'd become totally hyped about the many spiritual and supernatural stories about this sacred mountain. In fact, Gurunath had talked about great sages and saints visiting this holy mountain. Now they had the opportunity.

On their way back to the Sacramento Airport, they called me and filled me in on all the details of their adventure.

What made their journey even more special was an incident that occurred a couple of hours from Mount Shasta, in a wayside rest stop off Highway 5. They had pulled off to rest and met up with a woman who'd been at the spiritual retreat with us. She'd stopped at the rest area when an inner urge compelled her to wait, to take her time.

They embraced, excited to see each other. When she had left the retreat, she had taken fruit and flowers left over from the celebration. Once she met up with the guys, she gave the fruit and flowers to them to take as a spiritual offering for their sacred journey. The timing was perfect.

The guys made it up the mountain, looking for the source of the Sacramento River starting at the base of Mount Shasta. They bathed in its cold, sacred waters and spent several hours in meditation. I was happy for them. They had been truly guided and blessed on their journey.

## Head Surgeries – Healing in Hawaii

I had been promised more pain, most likely through health issues, in my delusional dream/vision, but I certainly did not expect the top of my head to begin bleeding.

I'd had a large cyst on the top of my head since birth, a noticeable bump I was used to, but it began to bleed, form discolored scabs, then bleed again.

I went to see my dermatologist, who decided to take quick action. She had me sit in the exam chair, then numbed me up. The next thing I heard was an electrical buzz over the top of my head. Holy smokes! She promised not to go too deep; affirmed she would just "saw off a thin slice of it."

*Saw it off?*

And she did just that, then sent the entire piece to the hospital lab.

A few weeks later, she got the results. It was a dangerous kind of cancer embedded in my skull. Surgery was scheduled right then to remove it.

In a 'small world' kind of way, one of the two women doctors who worked on me had been a classmate of Danica McKellar at UCLA—Danica, the daughter of one of my best friends, whose wedding I had attended. I found this out in conversation as they went about burning and cutting my head.

They went deep, as promised. It took a lot of stitches to close the wound. The good news was it gave me a macho-looking scar, but also a slight dip in my skull. I could not resist taking a photo of it from my computer to show a few friends. I mean, what is the point in having your head cut open and going through horrific pain without some evidence? Carol, of course, thought I was a little nuts. It made her uneasy to look at my head.

When the drugs wore off, and I was back at home, the pain was intense. I embraced it all and let go; no painkillers. I figured the worst-case scenario was a day or two of pain. I was wrong. It lasted over a week, but I held firm and survived.

Following the head surgery, I had a dream. Not a vision or anything supernatural, but it motivated me nonetheless. I dreamt Gurunath had come to me and told me to go back to Hawaii. He said, if I spent some time there, I'd feel better.

So even though it was just a dream, no doubt a product of my own imagination, I trusted Gurunath's words.

I acted and booked a three-and-a-half-week round trip to Hawaii online the next morning. I had already promised my good friend, Frank, to one day visit and help him work through some personal issues he was facing. He needed me and I could take care of my own healing in the same trip. Yet there was something more serious with Frank; something of urgency.

I arrived in Honolulu and connected with Frank. Though I'd changed locations, and was in tropical surroundings, the pain had also traveled with me. My hip, back, neck, shoulder—my whole body hurt. I could not walk more than a block from his apartment without having to stop and rest; pain and shortness of breath.

My friend asked me how I'd be able to see any of Hawaii's sights in my condition. His concerns shifted quickly to whether I was even going to survive. But I had faith.

He decided to take me to a Hawaiian culture store whose artisans made, then sold, native items. The store also sold books from local authors. When we arrived, an old Hawaiian man—actually, a few years younger than me—was just outside the store. There was an instantaneous connection. An old warrior, his name was Bert MacDonald. He had one of those massage chairs, like at airports and malls, and off to the side he had a cup for donations. He had the ability to channel the same old, Hawaiian healing energy I'd personally experienced when I'd lived in the islands in 1964.

I sat in his chair and told him my body was falling apart and, if he could do anything for me, I was open. We talked as he set up; turned out he was a fellow Vietnam War Veteran.

He became quiet when he started to work on me and did something I'd only seen fifty years before, when I began learning about the Kahuna religion from one of the great Kahunas, 'Daddy' David Kaonhiokala Bray.

An interesting sidebar: I had found a book about him in the store sitting on a shelf, right there in front of me. I'd picked it up not realizing it was about him until I'd paged through the book. What a pleasant surprise! I'd not seen him before he died, which was when I was in Vietnam.

Bert was practicing old school healing, but I do not think he was even aware of it. I think he'd stumbled onto this method while learning other massage styles. The important thing is not so much about what one does, but one's ability to channel energy. Bert was for real. He had his own style, but it was in harmony with the old Kahuna ways. Pure energy ran up and down my spine.

He'd placed one hand on top of my head and the other at the bottom of my spine. I heard his breathing change to coordinate with the energy he visualized moving up and down my spine; twenty minutes of massaging my back and shoulders.

I mentioned the energy part to him when he was done. He nodded in confirmation. I pulled out a couple of twenty dollar bills for his cup, but he stopped me quickly. Taking only one, he said, "That is all I need."

I was amazed at the generosity from my fellow warrior. I understood I was dealing with a real healer and not someone trying to make a few bucks.

Miraculously, I was pain free. Just like that. So, Frank and I decided on a hike in the mountainous jungles above Honolulu. We started off on a steep, muddy trail leading us though lush forests. All around us were nature spirits! The place was loaded with them! The energy was high. I was immersed in love. I tried to jointly experience this with Frank, but he felt and saw nothing.

So, we walked along on the muddy trail together; in the same place, but having totally different experiences.

He complained about the mud and wanted to go back to his car. We had hiked about three miles round trip by the time we got back and cleaned off our shoes. I had to smile. The day before I could not walk half a block without stopping in pain and being out of breath. Now I had just taken a hike and was charged with energy.

Over the next few days, I took several long hikes from Honolulu to Diamond Head Crater, and up to the top of it. I hiked to a waterfall and across all kinds of jungles and beaches—eight miles a day and enjoyed every minute of it.

Frank had been studying to become a Buddhist Monk in California, and had been working successfully toward his goal, until he'd returned to the islands, about six months previous, to help his aging parents cope with their lives.

Frank had traveled to Hawaii to fill the role of the good son. Frank's Japanese-Hawaiian father had married Frank's Japanese mother after WWII, when Frank's dad was stationed in Japan with the State Department, working on rebuilding the country, and for the war crimes trials.

Frank's family had lived in Japan for more than thirty years. It was only when he attended college in Washington he'd traveled to the USA. This background made Frank totally anti-war and against warriors. It was a serious topic of discussion between us. He was beyond righteous about his stance: no one spiritual could be a warrior of any kind. He went further to say his temple and his teaching did not glorify war in any way.

These conversations would lead into my storytelling—tales of sages, saints, and men of peace who were great warriors. In passing, I mentioned I considered myself a spiritually-based person, and yet I was not just a veteran, but also the founder and former president of The Military Writers Society of America. From time-to-time, I would endorse books, and write blurbs and forewords for military fiction and nonfiction.

He was not impressed, expressing he believed I was enhancing a war-based organization. He decided to take me to his Buddhist Temple to show this "old warrior" what peace is all about.

When we arrived, we went into the gift shop before heading inside. The shop held all kinds of things one would normally expect to find at a temple gift shop: books about religion and meditation, prayer flags, incense, small statues of Buddha.

And right there, in the dead center of the store, was the largest display of all: an organized exhibition showcasing books. And not just any books, but a series of books by an Admiral friend of mine.

The books were a series about WWII in the Pacific. I picked up one of the out-of-place books and showed him one. He looked at it, noticing the back-cover blurb written by me. I smiled. Then I pointed to the wall by the door where they displayed a framed book award from The Military Writers Society of America, signed by me.

He stood staring at the award, holding the book and shaking his head. It left him speechless. It was *not* something he'd expected to find in his temple.

I returned to Bert several more times for a recharge. On my last day, I went to see him and he gifted me a send-off massage; would not take any money. He told me it was from one warrior to another, stating it was not about money, it was about healing. We embraced and said good-bye. I later sent him a copy of my first book *A Spiritual Warrior's Journey*. I followed up with emails, and since, our friendship has grown.

Author's note: I recommended Bert to my friend, Linda. She flew to the islands just to experience his healing hands. He worked on her damaged back and shoulder. She went back home to Arizona feeling much better.

My friend, Frank, died unexpectedly less than a year after I'd visited him. When I went there, I sensed his need for spiritual change and his limited time. He did not exhibit any signs of danger from disease or illness, but I picked up something coming his way. A memorial service was held in Sacramento, at his old Buddhist Temple, where his family paid their respects. I was honored to provide a fitting eulogy, and bid him Aloha from this world.

## The East Coast with Gurunath – 2012

How often, in any lifetime, does one get the opportunity to spend close and personal time with someone who reflects the light and love of God? When I received the invitation to spend over three weeks with Gurunath, in the summer of 2012, on the east coast of the USA, I decided I'd be there, even if I was dying.

Though I was not feeling well, and considered seeing my doctors before I left California, I held off, fearing they might not allow me to travel. I booked my flight to the east coast, and made medical appointments for after I returned. I was determined to see my guru. I believed I would be okay as long as I was with him.

I landed in Philadelphia and was driven to the suburbs, where my wonderful journey with Gurunath began. It was like I had never been away any time at all. I was made to feel totally welcome. I was invited to eat with him and spend lots of time doing nothing; one of the best ways to spend time. We toured parts of Pennsylvania, New Jersey, New York City, and even had four days up in Niagara Falls; took a sailboat trip around Manhattan Island at sunset, and attended a short spiritual retreat in the Pocono Mountains of Pennsylvania.

Among my fondest memories was the honor of introducing him in New York City. It was a gathering of around 650 people at a Manhattan church. A massive crowd, he held their souls in his hand—total silence, each attendee locked in full attention and focused on every word he spoke, and was even more focused when he was silent.

Every individual was moved by his talk, which was a series of answers to questions from the audience. In India, this type of gathering is called a satsang. Gurunath amazed people as he took basic questions and delivered unexpected, divine wisdom. As always, his words came from another world.

I enjoyed those days and will always treasure them. Personal in nature, the challenge for a storyteller is balance: sharing many stories and overviewing the experience. That east coast journey was one where a summary works, and the deeply personal is held in a respectful inner-chamber.

When I returned home, I became terribly ill. I'd pushed my body on the east coast. No one truly understood the depth of my pain. My diabetes and heart issues were primary concerns, but not the only issues I faced the first two weeks.

Right off the bat, I had an appointment with my dermatologist to remove about a dozen more skin cancers, including several on my nose previously repaired with plastic surgery. Fortunately, the cancer could be removed with liquid nitrogen. I had treatments all over my body, not just the face.

A few days later I had to have another colonoscopy to remove several growths inside my colon. No big deal, except for having to prepare for the procedure. One drinks about a gallon of nasty tasting liquid to cleanse the colon before scoping. Thank God, all the growths tested negative for cancer.

Then I had to see my heart doctor, followed by an appointment with my regular doctor for diabetes issues. My glucose numbers had been running super-high while I was back east with Gurunath. When I went to see the heart doctor, she took one look at me and ordered me delivered, by ambulance, to the ER. She would not allow me to leave and drive myself.

The ER personnel, by that time, were well-acquainted with me. Medical staff poked me with lots of needles and ran all kinds of tests. I was kept there for twelve hours, then admitted into the hospital for a short stay, after which I was finally stabilized and released for home.

The next week, I had surgery on my left shoulder. Basically, specialists cut and cleaned my torn rotator cuff, chiseled away at several impingements—degeneration or compressions caused by friction from my arthritis—then they "shaved" away half an inch of bone.

My wife was advised to stock-up on pain medication as I would need them once the drugs administered at the hospital wore off. But as I'd promised myself, I coped with the pain. I had a clear understanding: only my body has pain, and that is not who I am.

*Note: The third colonoscopy I had was at the VA in 2014. They removed seven more growths, two of which were pre-cancerous. Then I had two more colonoscopies(2016 & 2017) and all of them found growths to be removed. The good news: I was staying ahead of this issue.*

## Spiritual Hug

Taken from an email I sent out on Sunday, November 3, 2013:

*To: Robert; cc: Cabot & Dan*

*Good talking to you again on the phone yesterday, Robert. I need to call you from time to time to see if I am crazy, or just insane. I decided I am only a little nutty on the inside. But let me tell you about what happened this week, then you might wish to declare me delusional, or whatever.*

*I had a strange experience several nights ago, while lying in bed trying to sleep. It was a little after four in the morning. I was feeling quite unloved. Yes, even I can feel this way sometimes. I was missing my lack of private time and physical connections with Gurunath. I've not seen him much this past year. Then something lifted my head and shoulders off my pillow into an almost sitting position, and I was hugged —yes, actually physically hugged! Two real arms wrapped around me gently but firmly, in a loving embrace. I languished in peace and love, like a breeze of divine bliss had traveled into my heart. This lasted an unknown amount of time. Time had kind of escaped my attention, but I found myself smiling and happy. I relaxed and rested there the rest of those early morning hours KNOWING I was loved!*

*I am amazed at the power of love our Master has for his disciples.*
*Bill*

I sent the above email out half expecting to get a little kidding and a few laughs. But when Dan, in India, received a copy of the email, he printed it and took it with him to the ashram to see Gurunath. Apparently, Dan read my email or paraphrased what I had sent to Gurunath as he was with a small group of devotees.

When the information was given to Gurunath, some of the group thought he might discount the information or even laugh; perhaps say something to the effect of "poor crazy and delusional Bill." But he didn't, of course. That is not Gurunath. What he did do was more confirmation for me, when Dan reported back to me, than I could have ever asked for.

Gurunath looked at the group and said, "Yes, this *did* happen. It was around four in the morning, his time, and I was there with him." He went on to lecture about how he could, and does, appear to "any truly sincere devotee who has the same kind of love, faith, and loyalty Bill has for me."

According to Dan, the group response was one of silence, and an added level of love for such a master who could and would appear to his faithful followers when they needed him.

When I learned about his response, I, too, was silent and in even greater awe of my guru. He really had been there with me. I did not need such personal confirmation, but others did. That was why he made it public.

Usually, Gurunath does not talk about the spiritual experiences of others, nor does he encourage them from anyone. Yet, I am his one exception. He has asked, even ordered me, to keep telling my stories publicly.

## Mount Shasta

It is said Mount Shasta is one of the seven sacred mountains of the world. It's listed on various 'best' lists and was recognized by Gurunath as a hallowed place. Mount Shasta is now a gathering place for many New Age groups looking for a connection to its energy. Known to be a place where highly evolved souls congregated for many years, Babaji himself is said to appear there. Many stories in numerous books recount the mystical and spiritual events that people have witnessed over the last century-and-a-half there.

My buddy, Dave Nye, and I decided to go there in 2014 to celebrate Gurunath's May 10th birthday, but also to evaluate it for Gurunath's planned, late-summer retreat; a first time for that location. We left at the last moment, making no accommodation plans and having no idea how long we'd be gone.

When we drove into the small town of McCloud, at the foot of Mount Shasta, we were gifted with a spectacular sight: the mountain was snow covered, a glittering spectacle. We parked outside the first hotel we saw on the main street, but found the door locked; no one there. Seeking assistance, we saw a man standing by his pickup, near the front of the hotel.

I was drawn to him, and so walked right up and inquired about the hotel.

He smiled. He'd already figured out we were connected to the upcoming summer yoga retreat, and that Gurunath was our guru. Though he said he was not part of the organization, had never met Gurunath, or studied any of his meditation techniques, he said he'd been distributing flyers around town in support of the retreat; that he was very knowledgeable about Kriya yoga itself.

He then took it upon himself to help us out; got the phone number for the woman who ran the hotel and called her, explaining we were looking to rent a room for a night. It turned out she was at the local baseball field, watching a youth game. She drove over and got us settled in. We learned she had bought the old hotel after moving to McCloud from Elk Grove. Small world, I live in Elk Grove.

Our new friend became our personal escort and guide around the town later that afternoon. When we got back, I invited him to our room and we all sat around talking about spiritual matters. I was compelled to teach him the meditation techniques, with the possibility he could be initiated by Gurunath at the summer retreat. Dave left the room and let me spend the next hour going over the process.

Early the next morning, Dave and I followed through with our plan to celebrate Gurunath's birthday on the mountain. We wanted to take a short hike up the trailhead and find a spot to meditate and watch the sun rise. At 8,500 feet on the mountain, deep in snow, it was freezing. We were totally unprepared for the wind chill at that altitude. Although it was Gurunath's birthday, and we so wanted to pay homage, we ended retreating to the parking lot and meditated in the car. Not quite what we'd envisioned.

Our next trip back to Shasta was for the Yoga Retreat at the end of the summer. All the snow was gone. Strange, none of the locals could remember a year in their lifetimes without some snow on the mountain. The town of McCloud became like an ashram when a couple of hundred people arrived for the retreat with Gurunath. There were no other visitors, and the locals not working became invisible. It was an amazing experience for all of us.

At the beginning of the retreat, Dave and I went off for a short drive and then a hike early in the morning. There were majestic waterfalls, clear streams, and tall trees. We were surrounded by the grandeur of nature for as far as we could see; life-giving trees breathing around us. We were enjoying our drive back to McCloud when we saw a black bear walking down the middle of the road. I had never seen a local bear in all my years of traveling in Northern California. Excited, I grabbed my iPhone, fully charged from the night before, and rolled down the window, ready to shoot video of the bear. I asked Dave to get as close as possible. As we pulled close, the bear cleared off the road and lumbered into the woods. I figured I'd hop out of the car and pursue, video running; not the safest or sanest idea I'd ever had, but I was determined. I opened the door, then stopped myself when I saw my iPhone battery level flashing a warning; that it was about to shut off. The screen went dark; my phone and camera were totally without power. It had gone from eighty percent to nothing in less than one minute.

I had to laugh. If I had chased the bear down I might have been in huge danger. Why my phone powered out was inexplicable, but it had stopped me from doing something extremely stupid.

Later that weekend, I found I had become a beacon for those needing to deal with personal and family issues. About thirty-five people sought me out for individual counseling. Part of this may have been due to the fact that at the retreat Gurunath had introduced me as his 'people person' so others could come to me for help. This opened the floodgates! No complaints. I finally felt like I was serving Gurunath again.

On the Saturday night of the retreat, at the ski lodge on the mountainside, Gurunath gave a wonderful dissertation about life, yoga, and love. I cannot recall any of his words, but when I looked at him—and others reported this too—he kept disappearing from our view.

I wondered at the time if he was actually disappearing or if we were all somehow hallucinating. After the retreat was well over, a time-lapse photo was posted on Facebook showing the chair where Gurunath was sitting. You could see his clothing, but not his hands, feet, or head. It was a most amazing and untouched photo that left one wondering what was captured by the camera.

Over the retreat weekend, a woman named Melanie, one of the key organizers of the event, lost her sweet little dog. The dog had been a delight, greeting people, and giving lots of love, and enjoying the attention. When the group learned, her dog was missing, everyone volunteered to search. Unfortunately, the dog was found dead. Somehow, the dog had made its way to the highway and been hit by a vehicle. She was devastated.

When I heard about the situation, I headed straight over to provide spiritual comfort. I spent about an hour with her, mostly listening, allowing her to find meaning to all that had happened. Later, when the retreat resumed in the afternoon, she asked me to speak to the group. She wanted me to talk about the death of her dog. This opportunity allowed me to bridge the meaning of the dog's life and death, and the spiritual lessons for all of us. I believe she was appreciative of the words flowing from me. Again, those words came from beyond my heart, and I am unsure of what I actually said.

The retreat ended early Sunday evening. Dave and I had planned on staying an additional night in town. After most of the attendees left, a few of us went to the city of Shasta for dinner, including Melanie. While we were all talking, I found out one of the older ladies who'd attended the retreat had been taken to the hospital emergency room, right there in Shasta. I suggested we visit and give her some support. We were so close, only five blocks away.

We left the restaurant and went directly to the ER, but they would only allow me to go and see her since I was a minister. Everyone else was asked to wait in the lobby. But before I went in, while I was with Melanie in lobby, I noticed she picked up a magazine from one of the tables. She flipped open the randomly chosen magazine to no particular page and her expression changed to one of complete peace and love. There on the page was a photo of a woman walking away from the camera with a dog in her arms. The dog's pose was such that it was looking at the camera. And it was not just any breed of dog, but exactly like her beloved pooch. I pointed out how happy the dog was, even though the photo showed someone taking the dog away from the foreground. That pup was smiling!

Melanie saw the photo as a symbolic way to say goodbye. It brought her great peace. A message from the universe. There must have been more than thirty magazines scattered around the waiting room, yet she happened to pick *that* one and turned to *that* page with a comforting image of a dog exactly like hers. I gave her a big hug, knowing she would be okay.

Next, I went to visit the woman taken ill with breathing problems. When I saw her, she was hooked up to machines monitoring her vital signs. She had needles in her arms and was wearing an oxygen mask. It was said she was not doing well, and it might be several more days before she could leave the hospital. Her husband was at the end of the bed. He looked concerned, scared. I walked to the head of the bed and spoke softly as I stroked her hair and held her hand. I wanted to comfort and relax her.

I watched the monitor with its crazy-high numbers for blood pressure and pulse. But the longer I held her hand, the lower the numbers went. Her breathing became less labored. I decided to tell her about Gurunath and how he'd helped me with all my medical issues over the years. I could feel Gurunath's love flowing into the room, making it feel lighter, filled with more love and peace. Yet, it was not my doing.

I spent about half an hour with her, staying until it was safe to leave. I gave her husband my cellphone number, in case they needed anything or wanted some support.

I returned to the waiting room and informed the group how she'd improved. We later learned, a few hours after we'd left, she was stable enough to go home.

The next morning, on the way out of McCloud, a massive owl swooped down from the skies and led our car out of the Mount Shasta area. It stayed low enough overhead for us to see.

It pleased me to know the woman in the ER was going to be okay and Melanie was at peace. The best feeling of all was that I got to spend cherished time with Gurunath. It was, all in all, a perfect retreat!

*Author's note: I toyed with NOT including this story in the book. Then my fingers began to dance on the keyboard and the story wrote itself. Still, I did question myself as to whether it should be included; if I was supposed to or not. Then, at the very moment when I was typing about Melanie and the dog in the magazine photo, my doorbell rang. I went to the door and received a small parcel delivered to my home. I picked it up and saw it was from the newly married Melanie, and her husband George. They had sent me a gift in appreciation for helping her with handling the grief over losing her dog. The package was filled with an assortment of wonderful, sacred items for my personal altar, and some books for my bookshelf. There was even an owl feather inside the box! It was perfect! When I called, and told her what had happened, I mentioned I'd tried to keep her name and life private, but she said to go ahead and tell others about all what happened.*

*It meant a lot to me, both the gift and her permission. I wished them well on their upcoming trip to India.*

## The Hunter and the Deer

Due to ongoing health issues, I was unable to return to India in 2015. Yet the need was great to reconnect with my guru in spirit, to find a place where I could participate in the Indian celebration of Maha Shivaratri. Even though Gurunath was at his own ashram 13,000 miles away, I wanted to make a symbolic gesture to be closer to him for the annual Hindu festival celebrating the day Shiva was married to the goddess Parvati.

My fellow devotee, Dave Nye, and I went to an ashram in the hills above Napa Valley where there is a wonderful Shiva Temple, which hosts an all-night celebration just like the ones in India.

We arrived early, while it was daylight to beat the crowds, and have some personal time in the temple and at the outdoor shrine to Lord Shiva, located in the woods.

We walked to the area of worship, paid our respects, and gave our hearts to Lord Shiva. Dave chanted a new chant he'd learned from Gurunath at the 2014 Mount Shasta Retreat. It was so peacefully quiet. All was holy. When we finished our personal devotionals, we proceeded back to the temple so we could participate in the beginning of the service.

Walking along the path, we could feel eyes on us. About ten meters away, a striking young buck was staring at us with his Bambi eyes. He watched us carefully, gracing us with his presence for several minutes. Then he was nudged away by a sibling—female energy, maybe his sister—who took his place, also watching us intently.

Moments or minutes later—the experience was so enchanting—a larger deer, perhaps the mother, replaced the youthful doe. She faced us, unmoving. Several minutes ticked by. Absolute silence and total wonder. Then another interruption occurred. This time a large buck came into view. As he moved into our sightline, the younger deer and larger female walked to the other side of the trees, joining the male.

None of them acted frightened. Dave and I were almost hypnotized by the large male's eyes glistening in the setting sunlight. We assumed, at the time, this was the father to a family of deer. As the large deer's eyes locked on us, we wondered if he was ever going to move.

Realization kicked in. The ceremony was only minutes away, so we reluctantly left the male deer.

When we arrived at the temple, the chanting had already begun. We quietly found our seats and settled in. When the chanting ended, the guru told a story straight from the Shiva Purana about a hunter and a family of deer. I had honestly never heard the story before. Yet, from the reactions of others, the story was most familiar to Indians.

I sat there next to Dave, who nudged me when the story sounded much like what had happened to us. The only difference was we were not there to hunt, only to discover the love of Lord Shiva's heart and to connect with Gurunath.

The actual story deals with a hungry hunter who has gone without food all day. By nightfall, he takes refuge on a branch of a Bilva tree. Beneath this tree just happens to be a shivalingam—a symbol of Lord Shiva's absolute form.

Every time the hunter moved around in the tree, his water jug would leak drops onto the shivaligam below and disturb the branch enough to shed several leaves onto the symbol. Unintentionally, he was worshiping Shiva in the scripturally correct manner by offering Bilva leaves and water all night long.

Later that evening, the hunter encountered a young buck wandering under the tree, who pled for his life when the hunter took aim with his arrow, saying he needed to go find his sister. He promised to return at sunrise and sacrifice himself for the hunter's family's needs. Trusting his word, the hunter allowed the young buck to go.

Then the sister comes along and the same scene unfolds, except she said she was looking for her brother. She said she would return as a willing sacrifice, if he let her go. Then the doe arrived, stating she was looking for her children. The hunter listened to her plea and let her go, based on her promise to willingly return.

Finally, the stag arrived and told the hunter not to shoot his arrows as he was looking for his family; pled for the hunter to let him go, and promised to bring his entire family in the morning if he would only let him go and find them. By this time, the hunter had little desire to kill any animal. As the night progressed, the hunter had grown more compassionate; his heart had become purified by his accidental worship, and by Shiva's grace.

When the deer family returned, he could not take their lives. The hunter asked the deer for forgiveness for having wanted to kill them. As soon as these words came from the hunter's mouth, Lord Shiva appeared out of the Lingam in a blaze of bright light. The hunter fell at Shiva's feet in devotion, who in turn granted him liberation to live in awareness of being ONE with HIM. Shiva said, "Because of your actions, from this time forward, the benefits of worship performed on this night will be multiplied a thousand-fold."

Dave and I listened to this story, jaws dropping. Our deer sighting was no accident. We had been blessed. We'd made a mystical and spiritual connection with our own guru in India.

A week later, someone sent me a photo of a new painting Gurunath had commissioned for one of the ashram walls. It depicted the story of the deer with an image of Gurunath sitting under the tree. When I saw it, a wave of warm love consumed me. Dave and I *had* been blessed by this connection. Neither one of us had ever heard the story about the ashram painting, nor of Gurunath telling this story at the ashram.

## The Prodigal Son

I thought this book was complete, with more than enough stories, and in fact, I had deleted many to keep the length comfortable for the reader. I was in the process of fine-tuning the content when I received a phone call from my good friend, Robert.

I'd entrusted him to have a look at a rough draft of the manuscript. His views and opinions on the content were important, and I wanted feedback on how others would receive the stories.

While talking to him, he'd causally mentioned something about his son, Isaac. I'd known Robert for seven years and this was the first time he'd mentioned having a son. They'd had a misunderstanding and not spoken to each other for at least a decade; about the same year I began writing this book.

A previous dream/vision flashed into my mind. In an instant of KNOWING, I strongly urged him to make immediate contact with his son. Not question why, simply not to delay. 'Instinct' told me his son would be open to and ready to hear from him now. *Now* was the time to begin a dialogue. His son was waiting. This would be a healing for both of them.

Robert, acting without question, typed a Facebook message to his son while he remained on the phone with me, and sent it off before we hung up. It was the right thing to do. More importantly, it had to be done *right then*. I told Robert to trust me and not ask why.

When I heard from Robert again, he went on to tell me the following:

At the time, I'd demanded Robert contact his son, Isaac was in Costa Rica with a shaman taking *Ibogaine* to cure his marijuana addiction. At the beginning of the ritual, the shaman had asked everyone to say something personal about their lives before ingesting it.

Isaac stated he hadn't spoken to his father for ten years. After which, the shaman abruptly said it was because Isaac had been using drugs; that his father, Robert, did not approve; that even though his father was trying to help him, Isaac had been disrespectful.

Isaac did not like what the shaman had said, but out of respect for him proceeded with the ritual, then told the shaman he was going back to his room to message his father on Facebook. As Isaac entered his room and went online, to his amazement, he found his father's message to him.

Isaac was so stunned by the synchronicity of this event he ran back to the shaman announcing that when he went *to* message his father, he'd found a message *from* his father waiting for him instead.

The shaman simply replied saying Isaac had opened the door and the Universe responded. "Life is simple, you make it complicated."

Isaac and his dad reunited as if the estrangement never happened. They had both been ordered to contact each other. More importantly, they had both listened to the "other voice." In my case I was just a messenger, and the voice was Gurunath's and the shaman whispering visions into my mind's eye.

For Robert, it was my commanding voice telling him to act without hesitation and to trust me, and the voice Isaac had followed was the shaman's, who'd ordered him to reach out and contact his father. In the end, I *know* all the voices were ONE voice.

Robert informed me his son was going with him the next Sunday to learn Kriya Yoga meditation techniques from one of the teachers of HYS in Los Angeles. Not only were father and son getting back together, but they would become one with the same guru.

I listened to the full story of how all the pieces of this mystical puzzle had come together, knowing it was all part of the Universe's Divine Plan. It seemed only fitting to make this my last story, ending my ten-year voyage across the inner cosmos and the physical world through my written words.

The Prodigal Son was finally home.

## *Epilogue*

# LAST WORDS AND THOUGHTS

I finished this book well over 3 years ago and yet, I have waited until the time felt right to publish it. I was struggling with my own inner concerns about how people would react to my book. I knew that once I went public with this book there was no going back. No putting the metaphysical toothpaste back in the tube. Opinions and emotions would open up from all sides of the religious and spiritual spectrum. I expected to be criticized, analyzed and judged by even the most devoted followers of Gurunath and certainly by those who saw him as something much less then divine. There is some personal risk in sharing these personal stories but I knew that this was what I was destined to write. My hope is that those seekers who needed to read this will find some inspiration for their own personal spiritual journey.

I personally placed a printed copy of this book's manuscript into the loving hands of Gurunath to read, approve and to bless. He instructed me to give copies to his youngest son Rudra and to Runbir Singh, who is not only a well published author, but also one of his organizations most faithful long time devotees. Their task was to read it through thoroughly and make sure that it was an honest and accurate telling on my relationship with Gurunath and what he stands for.

They had the power to delete and change anything I had written in this book. This book and that original manuscript are virtually unchanged except for minor editing.

What I personally experienced and understood was totally from my own point of view. I am sure that there are some people who do not hold the same views on Gurunath as I did. This telling of these experiences was how he related to me personally. This was how I saw him and our relationship. I am humbled to share this book which I was fated and directed to write. I finished my task as requested and predicted in my Naadi reading and by Gurunath himself when he first met me in August of 2008, a decade ago.

Hamsa Kriyacharya Bill McDonald

> *"Guru reflects the form of whatever one assumes him to be. If one regards him as a liar and a cheat, he is that; if one regards him as wise and noble, he becomes that, Guru can even assume the form of God if one's faith and devotion lead one to believe that he is God. We have to realize that in guru we are only reflecting ourselves. That is why it is said that only those who see their guru as God are fortunate enough to see God face to face."*
> **Swami Sayasangananda Sarawati**

# About the Author

Rev. Bill's life has been on a spiritual journey, spanning over 7 decades. His whole life has been a mystical trip in search of gurus, the paranormal, and self-discovery. He has written about his many spiritually transformative experiences and "near-death-experiences" including supernatural events during his combat tour of duty in the Vietnam War. In his books, he has shared some incredible spiritual events that are beyond both common understanding or explanation.

His autobiography *"Warrior A Spiritual Odyssey"* takes us on a life quest for love, understanding, forgiveness and enlightenment. What he knows for sure after all these years is that the only thing that is real is LOVE.

He is not just an author and an award-winning poet, but also an international motivational speaker, artist, film advisor, veteran advocate, a yoga meditation teacher, and a Vietnam War veteran. He has spoken around the world including Germany, England, Wales, Bolivia and India.

Rev. Bill has been on over 600 radio and TV shows over the last 20 years and has stories about his life featured in over two dozen books by other authors and hundreds of magazine and newspaper articles. He has had articles published in such diverse publications as *"Parade Sunday Magazine"* and *"The Self-Realization Fellowship Magazine"* as well as military magazines and new age publications.

Rev. Bill McDonald was born In San Francisco and raised in California, Oregon and Hawaii. His childhood was an emotionally painful one. He even spent a year in the county hospital when he was 8/9 years old for major illnesses. At that time, he had the first of his 3 near-death-experiences in which he was foretold major life events some 50 years in advance. In his

*Photo by Rev. Jean Balthazar Qualls (Hollywood CA 2009)*

## ABOUT THE AUTHOR

childhood, he had many encounters with divine beings, ghosts, angels and aliens. He met many monks and spiritual people growing up and was gifted with paranormal abilities that can only be called supernatural. In high school, he predicted the assassination of President John F. Kennedy days before it occurred even saying it would take place in Texas.

He went into the US Army. He served in the Vietnam War as a crew-chief/door-gunner on a Huey helicopter. He was wounded and survived several helicopter crashes. In the process, he was awarded several medals and ribbons including *The Distinguished Flying Cross*, *The Bronze Star*, *The Purple Heart*, 14 *Air Medals*, *The Vietnamese Gallantry Cross* and many more.

Unfortunately, many of his old war wounds along with the effects from Agent Orange have caused him to have major health and physical issues at this stage of his life but he still battles on for other veterans.

He graduated from *San Jose City College* with an AA Degree in Labor Management and later from *The University of San Francisco* with a BA degree in Public Service Administration. He spent over 30 years working for the USPS and retired as a safety and health manager in 2001. He has spent his time since then volunteering for 5 different non-profit organizations helping veterans while serving the purpose of world peace. He works with PTSD veterans and is an unpaid lobbyist for veteran issues in California. Has also worked as a volunteer chaplain in Folsom Prison. He also worked for a time answering phone calls for *The National Suicide Hotline*. His life is filled with service. He works more hours now as a volunteer carrying out his mission then he did at his old job before he retired. He is still married to his high school girl friend, close to 50 years. He saw her in his near-death experience vision as an 8-year-old boy and found her and married her. He continues to live in Elk Grove, California close by his family.

### How to Contact Rev. Bill McDonald

His public email address is: Huey576@gmail.com
He has a *You Tube Video Channel* where he is listed as **Bill McDonald** and many of these stories from this book and his other books, are talked about on short videos. He is also on *Facebook* – listed as **Rev. Bill McDonald**. His books are available on **Amazon.com**

*Photo by Arden Kamille Varnel (Cupertino CA 2014)*

# Acknowledgements

To my wife, **Carol** for loving me through all these crazy years. Thank you for allowing me to travel so often to India so I could grow spiritually. These were not easy times for you watching me go through all my health issues. You are my rock and my hero.

Love to my daughter, **Daya**, and my son, **Josh**, and to all my grandchildren, **Colton** and **Callee Marlow**, **Spencer McDonald**, **Jesse**, **Daylan**a and **Gianni Beard**. My deepest thanks to **Lori McDonald** and **Mark Beard** for being part of this family.

A spiritual hug goes to my "*literary guru*," **Gayle Lynds**, for her longtime personal friendship and support. I am grateful to my German brother, **David Schulz**, for his fellowship and hospitality, and for coming all the way to California to spend time with me after my open-heart surgery. Love and appreciation to my three "*spiritual sisters*," **Karen Wilson**, **Mahaila McKellar**, and **Linda Provance**. To my good friend **Dave Nye**, aloha. Thank you, **David Gallo** for traveling with me to India in 2004 and back to Vietnam in 2002, and **Bill Gunther**, for driving almost one-thousand miles in a round trip from Hollywood, just to see me in the hospital for a twenty-minute visit. Huge thanks to **Shadoe Stevens**! You *always* make me smile and laugh. <u>You truly are a Spiritual Warrior</u>!

Thank you to this list of amazing people who have influenced my life journey this past decade and thus contributed to this book's energy in some way: *Robert Mackie, Jay Ponti, Dr. Dan Kogan, Linda Smith, Bert MacDonald, Nadia McCaffrey, Chief Sonne Reyna, Ratna Chandra, Lars Rimoeck, Danny & Carly Murawsky, Melanie Sako, Lynn Wade, Marie Edwards, Maureen McGill, Gary 'Morning Sky' Bibb, Malcolm High, Rev. Jean Qualls, Holly Campbell, Romilla Bhagat, Dennis Mar, Ed Stevenson, Patrick Vath,*

*Christopher Martini*, *Arden Kamille Varnel*, and my good friends in the U.K. *James Thomas*, *Suerena Haley*, *Anthony Somers*, *Richard Munn* and *Peter Lee* – thank you for saving my life while I was there.

Thank you to **Brian Yosowitz** for sharing a sacred vision at the ashram in 2011; to **Cabot Smith** my trusted spiritual confidante and friend. *Brahmachari Carl*, fellow Vietnam Veteran and SRF devotee; almost fifty years of friendship, but who's counting? I treasure our friendship.

In heartfelt, loving memory: *Dondee Nettles*, *Bob Amick*, and *Mike Domich*— old friends never forgotten, your legacies are daily reminders of the gift of life. Good bye and aloha to my nephew **Bill Swift**.

Thank you to my old high school principal, *Adrian Stanga*, who touched my heart and soul by honoring me at my 50th High School Class Reunion. You told me that I was your personal hero – well Sir – you are mine! Thank you for all that you did for so many in your lifetime. You are missed greatly!

And thank you to my editors and friends: *Marie* & *Richard Beswick-Arthur*, *Nistara Randhawa* (for all the work you did at the ashram in India on my manuscript) and **Manjot Singh** for his last minute editing suggestions. A special heartfelt thanks to *Tom Heffron* for formatting my book and making it what it is. I feel extremely blessed to have had all your individual talents and energies attached to my storytelling. You were all used by the universe and rose to the task!

A huge thank you to *Mario Arturo* from Barcelona, Spain for his work and great patience in designing my wonderful book cover.

Of course, no list would be complete if I did not honor my guru *Paramahansa Yogananda*, The Pole Star of my life.

*Photo by Henry Sanchez (Elk Grove, CA 2017)*

**Other books by the author:**
*A Spiritual Warrior's Journey*
*Purple Heart: Poetry of the Vietnam War*
*Sacred Eye: Poetry of in Search of the Divine*
*Warrior: A Spiritual Odyssey*


**Contributing author:**
*Spinning Tales: Helicopter Stories*
*Angels in Vietnam: The Women Who Served*
*Stories of Faith and Courage from The Vietnam War*
*Divine Moments: Ordinary People Having Spiritually Transformative Experiences*
*Gottliche Momente (*German Edition of *Divine Moments)*
*Our Voices: Military Writer's Society of America – an anthology*
*Silent Battlefield: 2012 MWSA Anthology*
*Spiritual Teachers of the World*
*God in the Foxhole: Inspiring True Stories of Miracles on the Battlefields*
*Baby Its You: Messages from Deceased Heroes*
*Chopper Warriors*
*Warrior Men With Angel Wings: Stories Of Love, Hope, Faith, Courage and Angels*


**Partial Listing of Films Associated With:**
*In the Shadow of the Blade* (Military Channel – Discovery Channel)
*The Art of Healing* (PBS TV)
*The Trooper* (Indie Film)
*Veterans Village* (Indie Documentary)

*Blessings and peace…*

Printed in Poland
by Amazon Fulfillment
Poland Sp. z o.o., Wrocław